GAME
WITHOUT
END

GAME
WITHOUT
END

STATE TERROR
AND THE
POLITICS OF JUSTICE

By Jaime Malamud-Goti
Foreword by Libbet Crandon-Malamud

University of Oklahoma Press
Norman and London

This book is published with the generous assistance of Edith Gaylord Harper.

ISBN: 0–8061–2826–7

Text design by Cathy Carney Imboden. Text typeface is Palatino.

The paper in this book meets the guidelines for permanence and durability of the Committee on Production Guidelines for Book Longevity of the Council on Library Resources, Inc. ♾

1 2 3 4 5 6 7 8 9 10

A Bettina, por todas las casualidades que vendran.

A Anna y Geri, por lo que vale la vida que ha quedado.

Para Juancho, por tantos años juntos de hacernos y de rehacernos.

Y, por supuesto, para Hugo y Soledad.

CONTENTS

FOREWORD, by Libbet Crandon-Malamud   *page* xi

PREFACE   xv

**INTRODUCTION: WHY I BECAME INVOLVED
IN THE HUMAN RIGHTS TRIALS**   3

How the Trials May Have Eroded Democratic
  Authority   4
Why Try State Criminals?   8
Political Contingencies vs. Structural
  Constraints   20
Misconceptions about When the Violence
  Began   22
The Role of Blame in Rewriting History   24

Rewriting History and the Perpetuation of
  Terror   26

CHAPTER 1. TRAGIC ARGENTINA   29
  Two Main Groups: Montoneros and the ERP   30
  The Army Enters Antiinsurgency Operations   40
  The Cultural War   51
  The Inevitability of the Military's Demise   54
  Argentina's Brief Spring: *Nunca Mas*   59

CHAPTER 2. SELF-SEALING PROOFS   71
  The Original Misconception of Subversion   72
  The Role of Language in the Struggle with
    Subversion   77
  Argentina's Subversion   79
  The Official Bipolar Logic   83
  Bipolar Logic and the Game Without End   89
  Self-Sealing Proofs: How They Work   89
  Self-Sealing Proofs   91

CHAPTER 3. TERROR   100
  Why Terror?   101
  The Nationalist Spirit   114
  The Isolating Effects of Terror   119

CHAPTER 4. POWER AND TERROR   122
  The Postwar Confusion   123
  Power and Discrepant Versions of Reality   124
  Authority, Power, and Meaning   128
  The Role of Blame and Blaming   139
  A Recapitulation   145

CHAPTER 5. LEARNING TO LEARN   146
  Is Terror Back?   147
  Conditioned by a Theory of Terror   156

Chapter 6. THE OUTCOME OF THE
HUMAN RIGHTS TRIALS 167
   Support for the Trials but a Blind Eye for
     Violence 168
   Lack of Judicial Authority 178
   A Fragmented Community 179
   The Courts as the Center of Transition 184

NOTES 199

BIBLIOGRAPHY 219

INDEX 227

FOREWORD

Since the 1980s,
Latin Americanists have celebrated the area's transition
from dictatorship to democracy . . . in Brazil, in Nicara-
gua, in Chile, and most of all in Argentina, where dictatorship led to the worst bloodbath of all in the hemi-
sphere: the "disappearance" of ten thousand to twenty
thousand people. But after the so-called dirty war was
over and amends were to be made, Argentina's resolution
was the first civil self-examination through trial in human history (the case of Greece was tried by the Greek
military.) Jaime Malamud, with the rank of secretary of
state, was one of the two architects of those trials. In this
book, he criticizes those trials, not from the political perspective that all other critics have taken ("trials destabi-

lize democracy by inciting the military to rebel"), but from a structural perspective. What, he asks, was inherent in the process of the Argentine trials that would weaken, rather than strengthen, the judiciary, and strengthen, rather than weaken, the very authoritarianism that led to the dirty war. To do so, he takes an anthropological approach to a wealth of data, and a political-philosophical approach to their analysis. Neither perspective has ever been applied to a human rights trial before.

Although much has been written about Argentina's dirty war and the subsequent trials, nothing before this remarkable book has been written by an inside player. Jaime Malamud lived through the Dirty War. When he defended "subversives," he was himself suspected of subversion. He was constantly under death threats. He saw friends disappear. As a survivor, he gives us an inside view of what it was like to live through the terror of death threats, of knowing what went on behind closed walls, of losing faith, having to calculate all conversations, and staying awake at night worrying about the unknown. He calls upon himself as well as a wealth of other informants, newspapers, magazine articles, and documents left by the military regime, which mistakenly assumed they were worthless, to engage the reader in the horror that took place. And engaging it is. The reader both lives the terror through the author and follows the logical consequences of that terror—a game without end—to the conclusion that it is not yet over, and may never be.

As one of the two architects of the trials, Jaime reevaluates what he did, reassessing his work negatively as contributing to the "game" that rewrote and thus simplified Argentine history. Carlos Nino, the other architect of the trials, died of a heart attack defending their work: Nino continued to insist, as both he and Jaime had done in 1983, that the establishment of trials would reinforce the nation's judiciary and thus serve as the backbone of democracy. Jaime exposes a judiciary that is fragile at best, and often lacks authority, rendering a real democracy impossible in Argentina. What he has to say about the structure of human rights trials is of the utmost importance to those involved in transitions from dictatorship to democracy—especially to what we see happening in Eastern Europe today.

Indeed it is the irony of the Argentine trials and their outcomes and consequences that renders this book so valuable. Argentina has always been a violent society; to scapegoat the military for the dirty war is not only to rewrite history but to deny the wide support the military enjoyed and the extent to which nonmilitary people were directly or indirectly involved in violence. Many acquaintances told me; Susana is a case in point. Married to a Montonero (Peronist militant) whose participation in violence escalated, she fled with her children to Brazil, where the Montoneros kidnapped the children. The distraught mother returned to Argentina, where she was caught and tried for treason to the Montoneros by a clandestine "revolutionary" court. She told the court that she had not fled from the Montoneros but merely from her crazy husband. Her husband, being present at the trial, was enraged by her accusations and his hysterical antics convinced the members of the court that Susana must have been right, and they then went after *him.* To survive under such circumstances, Argentines were condemned to merge their political and their personal lives: the terror was ubiquitous; it was not simply the military.

This book is a remarkable feat, both for what it cost the author to write and for what it implies about Argentina and all those countries currently following its footsteps. The author lived through the experience three times: first when it happened; second when he designed the trials; and third when he reappraised his achievements while writing this book—a painful experience that took enormous courage. The book's conclusions—that the trials, as they were designed, reinforced the very authoritarianism they were designed to eradicate—are more than disturbing: they are immensely valuable.

What the book has to offer is a rich argument that confronts most of what has been written about recent Argentina. This argument emerges from a lived experience and a flawless logic that begins with a closer look at history and how it was rewritten by the trials, a reexamination of the terror in this new context and the role of blame in rewriting that history in the public mind, the emergence of a structure of power that creates a game without end, and the inevitable conclusion that transition to democracy is even more difficult than we had already concluded. It is an essential document for anyone involved in the transition from dictatorship to democracy.

LIBBET CRANDON-MALAMUD

PREFACE

Writing this book has been as painful as it has been enriching. The adventure of turning scattered, painful memories into a book has changed my perception of Argentina, of terror, and, of course, of myself. Indeed, the process of writing itself has dispelled some memories and engendered new ones.

In trying to make some sense of past events, I have talked to people, hassled some friends, and, in spite of their goodwill, exhausted the patience of others. I cannot adequately express my gratitude to Libbet, who gave me so much of the little time she had. Old friends and tireless discussants Martin D. Farrell, George P. Fletcher, and the late Carlos S. Nino inspired many of ideas this book is about. Andres D'Alessio's incredible memory has been a source of many recollections. In Buenos Aires, members of the CEDES generously lent me their ears and their opinions at a very early stage of thinking about terror and Argentina. I am specially thankful to Carlos Acuña, Laura Gingold, and Catalina Smulovitz. In the United States, I took advantage of my dialogues with Kay Warren and Irwin P. Stotzky. Kellie Masterson, Barbara Price, and Hal Scheffler managed to turn my English into English, thus rendering the text intelligible. Actually, they not only clarified the text, they also clarified my mind: their opinions had bearing on the way I now think about many of the topics this book is about.

Some of my students took special interest in my work and were extremely valuable interlocutors. I am extremely thankful to Joseph Emmel, Hilary Goode, Tim Joyner, and Kati Suominen for their suggestions and, most of all, for their revitalizing friendship.

I would not have had the opportunity to write this book without the financial help of the MacArthur Foundation and the United States Institute of Peace. Their support gave me the spiritual and financial peace that make thinking and writing a little easier. The writing stage of this book was made possible by the Harry-Frank Guggenheim Foundation. I am very thankful to the program officers who supported me with contagious enthusiasm and am particularly indebted to Karen Colvard, the foundation's senior program officer, who helped me see how many issues out there are worthy of exploration.

ORGANIZATION
OF THE BOOK

Following the Introduction, which tells how I became involved in Argentina's human rights trials, the book is divided into four parts. The first part (chapter 1) is descriptive. It sets the political scenario in which, for an authoritarian logic, implanting terror becomes the right approach. It briefly describes insurgency, ultraright-wing violence, and the trials of military officers indicted for their role in torturing and assassinating thousands of victims, most of whom were alien to violence. It also discusses the aftermath of the trials and the military revolts staged to protest the indictment and convictions of military officers.

The second part (chapter 2) exposes the conspiratorial logic that leads to state terrorism. It depicts how defining the enemy as "subversion" guides the authoritarian mind to split Argentine society into one of friends and foes, and the reason that this bipolar logic seals the mind against criticism. In such a world of black against white, the mortal enemy becomes ubiquitous. Its omnipresence neutralizes otherwise elementary distinctions between enmity and apathy, between hostility and criticism, between indifference and disdain. This black against white tack also blurs the difference between insurgents and their lawyers, guerrillas and confessors, critics and instigators, disapproval and hatred.

The third part of the book (chapters 3 through 5) explains the institutionalization of terror and the perpetuation of this terror. It explains how violence and uncertainty lays strong roots in society, shaping its practices and beliefs. Terror, I claim, molds the structure and behavior of political power and patterns basic moral practices.

Chapter 6 attempts to untangle the apparent contradiction between the present appeal to violence of Argentina's citizens and the sizeable popular support of the human rights trials of military officers set up by the 1983 Alfonsin administration. This final chapter explains the reasons why the human rights trials deepened and protracted the authoritarian propensities they were devised to terminate. The book's underlying thesis is that the 1970s in Argentina were but the stretch of time in which terror made itself visible in Argentina. Argentine social practices and institutions are not only the outcome but also the cause of the ongoing reign of terror, behind different labels and with renewed parties.

JAIME MALAMUD-GOTI

GAME
WITHOUT
END

WHY I BECAME INVOLVED IN THE HUMAN RIGHTS TRIALS

Between 1976 and 1983, Argentina was ruled by a terrorist military regime. Under the de facto control of four juntas, military personnel made extensive use of torture and assassination in the name of saving the country from internal "subversion." During the same period, the military provoked and lost Argentina's disastrous conflict with Britain over the Falkland/Malvinas Islands[1] in the South Atlantic. Coming as it did on top of ruinous mismanagement of the economy, the fiasco so discredited the ruling clique of top officers that they were forced to step down and call nationwide elections for a president, legislators, and provincial governors.

The winner of the presidential election was Raul R.

Alfonsin, the candidate of the Radical Party, a party that had historically represented the country's middle class. Alfonsin had promised during his campaign that, if elected, he would see to it that those persons responsible for atrocious human rights abuses perpetrated during the military rule would be brought to justice. Many Argentines, myself included, agreed that the trials were a necessary step in establishing democratic rule in Argentina. Carlos S. Nino and I, as senior presidential advisers, were asked by the new president to draft legislation that would enable the judiciary to try (and, if they were found guilty, punish) those accused of responsibility for infringements of human rights. Eventually, some trials were conducted, and there were some convictions of high-ranking military officers. Some officers went to prison. But, as is shown in the chapters that follow, the consequences have not been what we had hoped they would be. Although to a much lesser degree, torture and other terrorist practices are still around, a flagrant part of Argentina's private and public life. With the benefit of hindsight, I now see that politics by torture and intimidation, which began well before the military de facto regime of 1976–83, could hardly be expunged from Argentine society and the elected civilian administration that took their place in December 1983.

HOW THE TRIALS
MAY HAVE ERODED DEMOCRATIC AUTHORITY

Trials of persons accused of human rights abuses are widely proclaimed as essential to transitions from dictatorship to democracy. There are sound reasons indeed to maintain that punishment is a political tool to raise the consciousness essential to bringing about radical political change. Impartial allocation of blame to those who trample people's basic liberties—one may expect—will help restore belief in individual liberties and recreate democratic authority.

Most of the critics of this thesis condone the violent practices, arguing either from moral skepticism or out of a fear of deepening social conflict. The latter—those afraid of disruption—are concerned, for instance, that corrective justice may detract from the political acumen required to introduce the necessary amendments that, they claim, will bring about respect for rights and equality.[2] Recent experience in Argentina, however, suggests that trials of human rights abusers may have in fact reinforced the very authoritarian trends they were established to overcome. This book explores how structural features of postdictatorial communities turn human rights trials into a new source of conflict, rather than a means of "deauthoritarianizing" the polity. In fact, as current practices indicate, the trials, rather than consolidating democratic institutions and customs, perpetuated and encouraged state-sponsored violence. The Argentine populace, indeed, is so familiar with authoritarianism that any attempt to eradicate it from society's beliefs and practices in only a few years is unrealistic.

This penchant for authoritarianism can be illustrated by noting the political appeal of dictatorial figures such as Aldo Rico and Domingo Bussi. Lieutenant Colonel Rico, followed by a clique of ultraright-wing army officers, rebelled against the Alfonsin human rights trials—to "restore the dignity and unity of the army." "Restoration of dignity" for Rico meant coercing the civilian administration into stopping the human rights trials. It also meant the dismissal of the top army brass, who had allowed civilian courts to try military officers accused of violating human rights. It further meant that the media would be banned from reporting activities that tarnished the image of the army. After serving little more than one and a half years in a military prison for rebelling against the generals (together with a number of officers convicted, or only indicted, for human rights violations), Rico was pardoned by President Carlos S. Menem in October 1989.[3] Shortly after his release, Rico launched his candidacy for the governorship of Buenos Aires—and found that MODIM, the party he had founded, unexpectedly obtained roughly half a million votes—11 percent of the votes cast in Buenos Aires Province, the largest province in the country. This was a remarkable figure for a provincial election in a country of approximately 30 million inhabitants. In the election, MODIM gained four seats in the national lower house.

The second illustration is that of General Domingo Bussi's surprising electoral achievement when running for governor of the northern province of Tucuman. Bussi lost the race against his Peronista opponent, but by only 3 percent of the votes, in the province he had tyrannically governed during the 1976-83 military dictatorship. Bussi had ruled the community through a campaign of lawless reprisals. His despotic style, it is widely said,[4] ranged from the summary execution of abducted suspects of "subversion" and the violent removal from the province of shanty-town dwellers to the systematic extortion of money from industrialists to further his political aims. In the election, Bussi won 43 percent of the votes.

It is not only in the electoral success of dictatorial officers that the country exhibits its authoritarian inclination. This inclination is often reflected in dictatorial wording of official political rhetoric. In July 1992, for instance, President Menem claimed that students who rallied against his educational policies could soon become *desaparecidos* ("disappeared persons") as had thousands of suspected dissidents during the military dictatorship.[5] In 1994, the president reacted similarly to publicity given to the alleged murder of an army conscript by his superiors. He accused the journalists covering the case of promoting a "class struggle" and the "division of the armed forces."[6] Using oratory similar to that of his military predecessors, Menem said that those parts of society that now promoted an investigation had remained silent when the violence originated in ultraleft-wing sectors.[7] Menem's response, an authoritarian style that many of his also followers adopted, was not in itself incompatible with a working democracy. What seemed irreconcilable with basic democratic respect for dissent was the populace's apprehensive reaction. Immediately after the president's denunciation, "subversive" demonstrations shrank to roughly one-fourth of what they had been.

To summarize, the political appeal that ultraright-wing officers enjoyed in the 1991 elections, the president's intimidating rhetoric, the current indifference toward ongoing police abuses,[8] and the cowed response of the populace in the face of threats indicate that the trials of the Argentine military did not accomplish what was hoped for from them. The trials did not accomplish the goal of fostering democratic values in Argentina; namely, an understanding of the supremacy of the worth and responsibility of the individual.[9]

Three Negative Features

Three factors largely explain the failure of the trials to help bring about change in the direction of a rights-based democracy. First, by depicting the world as consisting of the innocent and the guilty, the trials reproduced the authoritarian view that the world is split into allies and enemies.[10] Second, by this same bipolar criterion, those who were not declared guilty were judged to be innocent of the terror campaign, regardless of their direct or indirect participation in creating or setting the grounds that led to state terror. Third, since the trials were necessarily restricted in scope, they reinvented history by pinning the blame almost entirely on a single social group—the military. On the one hand, this process led to the view that only a relatively small number of citizens were responsible for the extreme violence; on the other hand, it led to scapegoating: members of one sector were accused by, among others, those who should have shared moral and legal responsibility for the strategic violence they strongly supported.[11]

These three negative factors suggest that, in postdictatorial, fragmented societies, there is an indirect, and ironic, consequence of human rights trials: the trials tend to erode the very democratic authority they are devised to restore. It seems, at first, obviously plausible that human rights trials are a means to achieve democratic change in terrorized societies. But in this book I challenge that plausibility. It may be that the negative effects of such trials outweigh the positive.

WHY TRY STATE CRIMINALS?

When elected governments are reinstated after years of brutal dictatorship, it is assumed by most of the citizenry that new, elected administrations must promote the prosecution of violators of human rights. There is a deeply entrenched belief that punishment plays a central role in teaching citizens how to become democratic. This retributive idea is based on the assumption that moral blame for the gross infringement of rights in a dictatorship may be assigned to a clearly identifiable group. This belief was behind the popular drive to punish "state criminals" in Uruguay, Chile, and Argentina. In Czechoslovakia it was behind such measures as the lustration law that banned members of the Communist Party from office.

There are indeed strong reasons for claiming that corrective justice will contribute to establishing a rights-based democracy. Perhaps the most evident of these reasons is that a democratic system requires the consolidation of authoritative institutions; notably, the judiciary. Such consolidation is in fact both the cause and the consequence of minimally egalitarian law enforcement. It seems only too obvious that the trial of state criminals in unstable political systems affirms the principle that nobody is beyond the reach of the law, and that citizens have rights, the exercise of which is essential to a working democracy.

It also seems evident that punishment has a larger role than merely building and consolidating institutions. Most human rights activists, and some scholars, imply that convictions of human rights violators will contribute to the generating of democratic citizens, by instilling among members of the community a lost sense of self-respect. I, too, believe, that without prosecutions and punishment individuals who have accommodated themselves to state persecution are less likely to regain respect for themselves and others once the dictatorship is over.[12]

The oppressor kills our ideals, our self-respect, and the perception of our rights. Once we compromise our principles and goals, we feel shame;[13] deserting our loyalties, we feel guilt. Our sense of worthlessness, of shame and guilt, demands a "political remedy."[14] Only an authoritative admission by political institutions that we were wronged will legitimize us in our own eyes. Punishment of the violators of our rights is the clearest and strongest statement an authoritative institution may issue to that effect.[15] Citizens need to *learn* that they have rights, not only to be able to act on these rights, but also to respect other people's liberties. As an authoritative institution, punishment must play this role,[16] nevertheless, even as one who has argued thus, I now claim that the advantages of corrective justice may be, as the Argentine case demonstrates, overridden by the drawbacks inherent to prosecution and conviction of human rights violators. A conception of punishment is required that is not "perpetrator centered," as are the traditional theories of deterrence and full-blooded retributivism; it must be "victim centered," and in a particular way that I explain in subsequent sections of this chapter.

Authors who believe in the deterrent effect of punishment will find that the results of convicting state criminals hardly support their theoretical claim. Punishment may deter officers from staging a new military coup; being exposed as criminals at home and before the international community is a bitter experience, as some Latin American dictators have discovered—and not many officers would have liked to be in the shoes of the convicted Argentine military commanders.

But, even at their best, the dissuasive consequences of count convictions are applicable only to the generals at the top. It seems clear that the higher the rank, the weaker is the peer pressure to kill and abuse prisoners.[17] For the rest of officialdom, the deterrent impact of convictions is neutralized by immediate benefits. For the armed forces, violating others' rights wins the respect and support of comrades and seniors. In Argentina, hypothetical, remote criminal punishment was more than counterbalanced by immediate rewards from the transgressors' immediate circle. A very small (insignificant) number of officers retained their moral commitments; for the others, approval or disapproval of comrades was more important than the threat of possible punishment or future moral condemnation of society. Once an adequate climate of opinion had settled in, fear of future suffering from a criminal conviction was highly unlikely to carry much weight with an officer, in an authoritarian organization, committed by his peers to assassinate or torture.[18] Moreover, even what little deterrent effect there is in such cases for those at the top, this is limited by circumstances. Were the military to take over the government in the future, the deterrent effect of punishment would probably discourage them from surrendering their power to a democratic successor. According to some experts, after the Argentine trials were underway, the Chilean and Uruguayan military became reluctant to call for elections; and when they did they took the steps to commit politicians to grant them immunity.[19] Even if the heads of authoritarian power feel able to safeguard the continuity of their economic and political policies under democracy, the issue of personal accountability may still stop them from allowing a transition to elections.[20]

A sense of what little effect the Argentine trials had on the fanaticized military[21] can be gained by following the treatment meted out later to some of those few officers who supported democracy. During the apogee of state terror, those who deviated from the general policy of torture and assassination out of moral qualms were labeled as complacent, cowards, or even traitors. Officers who founded CEMIDA[22] in support of democracy were surprised by the strength of the hostility of their comrades.[23] Considered disloyal by their colleagues, they were subjected to bomb attacks and endless death threats. Then when, in 1991, President Menem pardoned the few officers who were still in jail, retired army Colonel Juan-Jaime Cesio was barred from wearing his uniform for having endorsed human rights organization complaints.[24] A similar sanction befell army General Carlos Dominguez. Dominguez was forced into retirement simply for airing his belief that, whatever cruelties left-wing insurgency had perpetrated, "law and order could not be established by breaking the law."[25] Perhaps the clearest signal of the futility of attaching deterrent effect to the conviction of military officers can be seen in the four rebellions in Argentina since its return to democracy. These mutinies were staged largely in support of suspected human rights violators, in attempts to force the civilian administration to go even beyond an amnesty. And the lower one looks in the military hierarchy, the weaker becomes the effect of the criminal convictions. There is a strong sense of loyalty to comrades.

Unstable institutions and political fickleness in Argentina further weakens any possible dissuasive effects of punishment. Officers assume that, even in the worst scenario, in cases in which punishment is actually imposed, the military will retain enough clout to secure amnesties or pardons in the short or the long run.

The Retributivists

Aside from the arguments of the defenders of deterrence, there are those of the full-blooded retributivists. These are no more convincing than the former. Retributivists who have advocated the punishment of state criminals have generally disassociated such punishment from its consequences. The message to the wrongdoer is: "This is how wrong your crime was."[26] Retributive factors—the harm done or the culpability of the actor—are seen as constraints on the treatment of individuals, and as tools for the promotion of social and the state's interests. Full-blooded retributivists will ignore all possible consequences of the criminal sanction as relevant to its justification. The value of retribution is simply that, by disregarding the effects of punishment, it does indeed place constraints on society. For a full-blooded retributivist, punishment is demanded of every military officer who participated in violations of human rights, even if the consequences are a military revolt.

For full-blooded retributivists, an individual is treated according to a specified set of rules; in this case, the Argentine criminal law. Every person who can be classified as meeting the conditions warrants an established consequence. For consistent supporters of such a thesis, punishment must be imposed on all officers who ordered, perpetrated, or aided a violation, on those who failed to avert or report such transgressions, and on civilians who aided and abetted the regime. In accordance with this view, some human rights organizations (e.g., the Madres de Plaza de Mayo) campaigned to have every officer who participated in human rights infringement punished.[27] There is, it is true, an appeal to consequences in the Madres rhetoric, but this appeal is not based on social effects; rather, it cites moral or evaluative consequences. In demanding that their children be returned alive and that all those responsible for the violations—whatever those violations may be—be punished, the Madres claim that societies, as *societies*, require minimal justice. Furthermore, if this justice is not carried out, by punishment of the abductors, the torturers, and the assassins, they cannot consider their children to be dead. If they did, they would be admitting that human rights abusers are accepted by society, and such society would become nonexistent as a moral community.[28]

I admit that it is plausible to maintain that those officers and their civilian advisers deserved to be punished by standard criminal law criteria. But the consequences of such a policy would surely have been a political and logistic disaster. Indeed, between one thousand and two thousand individuals were implicated in the abductions and assassinations. A high proportion of the two thousand were responsible for aiding and abetting the former, and almost every officer in the armed forces was responsible for not averting or at least reporting the deeds. The hands of so many Argentine officers were bloodied that, in certain units, no one would have been able to accuse anyone else.[29]

Retributivists stand essentially for equality of treatment and for constraints upon the state's power to repress individuals. A central feature of a system of constraints is generality: all guilty perpetrators ought to be punished even if, as Kant postulated, the sky falls. But this disregard for consequences disqualifies the full-blooded retributivist's answer to the question of "Why punish?" First, as H. L. A. Hart has pointed out, such a position cannot appeal to considerations of social usefulness.[30] Consideration of the social advantage of convictions makes the justification of punishment depend in part on its consequences. This contradicts the retributivist's basic tenet.[31] In overlooking the effects of the criminal sanction, a full-blooded retributivist must believe in the intrinsic value of the rules that render the act criminal. Just punishment presupposes that the rules that render an act punishable are also just. But the full-blooded retributivist cannot discriminate between rules that are just and those that are not without looking at the consequences of enforcing such rules as the ultimate reason for their existence. It makes no sense to elect to punish certain conduct as criminal without considering the consequences of this conduct and the expected effects of making them criminally relevant.[32] Second, it is not self-evident that the wrongdoing to which we attach a criminal sanction demands that the offender be made to suffer. If particular desirable consequences are not associated with the violator's suffering, we may prefer to refrain from punishing wrongdoers and elect instead to impose on them a duty to compensate the victim.

I do not here claim that the two approaches described above—the utilitarian (deterrent) and the retributivist— do not contribute reasons for punishing state criminals. Utilitarians are correct to expect criminal convictions to have dissuasive effects. But, at their best, these effects are, as I have explained, limited to a few officers at the top. And retributivists provide a cogent argument for protecting individual rights: persons who are not guilty of a wrongful act ought not to be punished, and no one should be punished beyond his culpability.[33] This negative aspect of retributivism is modest; it refers solely to restraints on the utilization of punishment. It does not offer a positive justification for criminal convictions. I argue that *punishment should contribute to the making of a rights-based democracy.* I also suggest that institutional regard for the victims of state-sponsored crime is crucial to the furtherance of that goal. In that respect, utilitarianism and full-blooded retributivism, as "perpetrator centered" theories, are intrinsically inappropriate. I propose a "victim centered" justification of punishment. This would be the most plausible, independent ground to warrant the conviction of human rights abusers.[34]

Redress for victims is not an essential part of a justification based on deterrence. By giving key significance to the dissuading of potential offenders, utilitarians have no qualms about overlooking the plight of those who have suffered degradation as a consequence of having their basic rights infringed or threatened. The notion of "justice for the victims" would be excluded from the utilitarian calculus when exercising discretion.[35] Full-blooded retributivists invite a similar criticism. By disregarding all consequences of punishment, proponents of this version of retributivism focus only on the wrongdoer's facing the consequence of his deeds.

But there is another, less popular variant of retributivism—a goal-oriented variant. According to this version, punishment ought to be directed at redressing the valued sentiments of those who were wronged. I am not referring to vindictive sentiments, but rather to the victim's loss of purpose and sense of worth. As mentioned earlier, those who endure unwarranted chastisement—actual or potential—from the oppressor experience shame and lack of self-respect for renouncing the personal ideals that made their life meaningful.[36] Goal-oriented retributivists will attach to punishment the function of restoring this lost trust.

There is a salient pragmatic difference between full-blooded retributivists and those who are goal-oriented. While the former are compelled, in the presence of a set of conditions that render an act criminal, to impose punishment such a generality does not apply to goal-oriented retributivists. In seeking redress for the victims, they may consistently choose to forego administering punishment, or content themselves with merely condemning the offender, or even only the offender's deed. If they believe that imposing pain on the perpetrator will do nothing substantial to improve the victim's sense of self-respect and confidence, punishment will be counter indicated. So if the victims of certain forms of state crimes have already regained self-respect and are confident that they will be protected against future violations because the heads of the criminal organization have been convicted, goal-oriented retributivists may refrain from punishing other members of the group. There is room for considerable discretion.

Although this victim-centered justification for punishment is certainly the most plausible, it is not intended to be an exclusionary viewpoint. Consequently, it does not attempt to displace other justifying reasons. A victim-centered view may exhibit the futility of imposing a criminal sanction on a given offender, yet find that punishing this offender may still be suitable. For example, it may be important to punish a perpetrator if, given the circumstances, it may deter would-be imitators. Rape of political detainees, for example, may have received a low enough degree of consensus among officials to make punishment an effective deterrent; politically motivated offenders may be seen by their peers and seniors as common criminals.

The applicability of a victim-based justification of punishment is not limited to establishing a rights-based democracy: it may also play a key role in improving the state of individual liberties in societies that are already rights based.[37] Since the approach is strongly connected with offences in which the perpetrator shamed his victim, the thesis may also serve to justify punishment of particularly humiliating transgressions, such as blackmail and ordinary rape. But I contend that a victim-centered theory of punishment is, prima facie, the most significant means for attaining the democratization of society.

There is no clear way to establish the degree to which the 1985 Argentine human rights trials have had a democratizing effect. If the thesis I have so far laid out is correct, by overriding respect for people's dignity and basic rights on the grounds of security and expediency, citizens reflect that they themselves have not recovered from the harms inflicted upon them by the past dictatorship. As I later explain, only an insufficient perception of our own rights may explain the appeal of violent solutions to social conflicts.[38] There are strong indicators that the trials of the generals in 1985 failed to teach the Argentine citizenry the value of their own worth as individuals.[39] This assertion may suggest that the reason for the failure lies in the meaning attached to the convictions. The failure, however does not result from grounding the convictions in retributivist or utilitarian principles. There are indeed powerful objections even against the victim-centered justification I espouse here.

The Question of Impartiality

For advocates of corrective punishment, like human rights activists, the criminal sanction is essential to citizens' democratic learning. A rights-based community is unlikely to emerge spontaneously where individuals have adapted to dictatorial violence by giving up their personal values and ideals. Two reasons to punish those responsible for this adaptation seem self evident. First, trials of human rights abusers may be expected to generate awareness of recent history, a requisite for effecting change. Second, anguish was felt by more than those directly touched by the assassinations; it also deeply affected the large majority of the population. Public admission that a sector of society was wronged will help legitimize governmental institutions in the eyes of the citizens; and punishment of human rights violators is the most authoritative and strongest statement to that effect. There are, however, several intertwined objections to this claim that I sketchily explain here and go into in more depth later.

To credit the prosecution and punishment of state criminals with having a democratizing effect presupposes that the courts' decisions are authoritative: that a large enough section of the citizenry believes in the judges' commitment to justice and respect for rights, including, of course, those of the culprits. Convictions may contribute to restore the citizens' lost dignity, insofar as the populace assumes that the courts are impartial and that convictions are grounded in shared notions of criminal responsibility. Indeed, one cannot expect the courts to instill any sense of worth and self-respect among citizens if the same courts fail to meet some popular sense of impartiality and prudence. At the trials of military officers, as I will later explain, the size and nature of the parties and the lack of an accepted system of prosecutorial discretion prevented the attainment of the desired democratic goals.[40]

The policy of trying state criminals has inevitable weaknesses. First, experience has shown the difficulties posed by selecting those to be brought to trial. There is an inevitable air of artificiality in establishing the boundaries of responsibility among members of a terror-ridden society. By pinning the blame on a limited sector of society, human rights trials reinvent history. The meaning of the resulting "truth" inevitably becomes controversial, if not plainly factious. Dissatisfaction with the 1985 Argentine trials was conveyed not only by those who vindicated the convicted officers, but also by frontline human rights activists such as the Madres de Plaza de Mayo and several international organizations.[41] While the former claimed the culprits were scapegoats, the latter protested that too few were actually convicted and that their sentences were too light. For both parties, the trials were "clearly political": far from being seen to administer justice, the judiciary was widely perceived to have merely adjusted to the political convenience of the executive. Accordingly, instead of reinforcing whatever authority the judiciary may have enjoyed, the trials had the opposite effect. Instead of contributing to bridging a fragmented society's multiple versions of reality, the courts generated the belief that the trials were a ploy to draw consensus from a compromised account of reality.

Some felt the government failed to do enough about past human rights violations. Others, including a sizeable number of military officers and right-wing civilians, perceived that President Alfonsin and a group of so-called acolytes (among whom I was counted) were determined to destroy the country's traditions (and the armed forces in particular) by bringing the whole military apparatus to trial indiscriminately.[42] This fragmentation of public opinion both brought about various kinds of popular demonstrations to press the administration to prosecute a larger number of officers and also provoked four military rebellions aimed at stopping the trials.

Such perceptions—that the justice system is compromised—deepens antagonisms between opposing groups. These groups are consequently further discouraged from entering democratic debate. The most striking feature about this fragmentation of public opinion was that hardly anybody, including lawyers, based their beliefs on the federal court 1985 decision on the criminal responsibility of the members of the ruling military juntas. The court found five of the nine members of the first three juntas responsible for the assassinations, torture, rape, and larceny committed by subaltern personnel during the military dictatorship. Not even the verdict of the supreme court, delivered one year later and mostly upholding the federal court's decision, was relevant to the citizenry's assessment of the country's recent political history. The citizenry's indifference to the proceedings shows that, in Argentina, the courts' decisions lack authoritativeness, both in establishing the facts brought to trial and in evaluating the significance of these facts. Thus, controversy about what should have been done about past human rights violations goes on and on, with no hope that any arbiter will bring it to an end.

POLITICAL CONTINGENCIES
vs. STRUCTURAL CONSTRAINTS

The debate over the appropriateness of the human rights trials has, by and large, given rise to two points of view. On one side there are authors who espouse the ideal of punishing state crimes: such writers have advanced an articulated set of moral reasons for applying criminal sanctions. Their opponents have largely argued from pragmatic grounds. Some advocates of impunity have maintained that punishment deals exclusively with the past. For the most part, they have appealed to ad hoc, compelling circumstances; namely, averting further conflict with what is a powerful sector of the polity. The numerous supporters of the trials contemplated this latter view as lack of political courage, moral skepticism, or both.

A Moral Quandary

Drawing on the Argentine experience, this book examines the structural arguments against holding human rights trials in postdictatorial systems. It will not claim that these arguments against holding trials are conclusive, but will demonstrate that there are genuine structural reasons to weigh against the politics of corrective justice. The reasons for not bringing human rights violators to trial consist not merely of "political contingent circumstances" but of genuine structural constraints upon notions such as moral and criminal "blame" and "responsibility" that are central to criminal punishment. It is naive, without first resolving the structural shortcomings that made military regimes and state terrorism possible, to use punishment as a central means for modifying a political system.

There are strong objections to such a policy. One cannot apply the notions of blame and responsibility to only a limited number of officers without implying that other forms of extreme violence—forms constantly used by army personnel and paramilitary groups—are not morally reprehensible. The fact that we decide to prosecute only murderers and torturers perforce conveys that state-sponsored abductions and assault are tolerable. To apply a broader standard of blame and responsibility for a large portion of the citizenry, including military and civilian collaborators, weakens the moral significance of *blame* and *responsibility*. To consider that millions of citizens who participated directly or indirectly in serious abuses were morally responsible would necessarily detach criminal blame and responsibility from the notion of crime as a social aberration. When crime becomes a common event, the moral condemnation necessarily loses the forcefulness required to warrant criminal punishment.

What should become clear in this book is that the adequacy of the criminal sanction is less than self evident. The impulse to convict human rights abusers is widely shared, but examination reveals that there is a genuine moral quandary here. Politicians and scholars must confront this quandry.

Both official and popular versions of recent Argentine history suggest that state-sponsored human rights violations were a result of the military regime's strategy following their 1976 takeover. However, situating the abuses between March 1976 and December 1983, when the military were formally in power, is misleading. State violence staged during the 1976-83 military rule was but an escalation of a wave of the brutality that started in the early 1970s. Furthermore, the number of abductions perpetrated after 1979, when the military were still in full control of the state apparatus, were relatively few, and there is no evidence that they were the result of a centralized policy.

What did not diminish immediately was the sentiment in favor of right-wing terrorism that was prominent during those years. Right-wing terrorism was felt to be a necessary response to violent left-wing insurgent groups, the activities of which were widely accepted—to say the least. These groups' escalating violence and their clashes with other exponents of the Peronista movement, and finally with Peron himself, dissipated a widely-held belief that they were a romantic movement. Opposing them, a large portion of the middle class increasingly supported the wave of assassinations and abductions carried out daily by paramilitary gangs directly associated with the ruling, elected, Peronista government. Peron's minister of social welfare, Jose Lopez Rega, ran the most prominent of these right-wing squads, the Triple A.[43] It consisted of factions of right-wing civilians, members of the police, and army personnel largely in retirement. Between 1974 and the end of 1975, hardly a day passed when disappearances and assassinations were not reported.

Immediately after the March 1976 military takeover, assassinations by the army and the security forces increased. A wave of abductions, many performed in broad daylight, rocked the country. The targets of this state-sponsored terrorism—labeled as subversives—came from many backgrounds: they were workers, students, writers, lawyers, and even priests and nuns.

The military were not alone in staging this so-called antisubversive campaign. A vast right-wing sector actively contributed to brutal repression under the guise of paramilitary squads and vigilante groups.[44] Conspicuous members of the Roman Catholic Church praised the assassination of students and workers, underscoring the spiritual value of the crusade and the "patriotic merit of eliminating those elements of society they considered 'unrecoverable'."[45] In addition to these organized groups, the middle class actively or passively largely supported state brutality. Widespread justification of the official strategy consisted of denying what was happening. Indeed, references to disappearances and torture were often dismissed with the phrase, "There is something she must have done," placing the blame on the victim, not the perpetrator.

The initiation of state-sponsored terrorism by right-wing activists (most of them, before the 1976 military takeover, civilians) demonstrated that responsibility was shared by many sectors of society. Civilians actively participated in the campaign of terror throughout the military dictatorship. Indeed, it can be said that by and large the citizenry supported the dictatorship's campaign of terror. The general appeal of violence indicates that the 1983 collective demand that the *milicos asesinos* (military assassins) be punished was based on a (conscious or unconscious) revised representation of past events.

The moral and legal responsibility for Argentina's tragic past is oversimplified by narrowly ascribing political terror to the military, and specifically limiting it to the abuses perpetrated by military officers during the 1976–83 dictatorship. This rationalized reinterpretation explains why one of the judges responsible for convicting military officers for human rights abuses confessed to me in private his belief that, in the 1985 trials of the generals, the sense of justice that supported the convictions was coupled with a belief in scapegoating. "It is now clear to me we have done nothing about the civilians who marched with the military and later turned their backs upon them," he told me.[46]

THE ROLE OF BLAME
IN REWRITING HISTORY

The outcome of the Argentine trials suggests the inadequacy of thinking only in pragmatic terms. Establishing *fault* is a way of understanding an array of social processes.[47] Although basically conceived as the result of our moral beliefs, fault plays a variety of roles, some of which reflect our attempt to come to grips with our existence. In many of these cases, the finding of fault is not the actual consequence of our causal findings, as we may be told, but rather an identifiable, "external," "aberrant," and "anomalous" element that makes social events intelligible and perhaps controllable.[48] For example, we establish that the "cause" of the train derailment is the conductor's behavior, regardless of the fact that we may attribute other factors to the accident. Blaming the conductor enables us to think we can control future possible mishaps— unlike factors such as poor visibility or the icing of the rails being named. In this sense, we frequently derive causation from blame, instead of the other way round.[49] Basing our judgment on faulty agents has practical consequences: it simplifies our task; it allows us to eliminate from our mental process other "normal" elements that also may have led to the derailment—for example, the management's decision to stick to the schedule in spite of the poor

visibility and the ice. Likewise, in the 1970s many Argentines "understood" the massive disappearances and torture by placing blame on the victims and their conjectured
behavior: "She must have been up to something." In the
1980s, this "understanding" changed radically. Blame for
the abuses shifted to the military as a group clearly dis-
connected from the rest of society: *milicos asesinos.* Closely
connected to our political interests, the social practice of
blaming is a selective process by which we attempt to control the behavior of those we blame. Intimately related to
the balance of power, blaming is essentially the practice
by which one sector of society seeks to change some other
sector's future conduct,[50] while disclaiming its own fault.
In Argentina, first it was left-wing students, trade union
leaders, and workers. Later, it was the military.

A clear example of the nature of the social practice of
blaming is Argentina's human rights trials. These trials
were indeed conceived by many as a means to redress the
human rights violations perpetrated between 1976 and
1983: the abuses that occurred when the military ruled
the country. But by zeroing in on the military in the 1980s,
a broader issue was overlooked; to wit, the pervasiveness
of individual rights violations that occurred in other periods of Argentine history, especially during the state-
sponsored terrorism in 1973 to 1976. Terror, one may say,
is a general and institutionalized feature of Argentina's
political life. The thesis of this book does not lie on the assumption that military officers lacked moral and legal responsibility; rather, it is the opposite. It claims that responsibility was more spread out than the populace is
ready to acknowledge. In maintaining that the human
rights trials served a generalized reluctance to accept responsibility, I imply that formalized blame contributed to
the unchanged situation in Argentina vis-á-vis attitudes
to terrorist power.[51]

When it became clear in 1979 that the military regime's

economic policies had led the country into severe unemployment and foreign indebtedness, the direction of blame changed. Human rights movements began to be heard. After Argentina's defeat by the United Kingdom in the Falkland/Malvinas war, the military regime no longer had even a minimum of consensus. The nation's cities were plastered with posters that read, Trial and Punishment to the Guilty, and a multitude of rallies conveyed a general desire that military officers be held accountable. The new focus of blame overlooked terror's origin under a civilian administration and the cessation of systematic human rights violations by 1980, more than two years before the military called for general elections.

Despite the restoration of civilian rule, the issue of blame in 1983 was tied to a host of political restrictions, the most important being the (conscious or unconscious) desire to avoid a direct confrontation with the largest opposition group—the Peronista Party, which ruled between 1973 and 1976. The fledgling democracy had too much to lose if there were to be a clash, with the Peronistas, when both they and the ruling party were temporarily allied to press for general elections.

The Argentine case suggests that the fabrication of recent history through limiting the focus of blame was, to a large extent, the result of partisan political interests. Thus, instead of the country benefiting from an open debate that would have reflected the far more complex and wider allocation of responsibility, blaming deepened political conflict and further fragmented the social perception of reality.

REWRITING HISTORY AND
THE PERPETUATION OF TERROR

I have already described President Menem's proneness to disqualify political and institutional challenges as "subversive" activities, a practice that, as I explain in chapters 2 and 3, led the military to resort to the use of terror. Menem was not alone in using extremely authoritarian rhetoric; others—senior officers in his administration—reacted similarly. When henchmen beat up political dissidents who dared to boo Menem at the 1993 Rural Expo, several of the president's underlings flagrantly explained that the victims had caused the violence by "provoking the president."[52]

Police brutality in Argentina has remained common currency in the 1990s and the majority of the population appears undisturbed by a renewed, flagrant contempt for basic liberties. The trials of human rights violators, which were originally confined to the generals in control of the state and to some torturers and assassins, did not achieve the goals envisioned by domestic and international human rights organizations. It certainly did not satisfy the expectations of rights-based democrats. Efforts to reinstate democracy have not dislodged the "foes and allies" bipolar logic embraced by the military rulers, nor the violence that such logic brings about.

The human rights trials had two prominent goals. First, they sought to instill a sense of individual responsibility basic to democratic citizenship by punishing those accountable for infringing basic individual rights. Second, they sought to reaffirm the authoritativeness of the judiciary as competent to provide an impartial version of political occurrences. However, the courts' decisions had the opposite effect, turning the judges into the centerpiece of what perhaps became the country's most afflictive political conflict. The outcome of the trials considerably eroded the authority of the judiciary. Almost every military officer I talked to labeled the trials "the judicial battle."

CHAPTER 1

TRAGIC
ARGENTINA

In 1970, large-scale left-wing violence appeared in Argentina. That was four years after a military coup had deposed the constitutional president, Arturo Illia. Perhaps the most dramatic sign of insurgency was the abduction by self-named "left-wing Peronistas" of former de facto President General Pedro Aramburu on May 29, 1970. One of the top leaders of the civic-military movement that deposed Juan Peron in 1955, Aramburu was convicted and executed in captivity by a Montonero mock revolutionary tribunal. The abduction perhaps was the event that marked the appearance of the Montoneros on the public scene.

As the 1970s progressed, radical clandestine organizations mushroomed under a variety of ideologies that encompassed a broad spectrum from progressive Peronism, through a refurbished version of the corporatist Peronism of the 1940s, to Maoism and Soviet Communism. There was a time of considerable confusion when, under numerous acronyms (many using similar combinations of letters) these groups tried to claim credit for abductions, bomb blasts, armed robberies, and assaults on police outposts.

TWO MAIN GROUPS:
MONTONEROS AND THE ERP

Two organizations dominated the scene: the Peronist Montoneros and the Marxist Ejercito Revolucionario del Pueblo (the ERP).[1] Organized in so-called secret cells and operating on similar targets, these two groups set the pace for what, to smaller organizations, was seen as a common struggle against "imperialism." Soon after their appearance, the smaller groups fused with one or other of the larger organizations—the ERP or the Montoneros.

The ideologies and purposes of these two groups varied considerably. The ERP, an offshoot of a small Trotskyite party, Partido Revolucionario de los Trabajadores (PRT), stood for a standard version of a Marxist revolution. Since the early 1960s, the ERP's top leader, Roberto Santucho, had sought to unite the "Latinamerican Nation" against foreign capitalist domination.[2] The Montoneros, on the other hand, were the armed branch of a young faction of Peronism known as the Juventud Peronista (JP), a renewed Peronism with left-wing understores. The JP/Montonero was a sui generis socialism consisting of a mixture of the corporatist and nationalist ideals inherited from Peronism and "antiestablishment" and "antiimperialist" rhetoric dominant among leftist groups. Montonero's tenet, which they labeled national socialism, was grounded on the word of their supreme leader, Juan

Peron, banned from politics since his ouster by a civil-military rebellion in September 1955. From his exile in Spain, Peron, once an admirer of Benito Mussolini,[3] had shifted his right-wing populist rhetoric to encourage a Castro-like, antiimperialist crusade. Peron repeatedly explained that ideological shifts within his Peronista movement were essential to its survival. "As the world changes, so do we," the Leader, as he was known, openly proclaimed.[4]

Consistent with his "left-wing" discourse, it was no surprise that Peron should espouse the then widespread revolutionary ideals. In the early 1970s, Peron endorsed left-wing violence and frequently referred to the Montoneros as his movement's Special Formation. "What other means but violence can a humiliated populace resort to?" he asked rhetorically.[5] "Violence already reigns and only more violence can destroy it," he explained, grounding his ideas in those of "my friend Mao."[6] In many ways, this rhetoric, the sincerity of which is seldom questioned, captured the hearts of many young, middle-class revolutionaries. Taking up Peron's discourse, Peronist and non-Peronist young left-wing militants of the late 1960s and early 1970s ceaselessly repeated: "Violence from the top generates violence at the bottom." By adopting a revolutionary rhetoric, Peron soon persuaded his followers that he was, and always had been, a socialist precursor. His old right-wing sympathies had now become intelligible only as a strategic move to veer left at the right time.

Peron's appointment of Hector Campora as his representative in Argentina further confirmed for people that Peron was now illuminating the country's road to socialism. Campora, the father of two JP militants, a man with very little charisma, won the 1973 elections. Peron's hand-picked candidate, backed by the lower classes and an almost unanimously enthusiastic youth, achieved a sweeping victory. He obtained 49.56 percent of the votes. Thus, both the Montoneros and the ERP could interpret the 1973 elections as evidence of their popularity. Campora's triumph was understood as the victory of violence by left-wing groups, and that included, of course, the ERP.

To finance their organizations, Montonero and ERP activities consisted largely of armed robberies and extortion, the latter by abductions of industrialists and financiers. Other targets of urban terrorism were police posts, military units, and military and police officers. On November 1, 1974, a Montonero group assassinated Alberto Villar, an anti-Semite, ultraright-wing chief of the federal police.

The most impressive of the Montonero organization's kidnappings was that of Juan and Jorge Born in 1974. Members of the family that owned Bunge & Born, the most powerful Argentine-owned holding, the Borns allegedly paid a record ransom of over US $50 million. Estimates have it that, by 1975, sixty industrialists had been abducted. Some of the victims of insurgency's kidnappings were assassinated. About three hundred policemen and military officers lost their lives in ambushes by, and in shootouts with, insurgent organizations.

The Ideological Differences

In spite of their similar procedures, there were deep ideological differences between members of the two groups. There was basic mistrust of each other. Like most nationalist groups, Montoneros had retained close connections with the Catholic clergy, an example of which was the Montoneros ideologue Padre Carlos Mugica. Mugica made it clear on every available occasion that his revolutionary ideals had no connection with those of Marxism. "To uphold the total equality of man," as Marxists do, Mugica cryptically maintained, "is to deny the reality of sin."[7] Padre Mugica maintained that only through Peronismo, a passion that "only Argentines can understand,"[8] could the people achieve the goal of "liberation." Like Mugica, most Montonero militants rejected the ERP's atheist Marxism; in turn, ERP militants despised the Montoneros' lack of commitment to the genuine left-wing cause. The former saw the latter's attachment to the word of their alluring Leader as the epitome of a populism[9] incompatible with socialism.

Discord between the two groups went beyond the ideological to embrace basic ethical beliefs. Former members of the ERP still claim today that Montonero militants occasionally turned in their comrades to the military. "Tactical purposes," however, drove the two organizations to bridge the gap between them, and Peron's death in July of 1974 contributed further to alleviate tensions. Peron's succession by his wife Isabel and the ultra-right wing clique that surrounded her ended the enduring speculation that, in the end, Peron would proclaim that the JP and the Montoneros were in fact his true followers.

There are no means accurately to assess the number of citizens who supported insurgency, but sympathizers of the ERP and the Montoneros were indeed numerous in the early 1970s. In an attempt to gain popular support, both the ERP and the Montoneros campaigned in shanty towns and at factories, distributing food and clothing to convert their clandestine operations into a widely supported political movement.[10] Because the young militants presented themselves as Peron's envoys, people with little affinities to the groups were lured into approving and supporting them. A 1971 official poll conducted in Argentina's largest cities of Buenos Aires, Rosario, and Cordoba indicates that 49 percent of the population sympathized with the insurgents.[11] Although the guerrillas were mostly from the middle class, they found in their beginning considerable receptivity among the disenfranchised and the working class. In the early 1970s, the members of these sectors believed that the young militants were bringing the word of Juan Peron in his attempt to reestablish social justice in Argentina. This approval lasted until constant clashes with the traditional right-wing Peronista movement undermined the popularity of the organization's image. This image was definitively eroded by the eventual confrontation with Peron himself.

Insurgency in Argentina must be understood to have had two distinct, and different, contexts. For the populace at large, the strongest reason for the appeal of insurgency was chiefly the Montoneros' link with the idealized image of an exiled Peron. For revolutionary youth, violence was the consequence of a more complex set of circumstances: the country's pervasive right-wing authoritarian regimes, the 1959 Cuban Revolution, the Vietnam War, and the mythical figures of Fidel Castro, Che Guevara, and Ho Chi Minh. This element believed that only a violent revolution would enable the subjugated peoples of the Third World to free themselves from the imperialist yoke. "Liberation" had thus become the catchword of middle-class youths tired of ideological repression and censorship. This repression stemmed from an alliance between the military, their ultraconservative civilian friends, and the no less conservative hierarchy of the Roman Catholic Church. The latter acted as a go-between for the senior military cadres and their ultraconservative civilian advisers, who were friends with the bishopric. Shortly after the 1966 military takeover, the police contributed to the deepening of antiestablishment sentiments by raiding universities and indiscriminately beating large numbers of people.

Most of the members of the insurgent organizations were only improvising as guerrillas, operating with very little discipline or political commitment. Survivors acknowledge today that their training and organization were minimal. Many joined the Montoneros and the ERP for the most futile and romantic reasons[12]: some perhaps because a friend was already an activist; some because they admired the figure of Che Guevara; some to reform an unjust society. For the most part, members of the insurgent groups were exposed by incompetence. Former militants today recall weekend drills, target shooting in public parks while surrounded by curious observers. Their identity must have been known to all.

Although the presence of young insurgents was disturbing, neither the ERP nor the Montoneros were successful in establishing control over territory or in fighting army units. The ERP's attempt to impose their primacy in the Tucuman bush in 1974 was a clear demonstration of such limitations. A poverty-ridden northern province, Tucuman lies in the Argentine subtropics, amid thickly forested hills not unlike Fidel Castro's Sierra Maestra. Tucuman had a large population of disenfranchised sugarcane harvesters, whom ERP planners thought would be easily recruitable: the two hundred-strong group of ERP guerrillas saw their campaign in the bush as paralleling that of the Viet Cong guerrillas fighting the French and the United States.[13] The ERP's efforts in Tucuman, however, failed completely. The scant popular support they initially mustered dwindled in face of the intimidating presence of the army. Driven by military pressure, the acting president, Italo Luder, issued two executive decrees in 1975 ordering the army's engagement in counterinsurgency operations throughout the country. Luder, chairman of the senate, issued these decrees while replacing Isabel Peron, who was on an extended, mysterious leave of absence, taken for no visible reason. The army rapidly defeated the ERP in Tucuman, some five thousand well-equipped troops storming the province's forests.[14] It was during this campaign that clandestine torture-detention centers appeared for the first time in Argentina.[15]

Tucuman was but one example of the insurgents' military limitations. ERP and Montoneros attacks on army units invariably failed. In fact, the ERP was severely depleted in December 1975 when they attempted to take over the army arsenal, Domingo Viejo Bueno, near the city of Buenos Aires. Forewarned by military intelligence, army troops overpowered the 130 ERP combatants. At least 30 militants were killed in the skirmish.

These insurgent groups had to contend with other armed enemies, not only the army and the police. Familiar with gang violence since the Peronista trade unions consolidated in the 1940s and 1950s, right-wing union chieftains and other ultraright-wing Peronista groups saw the JP and the Montoneros as a threat to their influence within the Peronista movement. Among the most bellicose of these right-wing groups were Jose Rucci, a top trade union boss; the metal workers' leader, Lorenzo Miguel; Peron's private secretary, former police corporal Jose Lopez-Rega; and a retired army intelligence colonel, Jorge Osinde. These leaders had managed to organize heavily armed groups among trade unionists and ultraright-wing supporters. Allied to these groups were various members of the police and some army officers, most of them retired. The degree of violence these right-wing groups exercised was reflected in daily assassinations and disappearances. Peron's scheduled arrival from Spain at Ezeiza, on June 20, 1973, illustrates both the brutality these groups were capable of and the scale of the support they enjoyed from within the official sectors.

The Return of Peron

Peron's official return, after eighteen years in exile, made visible the intensity of the brutality between right and left. Members of the JP and the Montoneros and a number of their sympathizers were killed randomly by ultraright-wingers near the Ezeiza airport, where Peron's plane was scheduled to land. Strategically positioned henchmen, under Osinde's command, opened fire on a cheerful crowd approaching the platform where Peron was to give an address to the nation. Some of the surprised victims were killed outright by the barrage; others were captured and driven to a nearby hotel, or shoved inside ambulances that had been deployed throughout the area as part of the day's celebration. In most cases, the demonstrators were tortured and killed.[16] After nearly a three-hour shoot-out, the landscaped parks near the Ezeiza airport were turned into a gory horror spectacle. Many of the hundreds of bodies were mutilated or tied with wires to the dais from which Peron had been scheduled to speak.[17] Some of the left-wing activists present were armed, but many of the victims were shanty-town dwellers who were there to take part in the celebration. Peron's speech, of course, was cancelled.

The incident had two politically important effects. First, it showed the extent to which the right-wing assailants were protected by silence; although many observers agree that the victims numbered more than three hundred, no official estimates of the Ezeiza Massacre were ever published. Second, it displayed President Campora's lack of power when his instructions to investigate the event were never even attempted. Right-wing groups circulated a version of the events, according to which the violence had been the price of protecting Peron from a left-wing plot to assassinate him. This allegation drove the president obsequiously to submit his resignation to Peron. Peron accepted it. Suspected of having connections with the JP, following the 1976 military takeover Campora was forced to seek political asylum at the Mexican embassy. After a short interregnum, during which Raul Lastiri, chairman of the lower house and Lopez Rega's son-in-law, served as the acting president, Peron stepped in, with Maria Estela Martinez de Peron (Isabel Peron) as the country's vice president. Peron's support of his traditional right-wing followers was now in the open, inviting questioning of the authenticity of his earlier support of the left. For right-wing Peronistas, the Leader's endorsement of the Juventud Peronista and the Montoneros was taken to be aimed at badgering the military leadership into looking for an electoral exit. Some members of these two organizations continue to maintain that the Leader's heart was with the left but that Peron was coopted by an ultraright-wing group commanded by Rega and Isabel.

A former Montonero sympathizer, writer Pablo Giussani, convincingly argues that Peron used his Special Formation for two strategic purposes: first, to hasten the military dictatorship's call for elections and, as a consequence, speed his own return to power; second, to enable him to obtain the support of the middle class, a large segment of which had opposed him during his tenure in the 1940s and 1950s. Left-wing gangs in the streets, Giussani argues, would promote a generalized fear of anarchy that only a highly popular political leader could avert.[18] Thus, as boxers do, Peron had threatened to hit with his left, while striking with his right. A similar thesis is espoused by Donald Hodges in his book on the dirty war. Hodges claims that Peron had instructed his right-wing underlings to annihilate the members of JP and the Montoneros in a way similar to Hitler's and Mussolini's purges of the left-wing sections of their movements. In 1973, says Hodges, Peron launched an antileft witch hunt similar to those of the Nazis and Fascists in 1934 and 1935.[19]

The ERP and the Montoneros indeed hustled the military regime's call for elections in 1973, which must have generated a sense of strength among their ranks. The truth remains, however, that neither the Montoneros nor the ERP were ever close to an armed victory over right-wing gangs, let alone the army. There were several reasons for the weakening of both insurgent groups. Their amateurishness and lack of preparation enabled army and police intelligence to penetrate the cells' structures and identify most of the members of both groups. Insurgents were also becoming increasingly isolated. Events demonstrated that, in spite of their part in driving the military to call for elections, the popular support that was enjoyed by insurgent groups in the early 1970s was short lived. This support dwindled as Peron visibly supported his right-wing followers.

The closeness of Peron to right-wing gangs seems to indicate that he must have encouraged large-scale violence. The fact remains that even if he did not order right-wing brutality, he never opposed it. As a result, no arrests were ever made among right-wing paramilitary groups and their activities kept out of the media and out the courts.

June 12, 1974 was a momentous day in the history of the relationship between Peron and the JP and Montonero groups. At a mass rally held in front of the Casa Rosada, Peron referred to the Montoneros as "infiltrators" and "deceivers."[20] According to Joseph Page, an expert on Argentina and Peronism in particular, Peron sought to force the Montoneros to choose between (traditional) Peronismo and the ERP.[21] Despite his reputation as a nonviolent politician, that Peron would be unaware of the violence perpatrated by his followers is highly unlikely. His closeness to Lopez-Rega, Osinde, and Miguel and his denunciations of "left-wing infiltration" clearly show that he supported the right-wing violence.[22]

Isabel Takes Over

Right-wing armed activities intensified when, surrounded by an ultraright-wing court, Isabel Peron took over after her husband's death in July 1, 1974. In early August, Rodolfo Ortega Peña, a left-wing congressman, was assassinated in broad daylight in front of his home. Subsequently, the police brutally dispersed those attending Ortega's funeral. Soon thereafter, right-wingers shot down Alfredo Curuchet, a well-known labor and human rights lawyer. At that point, the killings by right and left (but most of them by the Triple A) intensified to the point that unofficial reports calculated that a political assassination took place every nineteen hours.[23] The victims were students, priests, lawyers, journalists, and teachers. One of the most impressive assassinations by the ultraright was that of seventy-year-old Silvio Frondizi, an intellectual and brother of a former elected president, Arturo Frondizi. In 1992, I interviewed army officers who agreed in their accounts of how Isabel's minister of defense had sought out army officers to organize civilian death squads.[24] The fact that not even one assassin was ever arrested, let alone convicted,[25] further suggests Peron's ultraright-wing sympathies. Civilian ultraright-wing activities abated when, under the subterfuge of two executive decrees, the military entered the dirty war in 1975. In 1976, the military takeover seemed to bring private violence to an end, the army arresting a number of trade union and Triple A henchmen. This belief did not last long.

THE ARMY ENTERS
ANTIINSURGENCY OPERATIONS

There are two versions about how and why the military engaged in the dirty war. Under the first, the so-called vertical conception, the resolution to engage in counterinsurgency operations was made at the very top. This account links military intervention with the Argentine military's adoption in the 1950s of the French *Guerre Revolutionaire* and, in the 1960s, of the United States' doctrine of National Security (see below). The military involvement in the dirty war and the subsequent coup d'état were steps aimed at controlling every aspect of the country's social life in which conflict might surface. Under the second version, the horizontal account of the full involvement of the military in counterinsurgency operations, constant pressure was exerted on the generals by officers in the middle and lower ranks. The question of which account is adopted is relevant to establishing the degree of moral and criminal responsibility of lower and intermediate ranking officers.

In the vertical version, the rigidity of the military chain of command considerably attenuates the responsibility of subaltern officers, who claim to have followed orders. In the horizontal thesis, responsibility for human rights abuses requires an individuated and complex approach to responsibility. Many junior officers acted, in this theory, out of their own convictions. These officers may have been wrong about the ethos of their actions, but they acted of their own free will, not blind obedience.

The standard version of Argentina's recent history espouses the vertical approach. In this account, as noted above, the generals were driven to engage in the dirty war as a consequence of their adoption of the doctrine of National Security. Under this doctrine, it had become the mission of the Latin American military during the Cold War to guard their nations' internal "peace" from Communist infiltration. This required more than quashing left-wing insurgency; it also demanded neutralizing all other sources of insurgency.[26] Guillermo O'Donnell wrote of this role that the army "must include among their specific 'duties' the execution of internal warfare against 'subversive' agents who attempt to wrest the 'underdeveloped' nations from the sphere of 'Western Civilization' and to bring them under their control. Since the 'enemy' is multifaceted, 'internal warfare' can be 'ideological, economic and political.'"[27] In this light, bringing about "internal peace" required a highly integrated society.[28] It demanded that the military exercise control over the country's political life. According to this thesis, involvement in the dirty war was only one step in the generals' gaining control over every conflictive aspect of social life.

This vertical version of military intervention was the official interpretation adopted by the Alfonsin administration. Most official documents drafted during the Alfonsin period assumed that the responsibility of officers was highly attenuated by their following superior orders. The exceptions (which included torture, rape, and assassination) were aberrant acts. The commanders' inculcated among their subalterns that the "subversive enemy" was less than human. This was, from this viewpoint, the principal cause of the brutality of the dirty war.[29] To mitigate the younger officers' responsibility, President Alfonsin stressed that they "had been trained in an authoritarian context in the light of principles that demanded blind obedience."[30] It was with this outlook that the president's advisers, including me, approached the issue of criminal responsibility on each and every occassion that we met with the generals. I had not realized that this version was an artificial extrapolation of a Prussian-type army structure. The commanders at that time did not challenge this conception: it was safer for them not to have junior officers stand trial.

Today, numerous midranking officers (who in the 1970s were young captains and lieutenants) reject the vertical version of the dirty war. According to them, it was the junior ranks' relentless pressure that caused the army to engage in the atrocities. This insistence overcame the generals' reluctance to adjust their old World War II mentality to the demands of the new times. It was the seniors' resistance to fighting the ERP and the Montoneros that ultimately led an unprepared military to extreme cruelty. Lack of moral and professional preparation to preserve the integrity of officers engaged in secret and undercover operations was the main reason for the countless abuses that bloodied the country and jaded the army.[31]

In this alternative thesis, the dirty war began as an almost private war with insurgency. Young lieutenants and captains of the early 1970s recall their anger when, out of fear of ambush, they were forced to give up weekend promenades with their families.[32] These officers were tired of living under the tightest of security measures, including having to display their credentials several times a day to be allowed into the lobbies of the apartment buildings in which they lived.[33] Perceiving the constant threat of ERP and Montonero attacks, young officers increasingly rebelled against the generals' design to keep the army away from the dirty war. They organized themselves into posses, to retaliate against insurgent attacks. "When we learned at the officers' mess that someone had killed—or attempted to kill—a comrade, we rushed to our vehicles to hunt the assailants down," an army major recalled in 1991.[34] It was the younger officers untiring pressure on the generals to mobilize against left-wing "subversion" that, in late 1975, finally succeeded, five years after the commencement of insurgent activities.[35]

It seems clear today that there was truth in both conceptions. Evidence of the validity of the vertical approach is the military's earlier adoption of the two above mentioned doctrines—the *Guerre Revolutionaire* and National Security. Infused into the army ranks from top to bottom, "national security" hinged upon the central role of the army in antiinsurgency operations. As to the second version, that of a quasi private war, it seems that there was considerable leeway for officers of middle and even low rank to abduct, torture, and assassinate suspects of "subversion." Divided into operational areas, the country was at the mercy of area—and subarea—commanders. Espoused by both military and nonmilitary sources, this horizontal view seems to be confirmed. Junior officers were largely free to abduct, kill, and plunder.[36]

There are further illustrations of the "privatist" approach to the dirty war: of officers taking personal revenge against imprisoned members of organizations that, they thought, were perpetrators of attacks against their comrades. In a conversation, the army's General Tito admitted that some high-ranking officers could justifiably be punished; yet he defended General Ramon Camps, one of the most cruel exponents of the dirty war. Tito's reasoning implied that because Camps's best friend, Colonel Ernesto Trotz, had lost an arm as a consequence of a left-wing organization's bomb attack, torture and murder of suspects of insurgency was warranted, as long as personal emotions, such as loyalty to comrades and solidarity, were the motives behind the violence. Whether lofty or base, the motives Tito appealed to were relevant only in a "private" sphere.

It seems now plausible to maintain that the generals' original design had consisted of having the army involved in a limited, two-pronged way. First, senior officers would plan and supervise the counterinsurgent campaign. Second, army intelligence officers would operate closely with the police and ultraright-wing groups and civilian intelligence agents to put to effect "antisubversive" operations. This seemed to be an ideal solution, in spite of the military's distrust of civilians: it would retain control, without exposing officialdom to the multiple perils of the dirty war. After all, they figured, winning the war would require no more than a well-organized combination of right-wing gangs, including of course the trade unions.

Thus, the ensuing, all-out involvement does not mean that the generals' originally intended to engage the three services. The way events unfolded seems to have been the consequence of the insistence by junior cadres on participating in quelling "subversion." What seems to have precipitated the full engagement of the military, first in the dirty war and second in taking over the government, was the abysmal lack of authority of Isabel Peron.

The Isabel Peron administration demonstrated its inability to control increasing social unrest and the whooping inflation caused by, among other reasons, an erratic economic policy. In 1975, it was a common belief that only a military coup could put an end to political violence and labor agitation. With left-wing organizations terrorizing industrialists, bankers, and ranchers, and right-wing gangs assassinating and abducting students, newsmen, and union leaders, the middle class felt that violence, combined with economic catastrophe, had reached its apex. How wrong could an assumption be!

Shortly before the March 1976 takeover, right-wing gangs, threatening politicians at all levels, had gained a decisive influence in political decision making. In 1975 and early 1976, right-wing union leaders managed to dominate some cabinet members. Unhesitatingly, they interrupted sessions of congress to inhibit the legislators from passing bills that they deemed contrary to their interests. A secretary to Antonio Cafiero, Isabel's finance adviser, has described how Miguel and other union chieftains would barge into Cafiero's office to interrupt whatever meeting the minister may have been busy with. Other members of Isabel Peron's cabinet were also harassed. The institutions of democracy had become mere forms; behind the forms, violence gradually deflated power.[37] Armed groups disputed supremacy in control of violence.

A few months before the March 1976 coup, the Isabel Peron administration appointed the army's General Albano Harguindeguy as the chief of the federal police. Assumed to be a move inspired by the army, this elicited general applause from the middle class. The sectors that, only a short time before, had viewed Juan Peron as the country's potential savior were now convinced that only the military could restore order. The citizenry considered that the motorcades cruising through cities brandishing Uzis and sawed-off shotguns were preferable to having left-wing activists in control.

The era of private armies was confusing not only as to

who was who; it also awoke middle class aversion to the Peronista movement of the 1950s. To the middle class, General Harguindeguy's rapid move to disassemble several ultraright-wing private armies was a promise to stop not only the left but also the old-time Peronismo.[38] After the March 1976 takeover, the military incarcerated some ultraright-wing hit men, giving rise to the notion that they were finally overcoming the political power vacuum. But thereafter, confusion increased. Random violence escalated, and the military liberated and even rehired people who Harguindeguy had arrested a few months earlier.

As mentioned above, a few months before the coup d'état, the military had pressed for two executive decrees (signed by Italo Luder), instructing the armed forces to "annihilate subversion." This wording was later invoked by the military commanders—when they were brought to trial—to claim that the forces under their control had only followed the instructions issued by an earlier civilian regime.

On March 24, 1976, five months after the decrees were signed, a bloodless military coup overthrew Isabel Peron, closed down congress, placed the judiciary under receivership, and banned all kinds of political activities. Labor activities were proscribed, ending the boisterous protests that had become a daily scene during the Isabel Peron administration. The heads of the executive were now General Jorge Videla, Admiral Emilio Massera, and Brigadier General Orlando Agosti. They were the three commanders in chief of the army, the navy, and the air force, respectively. Videla later became the president, being replaced as commander in chief by General Eduardo Viola. The president became the "fourth man."

Soon after the coup, the military divided the country into areas and subareas, and a wave of abductions and assassinations rocked the nation. Those abducted, as noted earlier, came from a wide variety of backgrounds. A small minority of those kidnapped were above the age of forty; many were extremely young. I know couples whose children were in their lower teens when they were taken away.

In most cases, the fate of the abducted was similar. They were kept, hooded and often fettered, in clandestine detention centers. They were systematically tortured and most of them never reappeared. The army packed improvised confinement centers, located throughout the country. Each controlled by one of the services of the armed forces, the centers housed people in inhumane conditions in the most varied places: military locations, factories, and abandoned rural elementary schools. The secret torture centers proliferated: there were more than 250 of them.

The National Commission for the Disappearance of Persons (CONADEP), created in 1984 by the Alfonsin administration, has collected testimonies that describe the mass execution of prisoners. Survivors related how their companions were loaded into the back of Mercedes Benz trucks and taken away; the truck returned empty a few hours later.[39] Further testimonies describe how the captives were sat on the edge of a ditch and shot, their bodies being dumped into the ditch.[40] A witness recalls seeing General Luciano Benjamin Menendez, the commander of the 3rd Army Corps, being personally present at these killing fields.[41]

The military employed a practice that had also been used by civilian death squads before the coup: they avoided identification of victims by dynamiting and burning the bodies. Some of the victims' faces were destroyed; fingers were cut off to hinder fingerprint identification. When the number of corpses became so great that burials were burdensome, the army dumped the bodies from airplanes and helicopters into the Rio de la Plata. Many cadavers were found drifting off the coast of Uruguay. Recent evidence from repentent officers reveals that some prisoners were doped and thrown alive from aircraft.

Children were not spared by the dirty war. Some were utilized as bait to capture their parents, who for whatever reason had been listed as subversives; in some cases, children were tortured and killed. One of the most dramatic episodes was the abduction, torture, and assassination of the "pencil children" *(niños de los lápices)* in September 1976 by order of the chief of the Buenos Aires Province police, the army's General Ramon Camps. The victims, whose ages ranged from fourteen to eighteen years, were abducted for organizing a school protest to obtain special bus rates.[42] About twenty boys and girls were kept, half naked, in dungeons. The girls were regularly raped. All twenty, with the exception of three whose families had direct connections with the authorities, were killed.[43]

Priests and nuns were also among the slaughtered. One of the most renowned cases was the assassination of Monsignor Angelelli, in a faked car accident in the northern province of La Rioja in 1976. The bishop had become a well-known critic of the regime's individual rights' abuses and, a few days before his death, hooded killers machined-gunned a layman who was working for him.[44] Revealing the political nature of Angelelli's death, Colonel Jose Luis Garcia, a democratic officer who opposed the dirty war from its inception, remembers a private conversation with a retired general who proudly proclaimed: "We have defeated liberation theology, we have killed Angelelli."[45]

On July 11, 1977, Bishop Carlos Ponce de Leon, of San Nicolas, died in a similar fashion. He was carrying with him evidence of state brutality, but by the time his body was found the evidence had disappeared.[46] The right-wing church hierarchy did not complain about these and other church-related cases. Human rights activists testify that the doors of most churches were closed to those who sought protection and help against state violence. The Madres de Plaza de Mayo claim that state terrorism was made possible by an acquiescent Church. Hebe de Bonafini, a leader of the Madres, has been quoted as stating: "We have 30,000 *desaparecidos* today because the leadership of the Church and the unions, as much as the political leadership, allowed it."[47] The fact is that, with some exceptions, Roman Catholic priests were supportive of the military dictatorship. Many of them went beyond support to collaborate in torture sessions or to hand over information to the intelligence apparatus,[48] and Bishops Mariano Perez and Monsignor Antonio Plaza who instigated the state terrorist apparatus by advocating the elimination of human rights activists.[49]

Political persecution was extended to the friends and acquaintances of those who belonged—or merely sympathized with—Montoneros and ERP groups. Physicians who aided members of such groups, and lawyers who sought to clarify abductions, were themselves threatened, incarcerated, and sometimes killed. Some lawyers of my acquaintance were themselves imprisoned on the occasion of visiting clients who were "institutionally held" political prisoners. Most of those held in official prisons had been arrested for subversive activities prior to 1975, a year in which, under the Isabel Peron presidency, right-wing terrorism intensified. Most official detainees were held in inhumane conditions. Visitors were not allowed; reading materials were interdicted. The military wanted to be rid of these prisoners; hence, they created a system of reporting assassinations as if the victims had attempted to break out. In fact, they took these prisoners to the front gate and shot them. The procedure was called Ley de Fuga, the "law of flight."

Sexual abuse of women in clandestine centers was common. Whether from lust, or to humiliate them, or to break

their will, young women were often the sexual prey of torturers. Sex sometimes became a compensation exacted
from detainees in exchange for subsequent freedom, or
the freedom of their loved ones. In her testimony at the
commanders' trials, Carmen Floriani explained in detail
the circumstances in which she acquiesced to having sex
with one of her captors (seemingly a civilian) in exchange
for her own release. The twenty-two-year-old, mother of
an infant and with her husband earlier disappeared, Carmen was left with no choice.[50]

Estimates of the number of victims of detention, torture, rape, and assassination vary considerably. The numbers for disappearances alone range from ten to twenty
thousand. CONADEP has documented nearly nine thousand cases of disappearances,[51] but even for its members
alone the true figure is higher than that. CONADEP
knows of victims and their families that elected to forget
their loss or were simply deterred by the idea that, should
terror reign once more, they would again become victims
of revenge or reprisals from paramilitary groups. Their
angst was more than justified: some paramilitary groups
remained active even after the December 1983 Alfonsin
inaugural. The victims of these Alfonsin period reprisals
were mostly young political activists. They resurfaced
one or two days after their abduction, but terror was still
present and some youths felt compelled to leave the country after threats of assassination.

During the state-terrorist period, looting became a
common practice. It is clear that immunity for exercising
discretionary violence generated a feeling of omnipotence in the perpetrators. In the wake of a terrorist oper-
ation, the affected neighborhood would witness military
trucks loaded with furniture and appliances that soldiers and their civilian allies had collected at ransacked
residences. Official abuses involving property went beyond petty larceny. On January 11, 1977, Victor Cerrutti,

a businessman from the western province of Mendoza, was taken captive and forced to sign the transfer of his lands in the locality of Chacras de Coria, in the same province. The beneficiary had a nonexistant name, but forged identification papers allowed him to sell the lands to purchasers in apparent good faith and recovery of the property by its original owners became legally impossible. Cerrutti, in his late sixties, had never been involved in any political activity other than conveying his conservative views. He was never seen again. A retired colonel, Jose Luis Garcia, described to me at a CEMIDA luncheon his revulsion when he learned from his wife that looting had become a part of everyday military life: not only were search-and-destroy officers involved, but also their wives. In 1977, while Garcia, then retired, was visiting a former comrade, who was ill, at an army compound, Garcia's wife was invited for tea with the officers' spouses. At the tea, her hostess and guests exchanged complaints about the booty their husbands brought home from antisubversive operations. Why confine oneself to a hair drier when somebody else got an air conditioner or a refrigerator?[52]

THE CULTURAL WAR

Throughout the years of repression, the authoritarian mindset also introduced reforms to the education system. Armed insurgent organizations, the military often emphasized, were only one piece of the subversive apparatus: the real enemy was that which taught and circulated ideas incompatible with Argentina's traditions.[53] This "cultural war" probably started during Juan Peron's presidency and was radically extended during the 1974–76 Isabel Peron presidency. At that time, the military intensified the educational campaign.

After the death of Juan Peron, Argentina's education system was placed under the control of nationalists—Catholic traditionalists. For most of them, tradition meant a confessional, dictatorial state—one epitomized by Spain's Franco. Isabel Peron demonstrated her sympathies for these groups by appointing Alberto Ottalagano as new rector of the University of Buenos Aires. No ordinary religious believer, Ottalagano stated at the outset that his mission was, above all, to cleanse the university, the largest in the country. His mission was not only to purge left-wing intellectuals but also those that he and his ultra-Catholic circle considered to be a threat to the country's heritage—ultraright-wing Catholicism. Ottalagano made evident the seriousness of his commitment when he had a priest exorcise the university's premises from what he said were lurking forces of evil.[54] According to a Nazi magazine, *Cabildo* (that many officers read as their favorite literature), these fiendish forces had been let loose by, among others, Artaud, Sartre, John Locke, John Stuart Mill, and Jean-Jacques Rousseau. In such a view, only certain citizens were qualified to pursue a humanistic education; only military officers, priests, and lawyers were entitled to study sociology and sociocultural anthropology.

High schools were also affected by this cultural crusade. Some teenagers were arrested and abused for expressing critical views about new school texts, the central topics of which were Fatherland, Church, and the Catholic family. Modern mathematics textbooks were banned for constituting a form of "subtle indoctrination."[55] The basic notions of constitutional law, the teaching of which had been a tradition in Argentina's high schools, shifted to the study of Roman Catholic morality. Debate of issues such as the Roman Catholic faith, sex, contraception, censorship, and political ideas was forbidden. Educational methods changed drastically: class discussions were replaced by rote learning. Students were not to elaborate on the texts they read but simply to memorize them. Those who overlooked the rules were severely punished, mostly with expulsion.

Under Isabel Peron and later the military, a host of terms related to politics were considered inadmissible. From speeches delivered by senior officials during these times, I collected the following terms considered incompatible with what were considered to be the country's traditions: *leftism, empiricism, positivism, rationalism, agnosticism, atheism, contractualism, materialism, utilitarianism, modernism, liberalism,* and *romantic egalitarianism.* Aware of the dangers of using the wrong terminology, students and parents alike became extremely self-conscious, quickly shifting their vocabularies. The emancipation rhetoric that pervaded society during the early 1970s changed into one devised to avoid political persecution. The use of *liberation* and *imperialism,* ceaselessly uttered during the early 1970s, became less frequent after Juan Peron's election in October 1973; they vanished totally during the Isabel and military regimes.

Carmen Ferradás describes the way in which, in Argentina's universities after the 1976 coup, teachers and students became increasingly aware of the dangers involved in even hinting at a left-wing bent. Self-censorship was coupled with extremely careful manipulation of speech. One consequence was the suppression of many words, including relatively neutral and indispensable terms such as *contradiction, structure, base, marginality, colonialism, dependence, Latin America, bourgeoisie, class,* and *consensus.* These expressions disappeared from people's vocabularies.[56] As for the middle class, to the extent that they felt beyond the reach of state terror, they adapted to what was now a familiar militarization of politics. After all, as noted in the next section, the new economic strategy seemed to be indeed promising.

THE INEVITABILITY
OF THE MILITARY'S DEMISE

For middle-class citizens who considered themselves to be beyond suspicion of left-wing militancy, the military takeover was associated with calm and tidy cities and economic prosperity. The military regime had immediately prohibited trade union and political activities, and the army was patrolling the streets. The country's towns had recovered the charm they had lost after the previous (1966–73) military regime. Gone were the boisterous, angry crowds protesting daily on the streets; gone was the frustration caused by strikes so common during the Isabel Peron administration. Coming in on a tide of petrodollars in the world market, a sense of financial well-being added to the military regime's appeal (although this bonanza was to be short lived). The military's finance team scheduled a devaluation of the dollar (U.S.) and liberated import taxes to force the domestic industry to keep prices competitively low. The immediate effect of these measures was the enjoyment of an artificially sustained peso. It became possible to purchase untaxed, imported goods and to travel overseas with profit. In 1978 and 1979, middle-class families spent their holidays and their money in Brazil and the United States, where reequipping their children was relatively inexpensive. Clothes and school materials were so much cheaper abroad that they made up for the air fare and hotel expenses. Argentines in fact shopped all over the world, and their celebrations of purchases became a familiar sight.

During those times of petrodollars the regime eased banking regulations to encourage investment in Argentine pesos. They invited inexperienced financiers aggressively to compete in speedily expanding their clienteles. In the late 1970s, financial speculation became a cottage industry. Some Argentines even sold the houses they lived in to invest in the unregulated financial system with its extremely high interest rates. Financial institutions, competing to enlarge their portion of the market, offered loans to insolvent borrowers who found it impossible to repay on time. This financial whirl quickly deteriorated. At the end of the 1970s, first-line banks such as Promosur and Banco de Intercambio Regional failed to meet their obligations. In desperate attempts to remain in the market a little longer, financiers improvised, offering ever higher interest rates. There was a wave of bankruptcies in financial institutions, the news often being preceded by the defection of managers and directors. Seventy-two such institutions closed down in March 1981 alone.[57] Investors' funds were swallowed. The IMF called this process the Financial Hiroshima.[58]

The high-interest economic policy also damaged the industrial sector. Extremely high financial costs rendered exports unprofitable. The yield of short-term financial operations was so high that, between 1979 and 1980, it tempted the business sector to funnel resources away from production and into financial speculation.[59] In those years, about U.S. $15 billion left the country; 90 percent of the foreign capital in the country was placed in the financial circuit. To make things even worse, the regime imposed price controls over some eight hundred major firms.

As a consequence of high public spending, the foreign debt increased at alarming speed. In 1980 alone, a $19 billion debt climbed to $30 billion due to public expenditure. A sizeable portion of the expenses was devoted to the purchase of military equipment.

Due to the contraction of the productive apparatus, unemployment increased. The average working-class salary lost 50 percent of the purchasing power it had had when Isabel Peron was overthrown.[60] Open conflict between the regime and wide sectors of the nation—industry, the ranchers, and the working class—was a sign that break-down of the regime was inevitable.

The military's sympathizers began to detach them-selves from a collapsing administration. A wage freeze de-creed by the regime to lower industrial costs forced union leaders to challenge the ban on labor activities by going on strike. The mighty Central Confederation of Labor (CGT) staged its first general strike in April 1979. In 1981, the long-established Union Industrial Argentina, proxy to the largest industrial complexes, warned the regime that continuance of the course set by its financial advisers would devastate the country's production system.

Affected by high production costs, the rural sector also began to withdraw its support of the regime. In 1981, the Sociedad Rural Argentina, the strongest rural association in the country, openly protested against the economic pol-icy. Economic complaints were not the only ones to sur-face; other criticism touched on the military's disdain for individual rights. It was no surprise, at this point, when a Catholic bishopric, a former ally, distanced itself from the military.

In 1981, General Roberto Viola replaced Videla as the de facto president. Nine months later, a palace coup ousted Viola and his financial advisers. General Fortunato Galtieri, who then succeeded Viola, attempted a new strategy: with the support of Admiral Jorge Anaya, the navy commander, he invaded the Falkland/Malvinas Is-lands (settled by British citizens) in the South Atlantic.

The war critically increased the country's political ten-sions. A wave of accusations broke over who was to bear the responsibility for the military debacle. The Falklands/ Malvinas conflict critically exposed the incompetence of the generals and admirals who, through the manipula-tion of the press, had induced the populace to believe that Argentina's troops were winning victory after victory. Military blundering became additionally evident when it was learned that young soldiers with barely any military training had been sent to the cold climate of the South Atlantic from the hot Argentine subtropics. The war also exposed the degree of corruption in the military: gifts sent to soldiers serving in the islands never arrived. Commandeered and sold by noncommissioned officers, some of the items were later found for sale at kiosks and stalls throughout Argentina. The putrefaction indicated that it was time for political change.

The three members of the military junta resigned soon after the war, to be replaced by three other general commanders, and General Benito Bignone replaced Fortunato Galtieri as de facto president. The government's rhetoric also changed, radically, after the war. Whereas the outgoing de facto president had proudly maintained that "the ballots were well taken care of" (he was pointing out that elections were out of the question) his successor, Bignone, made it clear from the start that he was presiding over a transitional regime. As a token of his purpose, the general invited the delegates of the major political parties to find an electoral exit out of the political mess. Elections were scheduled for October 1983.

Concurrently with increasing protests over the economy and the Falkland/Malvinas disaster, the voices of human rights organizations, previously inaudible, became increasingly loud. A formerly acquiescent middle class radically shifted its mood to one that was enthusiastically antimilitary.

With the October 1983 restoration of the democratic forms after more than seven years of military rule, the call for punishment of the military for abuses gained enormous popularity. Radical Party leader Raul Alfonsin won the elections with 52 percent of the votes, defeating the historically predominant Peronistas. Italo Luder, the Peronista candidate, had shown little interest in having military officers tried for human rights violations, whereas

Alfonsin's fervent image had loomed large. Alone among Argentina's first-line politicians, Alfonsin had raised his voice against the regime's brutality and its invasion of the Falkland/Malvinas Islands. A cofounder of the Permanent Assembly for Human Rights,[61] Alfonsin had consistently stated his intent to try military personnel responsible for torture, rape, and assassination. This commitment seems to have had a decisive electoral result. In a political climate in which millions of new militants were ready to demand "trial and punishment to those responsible" of human rights' infringements, it proved magnetic. By the time of the elections, the cities were covered with crayon silhouettes, each one representing a disappeared person.

Confronted with intensifying demands for human rights trials, the generals attempted to secure impunity for their activities during the dirty war. In September 1983, a few weeks before the general elections, the military regime passed what was, in effect, a self-amnesty bill, the Ley de Pacificacion (pacification bill). In what the populace perceived to be a show of omnipotence, this *in extremis* law granted impunity to insurgents, the military, and police personnel who had been engaged in the repression of 1973–82.[62] Only a small number of insurgents benefited from this law, which suggests that its true aims had little to do with appeasement and a lot to do with self-preservation. The public did not miss the irony when a former general, Jorge Videla, the regime's first de-facto president, welcomed the new bill as an "an act of love." From the military's own point of view, the self-amnesty was untimely: some of the judges appointed by the regime itself dared, as they would probably not have done at a previous time, to declare the amnesty bill unconstitutional. It was forseeable that only a few judges would uphold the validity of the amnesty after the democratic authorities stepped in.

Several polls carried out in mid-1983 revealed that the

three most unpopular institutions in the country were the military, the police, and the Catholic Church, in that order. It was now clear that to distance oneself from the military was strategically beneficial and nothing was regarded as more contrary to the military than the issue of human rights trials. Alfonsin was the most prominent of its advocates.

ARGENTINA'S BRIEF SPRING:
NUNCA MAS

Raul Alfonsin stepped in on December 10, 1983. Before the end of December, he had instituted a series of measures aimed at probing and prosecuting human rights violators and providing redress for the victims. Soon after his inaugural, Alfonsin created the National Commission on Disappeared Persons (CONADEP) and charged it with investigating the fate of the disappeared. Headed by novelist Ernesto Sabato, the members of CONADEP were citizens of the most varied ideologies and occupations. Although unable to subpoena witnesses or compel testimony, the commission produced 50,000 pages of evidence, documenting the utmost brutality. After piecing together hundreds of testimonies, CONADEP's underequipped personnel dug out bodies buried in secret graves and photographed torture chambers at clandestine detention centers. In September 1984, CONADEP submitted to the president a detailed and widely read report, *Nunca Más (Never More)*. CONADEP recorded 8,961 cases of disappearances.[63] The commission's task, however, was limited to establishing the fate of the victims of repression: it did but did not supply the names of those responsible.

Perhaps the central plank of the Alfonsin government's program was the trial of those considered responsible for the campaign of disappearances, torture, assassinations, and rape. Alas, his administration and the general populace's vision was limited to the military. Putting the military on trial required considering the self-serving "Pacification Bill" as void from the outset. The judiciary nullified the bill,[64] thus rendering it legal to hold trials of human rights violations.[65] The president also proposed legislation to modify the military tradition in which officers were tried by military tribunals. He further established that future offenses by military personnel be tried by civilian courts, with the exception of disciplinary transgressions; the latter were exclusively delegated to the military tribunals. In the case of past offences, including those committed during the 1976–83 military rule, military tribunals were now to serve as trial courts, but the final judgment would be that of the civilian federal courts. Enacted by congress on February 9, 1984, this amendment of the military justice code gave military courts 180 days to complete each trial; an appeal to the civilian federal courts became mandatory.

The new legislation exculpated those who had acted under orders, unless they had exceeded the scope of those orders. The senate widened this exception by making "atrocious and aberrant acts"[66] into presumed excesses. This initial "due obedience" clause did not prevent prosecutions. Whether defendants had committed the punishable deeds could be established only by trial, on the merits of the case. The original official strategy was to have the judges convict only those senior officers who had designed the state terrorist campaign, plus the military and police personnel directly responsible for the worst infringements, such as assassination, torture, and rape.

The idea behind having military tribunals initially try their peers was twofold. First, it would help the totally discredited military to regain some prestige. The military would be cleansing itself. Military judges would have the opportunity to rid the armed forces of the worst transgressors. Second, it would contribute to the development of a set of standards for prosecution, thus averting random prosecution of the entire military. This expectation proved to be mistaken, however, since the military courts dithered. After indicting some of the members of the first two juntas, they later refused to pursue the cases. Eventually, cases of human rights violation were removed to civilian courts, but valuable time, and a reservoir of political support, had been lost. The families of the direct victims and the victims themselves criticized the government's policy. To express objection to intervention by military courts, most grievances were filed at federal courts, instead of at the military councils.[67] Although judicial intervention secured a minimum of impartiality, the military tribunals' refusal to take testimonies and to collect evidence were at least partially accountable for time lost.

In deciding who to prosecute, the government focused on the commanders of the three branches of the armed services—men who were accountable as members of the ruling juntas. In December 1984, the Federal Court of Appeals of Buenos Aires took over the conduct of the trials against the commanders. After a highly publicized five-month trial, the court convicted five of the six members of the two first juntas on numerous counts of torture, abduction, murder, and rape. The three members of the third junta were acquitted. The court sentenced Jorge Videla and Emilio Massera to life imprisonment; the other three commanders were given terms of sixteen, eight, and four years.

Although the courts had attributed the criminal design to unleash the witchhunt to the commanders, it was also clear that "somebody" had had to carry out the plan. But whether or not the generals had responded to the pressures of their juniors, the legal responsibility had been assigned: the federal court considered them to be the actual perpetrators, the main characters on the criminal scene.

This thesis was based on the notion that the head of the three services had total control over the country's state apparatus. Only criminal intent at the top could explain two facets of the dirty war: 1. That the campaign was nationwide; variations of intensity in time and venue did not detract from the fact that the methods used were indeed similar; 2. That death squad members felt certain no official agency would ever interfere with them.

It is obvious that none of the abductions and assassinations could have been performed openly without the commanders' acquiescence. Only consent at the top could explain operations performed in broad daylight and only yards away from police precincts. Only consent at the top could explain the lack of interference by the police or other military patrols. No member of the death squads was ever singled out to stand trial; the operations were never officially acknowledged.

The accused commanders attempted to justify the violence as being necessary to a state of war; moreover, it was a state of war in which the enemy was not easily recognizable as such. Among defenses invoked by the commanders were those of due obedience, self-defense, and necessity. In waging the dirty war, the generals claimed to have followed legal orders; namely, the two 1975 executive decrees signed by the provisional president ordering the armed forces to "annihilate subversion." President Luder's directives, the defendants claimed, had not only called on the military to quell insurgency; to *annihilate subversion* meant, according to the commanders, the physical extermination of insurgents. Self-defense thus consisted of protecting society from the illicit threat of subversion. The violence exercised by the armed forces was the appropriate reaction to avert a greater evil.

The federal court carefully dealt with every defense brought by the commanders. It is absurd, said the court, to seek to justify brutality by claiming that it stemmed from orders issued by civilians. The same administration that had been ousted (by the military) for being corrupt and devoid of minimal authority was now responsible for causing the brutality by issuing the order to "annihilate"? It was clearly unsustainable to claim obedience to the same officials that the culprits incarcerated shortly after the executive decrees were issued. Self-defense and necessity were found implausible defenses because their purpose is to justify the use of violence by *private citizens*.[68] It is private citizens who are entitled to resort to necessary defensive violence when the police—the state—is not present. The federal court took a shortcut in dismissing the defenses of necessity and self-defense: it claimed that the grounds for justification lay in the necessary use of the violence; the defendants, the court maintained, had never demonstrated that the brutality employed was necessary.[69]

The supreme court largely upheld the convictions. There were, however, a few exceptions: for instance, it lowered some of the prison terms and modified the legal qualification of the commanders' role. Instead of naming them as perpetrators, the supreme court convicted the commanders for complicity in felonies committed by their subordinates. Both the supreme court and the trial court refused to convict the members of the juntas for conspiracy or participation in the criminal deeds of their colleagues, as the prosecution had requested.

Out of some two thousand formal criminal complaints, the courts prosecuted only a handful for the kinds of abuses the commanders had been charged with. In December 1986, the federal courts convicted two army generals, Ramon Camps and Ovidio Riccheri (former chiefs of police of the Buenos Aires province), to twenty-five and fourteen years in prison respectively. Also charged with murder and torture were General Luciano Menendez, former commander of the Third Army Corps, and Admiral Ruben Chamorro, head of the Navy School of Mechanics, the country's largest torture center. The courts also had Lieutenant Colonels Jorge Acosta and Roberto Roualdes arrested, the former for abuses at the naval school, the latter for ruthless repression in the Buenos Aires area. Although indicted and placed under preventive arrest for murder, other officers, too, were never convicted. After a slow beginning, the trials of these officers were interrupted by the Full Stop and Due Obedience bills (see below, in this chapter).

Very few officers, in fact, were convicted. With the exception of the trials of the commanders, legal proceedings were extremely sluggish. Two and a half years after the first indictments for human rights abuses, few trials had gotten off the ground. There were two main reasons for this. First, the slow pace of an inquisitorial judicial practice and the large amount of proof and evidence required for a conviction in the Argentine tradition. Second, the system of first having the military tribunals try the cases. This caused systematic delays. Furthermore, conflicts of jurisdiction became inevitable obstacles. Some progressive, democratic judges felt they had a duty to thwart the intervention of the military courts, which, in their perception, had been given unreasonable privilege by the Alfonsin administration. In spite of the supreme court's ruling that the military tribunals were the competent trial courts, these judges decided to try human rights violators themselves, and their stance produced endless delays. Conservative judges, too, were a cause for the sluggishness: by dispatching cases to the military courts with no further supervision, these judges granted power to the military courts to immobilize the proceedings indefinitely. Behind such actions by these judges lay the conviction that, even if some of the military had performed atrocities, human rights abusers were not "real criminals"; rather, they were some sort of misguided patriot.

For many right-wing Argentines, the issue of human rights was strategic, not moral. Menem's air force chief of staff, for example, said the convicted commanders were patriots who acted "for the good of the country and the (armed) institutions."[70]

As time went on, the bulk of the military became increasingly opposed to the trials. Challenges to the administration from ultraright-wing sectors were expressed by bomb blasts and in threatening speeches nationwide. Even officers with clean records began to express solidarity with their comrades under indictment. Under pressure, in 1986 the government pushed through congress the Punto Final, or Full Stop. This law placed a limit on the time in which new complaints about crimes committed during the dirty war could be brought: the cutoff time expired in sixty days. Existing complaints would be considered moot unless the courts took some action during those sixty days. The result of the Full Stop was a flurry of filings of complaints by human rights groups and victims' families.

The new law, however, proved insufficient to quell military unrest. In April 1987, a group of young army officers, led by a lieutenant colonel, Aldo Rico, took over a military compound after an officer accused of torture sought refuge in a military unit rather than face questioning before a civilian court. The rebels demanded that the trials be halted and that the commanding generals (that is, those in command then, during the Alfonsin administration) be removed from their posts. Officers in the lower and middle ranks considered that, in allowing the civilian administration to bring subaltern officers to court, the generals had forgotten the basic loyalty owed to their juniors.

President Alfonsin ended what became an impasse by agreeing to speak with Rico at the rebel-held barracks. It was now clear to him and some of his close advisers that to continue the trials involved too great a risk. There were clear indications that the administration would have to enforce the courts' wishes if officers refused to comply with court summonses. To demonstrate their hostility, groups of officers, in uniform, gathered at train stations and airports to express solidarity with comrades traveling to give testimony before the courts. The situation was critical, especially so when it became doubtful that officers indicted by the courts could actually be brought for questioning. The government decided to counter the crisis by drastically limiting the trials. A few weeks after the Easter rebellion, the president sent to congress for rapid dispatch the draft proposal of what is known as the Due Obedience Bill. It was, in fact, a new label for a new amnesty law called Due Obedience that affected numerous officers, some convicted and some standing trial. This revised bill was aimed at appeasing the intermediate ranks, who felt they were the victims of the arbitrariness of the civilian administration. Young officers claimed that their superior officers—who had neither designed the dirty war nor committed torture, murder, or rape—were sleeping safely at home or were promoted. The perception that they bore the brunt of the dirty war for being directly involved in torture or rape was, they said, inconsistent with the true situation in a hierarchical organization. It did not make sense to hold them accountable for deeds performed while their superiors ate dinner in the room contiguous to the torture chamber. To straighten up this situation, the new initiative, soon to be enacted by congress, ensured that officers below the rank of colonel—and some even above that rank who were not chiefs of areas—would not be criminally prosecuted. It created an irrefutable presumption that lower-ranking officers were following orders and thus were not liable. The supreme court promptly upheld the law's constitutionality.

The Due Obedience Law, however, did not nearly satisfy the rebels. They now claimed that the government was instilling among the populace the notion that they were automatons—not selfless patriots—whose simple-mindedness had driven them blindly to follow directives from their superiors. To their minds, the civilian government was spreading antimilitaristic sentiments, instigating the media constantly to arouse contempt for the armed forces. It seemed to them that, instigated by the administration's officials, the constant disclosure of discoveries of mass graves and secret torture centers were being used as a means to humiliate the armed forces.

Military mutinies were not over. At the end of 1988, a charismatic army colonel, Mohamed Ali Seineldin, staged a third revolt against the army generals and the trials. He had promised his juniors that, without the generals, the army would stop the antimilitary campaign of humiliation. A fervent Roman Catholic, Seineldin had earned a soldierly reputation in the Falkland/Malvinas Islands war. In spite of considering Seineldin a potential hostile leader, the Alfonsin administration did not force him into retirement, as some advisors had suggested; instead, the minister of defense in the mid-1980s sent him to Panama, where he trained Noriega's elite forces for several years. Allegedly helped by Manuel Noriega, Seineldin managed to sneak back to Argentina to head the December 1988 mutiny.

Seineldin gained control of an army unit on the outskirts of Buenos Aires, and, again, the rebels demanded that the government stop its campaign to discredit the armed forces. They argued that the reason the citizenry had never recognized the army's role in quelling insurgency basically stemmed from the administration's constant disclosures—every discovery of a clandestine detention center was announced; every secret graveyard. The Alfonsin administration, they said, was also publicizing the human rights trials and conducting a campaign of ruthless condemnation of military cruelty and turpitude. In 1992, Colonel Seineldin told me he found it no coincidence that, of the multiple projects the Alfonsin administration had set out to achieve, only the trials of military officers were actually carried through.[71] As things stood, the winners of the armed battle against subversion were losing the "legal battle." As an army colonel stated at the Seineldin trials in 1991: "The radio was supposed to issue reconciliatory messages"[72] Instead, many officers believed that what the public was told deepened the tension. This perception was still strong among the military in the early 1990s.

Seineldin felt that the "honor of the armed forces" was being damaged by the administration's policies. The human rights policy had stimulated disputes between junior and senior ranks; it had also led to a generalized lack of loyalty on the part of superior officers, who were mostly ready to pass on their responsibilities to subordinates. Another aspect of "honor," to Seineldin, was the officers' ghastly financial situation. It was the first time in the country's history, he pointed out to me, that to make ends meet army officers were looking for additional sources of income.[73]

This new mutiny (December 3, 1988) generated widespread anger among the populace. This time, unlike in the Easter mutiny, when massive demonstrations against the rebellion were staged in front of the government house, crowds surrounded the barracks, to hurl stones and shout insults at army vehicles blocking the gate to the compound. Army officers, both rebel and loyalist, viewed the angry crowd as an evidence of armed subversion. Each side of the military interpreted the bellicose civilian reaction as a subversive maneuver to deepen feuds within the army.[74] At the Seineldin trials, a colonel (Toccalino—see below) described the ardent civilians as "Marxist hordes assaulting the military institution."[75] Another military witness at the trials said the presence of hostile civilians demonstrated once more that the populace was still reluctant to acknowledge that the dirty war had made peaceful coexistence possible."[76] Yet another officer attributed the appearance of civilians as "a plan well known to them," adding: "They [the subversives] were planning to penetrate the barracks to provoke bloodshed."[77]

Until the third mutiny, the military did not take rebellions very seriously. Evidence of this is Colonel Jorge Toccalino's deposition at the 1991 trial of Seineldin and his followers. In his deposition, Colonel Toccalino recalls that when he decided to follow Seineldin he requested permission from General (Luis) Gassino, who was his superior and, a few months later, the army's chief of staff. Toccalino expressed to the general his decision to join the mutineers by saying "the honor of the army is being defended [by the rebels] at the School of Infantry."[78] Instead of having the colonel immediately arrested, according to Toccalino's own version, the general hugged him and said: "Go ahead Toccalino, if that is how you feel."

The barracks—the Villa Martelli—were quickly surrounded by progovernment armored vehicles, but Seineldin surrendered only after days of deliberations between the two factions of the army. An accord limited criminal responsibility for the mutiny to the commanding officers; in exchange, the administration committed itself to endeavor to "restore the army's dignity"—whatever those words may mean.

Seineldin's arrest after the incident did not stop him from heading yet a further (fourth) revolt in early December of 1990, during the Menem administration. That time, the insurgents took over the barracks of an army unit within the city of Buenos Aires and the building of the army's chief of staff. Several civilians, conscripts, and officers were wounded and killed. But loyalist forces were by now determined to terminate the rebellions and they immediately responded to the president's orders to quash the rebels. Buenos Aires residents witnessed a flow of tanks and infantry troops converging on the rebels' buildings. Without any negotiation, the rebels surrendered. Within a few hours, the revolt was over. Seineldin and his men were tried and convicted for mutiny by the federal court in Buenos Aires. The conflict seemed to be taken seriously this time, and all the participants, including some noncommissioned officers, were convicted by the civilian courts.

Seineldin and his followers are still in prison for their December 1990 uprising. However, all other officers convicted or merely standing trial for their responsibilities in the dirty war, the Falkland/Malvinas Islands dispute, and the first three mutinies were pardoned, by two executive decrees issued by President Carlos Menem on October 6, 1989, and December 29, 1990. Given the vagaries of the political context in which the commanders were tried and sentenced, the question as to the value of the trials is still a matter of speculation today.

CHAPTER 2

SELF-SEALING
PROOFS

In July 1992, thousands of teachers, students, and parents staged massive rallies in Argentina's major cities to protest low wages and the government's drive to cut back on public funding for education. In response, President Menem startled the population by announcing that "subversion" lurked behind the demonstrations.[1] Menem also warned that parents involved in the protests could "become Mothers of the Plaza de Mayo."[2] These ominous statements were widely taken as a threat, reminiscent of the country's most authoritarian periods. Many people thought Menem was saying that if students and parents protested, the students might be abducted and assassinated. His words were heard as similar to those of the

1976–83 military dictatorship. The president's message, coupled with the memory of the nightmare of the 1970s, shocked the populace: demonstrations shrank to less than one-third of their former strength. Thoughtful Argentines saw the president's reaction to those opposing his educational policies as proof that it would be a complex task to dislodge the nation's ingrained authoritarian logic—the bipolar way of thinking in terms of "allies or foes." To jolt that bipolar logic is essential to a democratic system. Argentine society has not yet rid itself of it.

THE ORIGINAL
MISCONCEPTION OF SUBVERSION

The notion of "subversion"—the word Menem used to label the protesters—has a special weight in reflecting and explaining state violence in the 1970s. This concept, I argue, played a central role in expressing and in fostering the widespread intolerance that still pervades Argentine daily life. Since "subversion" is strongly linked to the "foes and allies" type of logic that has deeply influenced the country's domestic and foreign policies, its origin and implications merit a brief inspection. In this chapter, I set out to explain how the right-wing's use of "subversion" developed an environment in which

1. The existence of only allies and enemies was conceptually possible
2. Valid criticism was rendered logically impossible

After the downfall of Peron in 1955, the military committed itself to preventing the return of Peronismo and to thwarting foreign "subversion," a subversion that was not acknowledged to emanate from any particular country: it was a "country-less subversion."[3] In a country where the great majority of people were still Peronistas, the "doctrine of National Security" became the banner in the struggle against an international Marxist conspiracy that could easily mobilize large segments of a disheartened populace. With the emergence of the ERP and the Montoneros, the extremely vague references to "subversion" became more habitual and significant. Guided by the ideal of a socialist revolution, left-wing organizations frantically sought support from the Peronista working class and the disenfranchised. In the early 1970s, "subversion" and "the subversive enemy" became the official catchwords to single out society's mortal enemy. Repression was carried out not against "terrorists" or "insurgents" but against the looser category of "subversives."

The term *subversion* was introduced into Argentina's culture in the 1950s, not by ultraright-wing nationalist officers but by Carlos Jorge Rosas, who in those days was a lieutenant colonel with the reputation of having been one the army's most brilliant officers and a staunch democrat. In 1966, Rosas demonstrated his commitment to democracy. At the request of the civilian president, Arturo Illia, he agreed to head the country's armed forces, should it become necessary in view of a looming ultraright-wing military coup.[4] A few days after his meeting with President Illia, Rosas, now a general, died in a car accident driving back to Paraguay where he was serving as the Argentine ambassador. Rosas's car was reported to have crashed after skidding on an oil spot on a desolate provincial road. Many people suspect Rosas was eliminated by an ultraright-wing clique that a few months later appointed a fascist general, Juan Carlos Ongania, as de facto president after a bloodless military coup.[5]

In 1955, Rosas had returned from France with the innovative view that the new role of the armed forces should be to foil international "subversion."[6] A student of the French army's campaigns in Indochina and Algeria, Rosas had become convinced that rural insurgency would soon turn into the principal threat in the Southern Cone; accordingly, he believed that the army's fundamental mission was to protect the region against Marxist revolution. These concerns led him, as subdirector of the war college in 1957, to invite French officers to instruct Argentines in methods to counter "subversion."[7]

Thus, the term *subversion* came into Argentina as a consequence of conceived similarities between the French attempt to uphold their rule in Algeria and a future Latin American war against Marxist insurrection. In the Algerian conflict, subversion encompassed an entire population's belligerent attempt to overthrow colonial oppressors. In Argentina, some officers, with their eyes on a disheartened and thus easily seducible Peronista majority, found the analogy with Algeria to be striking.[8]

Rosas's views on subversion and the army's new professional role against it were confronted with two sorts of objections. The first was strategic. It originated among officers who, like Rosas's follower Augusto Rattembach, found no plausibility in the predicted emergence of a rural guerrilla war;[9] the absence of an Argentine peasantry (unlike the situation in other South American countries, such as Bolivia, Peru, and Ecuador) indicated that insurgency was likelier to take place in the cities.

The second objection, although mostly couched in strategic terms, was essentially ideological. An agnostic who believed the army's role to be essentially technical,[10] Rosas was opposed by the nationalist, Catholic faction of the army. Ideologically corporatist and closely linked to the Church, this faction thought that to counter subversion, the country needed the rule of a spiritual elite—one that would confront the Marxist threat with national harmony acquired by upholding the values of the Western Christian tradition.[11] The idea was not new. For example, the right-wing factions of the French army had had close links with an ultraright-wing group named the Cité

Catholique. Not himself an observant Catholic, Rosas was unconvinced that only superior ideals would preserve the army's integrity and discipline in a fight against subversion. The army's morale was particularly threatened when engaged in unconventional underground operations.

The struggle between clerical and secular factions ended rapidly when the leader of the Catholics, General Juan Onganía, was given control of the army. In June 1966, the pro-Ongania military removed civilian President Arturo Illia without any visible popular resistance. Colonel Horacio Ballester, member of the military group that opposed the dirty war and a staunch democrat, recalls his surprise. When the infantry regiment under his command encamped in downtown Buenos Aires, across the street from the government house, instead of finding a hostile crowd he and his soldiers were offered food by a friendly populace.[12] Perhaps as a consequence of this welcome, the generals went beyond simply replacing the civilian government: they humiliated President Illia, having the police usher him out of the government house to a taxi. The junta that took over immediately designated Ongania as de facto president.[13]

The democrats of the early 1970s did not realize, when they labeled as subversive those behind the bombs, assassinations of police officers, and abductions of industrialists, that it would imperil whatever was left of democratic conviction in Argentina. Unlike terms such as *terrorist* or *insurgent* that denote organized mayhem, *subversive* does not necessarily indicate violent activity. As some military officers who actively participated in the antisubversive campaign have now come to admit, subversion represented just the first step in a strategy of destabilization in which most actors, they thought, would later turn to sabotage and terrorism.[14] These army officers now acknowledge that the armed forces committed "grave mistakes" during the dirty war. It is now clear to them that some so-called subversive elements would never engage in violence, let alone terrorism.[15]

It is instructive to examine the different contexts in which the word subversion has been used—contexts that have no connection with insurgency or terrorism. By and large, the notion of subverting the order (or subverting a lifestyle) depends on ideological assessment. For instance, many years ago the word was used to describe the increasing power of the Roman Catholic Church and the subsequent erosion of the monarchy: "It may be truly affirmed that he [the pope] was the *subversion* and fall of that monarchy, which was the hoisting of him" (Milton). It was also used to censure political corruption by the wealthy: "Wo, worth these gifts! they *subvert* justice every where" (Latimer, 1549). It even served the purpose of conveying shifts in our understanding of the world: "This would *subvert* the principles of all knowledge" (Locke). When, in the eleventh century, Peter Abelard came under attack by the powerful Bernard of Clairvaux—when Abelard defended the supremacy of *reason* in the understanding of God and declared *diversa non adversa* (diversity is not aversion)—Bernard defined Abelard's posture as "a shameless *subversion*" by a "shameless inquirer."[16] Abelard's theology became the work of a "destructive intellectual" and a wicked "progressive" who took pleasure in befuddling the wits of the students and destroying their faith; gambling away the certainties of faith, which seemed fixed for all time.[17] In the main, as Popper points out, *subversion* has been an expression used by enemies of freedom—authorities who have almost always "succeeded in persuading the guileless and well-meaning."[18]

The adoption of the word to define the enemy in Argentina coincided with the introduction into the country of the French military notion of holding the line against a hostile populace. The term, as we shall see, had the direct effect of transforming the campaign against insurgency into a struggle against the entire population. We shall also discover that, for the authoritarian mind, a war against an enemy of such magnitude invites the use of terror.

THE ROLE OF LANGUAGE

IN THE STRUGGLE WITH SUBVERSION

It is widely accepted truth today that language not only expresses our perception of our social and political environment, but also shapes it. The fact that "traitors" are denounced much more frequently in authoritarian contexts than they are in democratic systems communicates something basic about the way citizens and governments view certain forms of dissent.* When we call somebody a traitor, the relationship between those we label and ourselves becomes radically different from the relationship that emerges from calling somebody an opponent or dissenter. When we use the word traitor (in place of opponent) we are not simply expressing intolerant feelings toward the

---

*Some words have a particular forcefulness both in depicting our views of how we relate to other people and in reinforcing preexisting views. These expressions have strong normative implications. Declaring our love and hate not only exposes such feelings but also explains our behavior toward the object of our feelings and commits us to adopt or keep a certain attitude. In the realm of political relations, words such as *treason, war, enemy,* and *coward* (and in the Argentina of the 1970s, *communist*) imply moral condemnation, and those who witness our utterances will see us as committed by them to be consistent. The fact that we call a certain person a *traitor* limits our actions in relation to this person. We don't deal with *traitors;* we do not compromise or negotiate with them.

In expressing our revulsion and calling someone a *traitor* we commit ourselves to destroying that person. Thus, labelling someone a *communist* or a *subversive* in the Argentina of the 1990s commits us to be hostile to that person. Like the language of *war* and *enemies,* that of *treason* and *subversion* places the listener in a special situation. If there are no reasons to contradict the speaker we, too, become committed to his cause.

Once the climate of *war* and *disaster* settles, calling someone *subversive* clearly commits the speaker to abhor and neutralize the danger the

target person or group; we are implicitly invoking the power of language to generate a new relationship.

If we think that the elocutionary force of a word determines our feeling toward the people we speak of, such thinking presupposes a linear, cause-and-effect approach. This approach to social relations conceals how our own language both expresses and *redefines* the way we relate to people and ideas. Does use of the word traitor determine our intransigence? Or does our intransigence compel us to call someone a traitor? I will assume that a particular relationship exists between ourselves and the language we use. The words we elect are, on the one hand, the expression of our character and, on the other hand, a reinforcement or validation of that character. When accepted by our interlocutors, words such as *spik, wog,* and *broad* not only testify to the speaker's chauvinistic character but also reaffirm this racist or sexist trait as an expression meaningful to others.[19] One may argue that not everybody using this rhetoric is convinced of its appropriateness, but this argument is relevant only in part. Whatever the speaker's convictions, his use of such words contributes to engendering a particular, bigoted milieu. The rhetorician becomes one participant among many. When we label somebody a traitor for having frustrated our expectations, we are not only expressing our intolerance; in the absence of a strong verbal protest, we are also establishing a bond with the listeners that will not allow for compromise.

Drawing on words such as *fatalism, acquiescence,* and *guilt,* Bateson (among others) explains how religion and

---

person incarnates in spite of the vagueness of the expression. Once we adopt the language of *treason* and *subversion,* we cannot minimize its significance. We cannot state that someone is a "little *subversive*" or "rather *treacherous.*" Being the enemy in a war addressed to preserve the country, the traditions, and so forth, such as *traitors* and *subversives,* places those who share the language ruthlessly to eliminate them and neutralize the effect of their activities.

other "mass agencies" like philosophy and art "determine our epistemology—our theories of the nature of the reality in which we live and our theories of the nature of the knowledge of this reality."[20] Thus, we call someone a traitor because we are reluctant to consider his views as those of an opponent with whom we are willing to compromise. But our utterances acquire their own independent force, thus reaffirming our intransigence.

This relationship between our choice of words and our notion of reality is better understood as follows: a nonlinear explanation, in which words forge our character and define the way we relate to our opponents, is one in which calling things in a particular way "causes" us to view them in a particular way. Such a relationship is one of correspondence, in which adopting a certain language both reflects our character and also promotes and enhances some particular features of this character.[21]

Intransigence had installed itself in Argentina long before the 1976 military coup. And extrapolated from the wars in Indochina and Algeria, the notion of subversion encompassed a vast and undetermined sector of the population. It encompassed even those who merely did not favor the cause of the crusade. Novelist Ernesto Sabato described the setting as early as mid-1977 as one in which society had polarized. "Lack of scruples and extreme prejudice are placing the country at a risk of sterilizing or killing (which are the same) its soul in its most vital and durable expression: the ideas, the fictions, the creative explorations of the spirit, from the scientist's laboratory, to the painter's workshop, to the desk of the poet".[22]

ARGENTINA'S SUBVERSION

In Argentina, between 1973 and 1983 "subversion" became an extremely manipulable concept that embraced all agents of social and political nonconformity. Take the navy's admiralty for example: in 1976, Emilio Massera, the commander-in-chief of the navy, made it clear that the real "subversive enemy" was in fact ideological. Said Massera: "Subversion is not only terrorist organizations, whatever their ideology, but also the ideological sabo- teurs."[23] Vice Admiral Luis Mendia, Massera's subordi- nate, went even further to state that the navy's struggle was against "the ideologues, the corrupt and unauthentic leaders, the irresponsible, the economic delinquents and the false preachers."[24] Other senior naval officers defined subversion as "psychological aggression in its attempt to corrupt other people and debase the traditional forms of our lifestyle."[25] Subversion, others added, was also hin- dering the country's economic takeoff.[26]

Thinking and speaking thus, the military and their al- lies were the epitome of what Karl Popper calls "histori- cists." For historicists, history is a purposeful process, the truth of which is only understood by the gifted,[27] and only those who understand the truth that underlies so- cial events can lead humanity in the right direction.[28] For this "humanoid" notion of society, history is an "ori- ented" succession of meaningful events, the laws of which, if discovered, turn the discoverer into a prophet.[29] Thus, once the truth is unveiled, or revealed, the world can be split into two camps. To the first camp belong those who follow the dictates of the revelation, those who contribute to the advancement of true values. To the second belong those who defy the prescriptions of history, who betray the commands of a meaningful fate made available through revelation. In the case of Ar- gentina, believers in these "true values" have had a long- standing tradition. The slippery dogmatic of Peronism added its share to this tradition in the 1940s and 1950s. As Sigal and Veron write: "If Peronismo is the enuncia- tion of the truth, how do we explain that some Argentineans do not follow this ideal?."[30] Although the content had changed in the 1970s, the approach continued to be the same. The "truth" was now certain Hispanic traditions and the Roman Catholic faith. For the most part, the truth was "anti-communism," defined in a hundred different ways in Argentina.[31]

In the eyes of officialdom, this sense of history was the advancement of Argentina's unity through the observance of Roman Catholic traditions that embodied the real, right sentiments of the citizenry, at that time threatened by international subversion. Space limitations make it impossible to provide the whole variety of conceptions that defined "subversion." For Videla, subversion meant "attacking and destroying the eternal values of "Argentinity."[32] Admiral Antonio Vañek declared that subversion was "blurring and concealing the *real* face of the nation."[33] For former admiral Ruben Chamorro subversion was "inculcating values contrary to our national feelings,"[34] meaning the Catholic traditions as conceived by Argentina's right-wing religious hierarchy.

In fact, what was called subversion had little to do with violence. The preceding discussion of the word shows that the definition went far beyond armed insurgency and terrorism. Moreover, "subversion" excluded clandestine organized violence by right-wing terrorists. Admiral Cesar Guzzetti, at one time the regime's minister of foreign relations, made it clear in a speech delivered in 1976 that subversion did not encompass right-wing terrorist organizations. These organizations, the admiral emphasized, "were only society's defensive anti-bodies acting against a disease that is eating its entrails. These defenses or anti-bodies should not be considered microbes."[35] It is obvious that, the Triple A, among others, was not to be included in the notion of subversion.

The dirty war was indeed a war on a vast sector of the population. It encompassed the elimination of those who "simply stood on the sidelines."[36] The regime's adoption of an indeterminate and apocalyptic view of subversion foreclosed the possibility of remaining neutral. War on a vast and undetermined enemy blurs the distinction between active and passive negation.[37] While active negation indicates our rejection of a postulate, passive negation does not. It simply indicates that, for whatever reason, we do not hold a certain proposition to be true. Passive negation does not manifest any particular purpose or desire; it conveys detachment from either being for or against a certain idea or event. It is different to assert that we believe some thing to not be true (which is active negation) and simply not to believe something to be true (which is passive negation).[38] This neutral stance may result from our lack of evaluation and ignorance of, indifference to, a certain proposition. Not content with the mere absence of active opposition, the military regime confused active and passive negation. Only active support could satisfy its exigencies. These exigencies were reflected in everyday life: students endorsed obligatory religious studies (namely, Roman Catholicism at school and, more specifically, Aquinas at the universities): students also sustained a healthy uniformity, wearing similar, sober attires. In the early 1980s, I applied for a fellowship at the country's official research institute (CONICET) and was interviewed by a bureaucrat who questioned me about a right-wing Roman Catholic group devoted to studies akin to mine. When I confessed that I did not share this group's ideals, the bureaucrat immediately asked: "Is there anything you have against Catholics?"

Ideologies purporting to stem from ultimate truths are usually considered peculiar to totalitarianism; however, they also characterize authoritarian systems such as the Argentine, which unlike the Nazis and the Fascists did not formulate a coherent set of principles. However, dictators are frequently obsessed with the fickleness of the populace and its vulnerability to ideological and charismatic seduction. In their *Theory of Human Communication,* Watzlawick et al. describe the phenomenon of conformity in totalitarian contexts: this characteristic is easily detected in totalitarian systems, in which the dictators are not content with mere obedience to reasonable, common-sense laws (which is usually all that democratic administrations are content with). The Argentine dictators, although often defined as merely authoritarian, wanted to guard the country—and not incidentally themselves—against popular left-wing contamination by attempting to control the populace's values and outlooks. Mere conformity is not only not enough; it is in itself considered to be a form of passive resistance, and even that particular form of silence that under Hitler was called "inner migration" becomes a sign of hostility. One may not simply put up with coercion, one must want it.[39]

THE OFFICIAL
BIPOLAR LOGIC

Insofar as the world is seen as one in which a wide conspiracy threatens to steal away the ignorant, the indifferent, and the reckless, the thin line between authoritarianism and totalitarianism wanes. In Argentina, the regime's confusion between *active* and *passive* negation increased the people's anguish. The process of equating ignorance and skepticism with positive opposition to the antisubversive crusade made neutrality (between state right-wing extremism and concocted "subversion") impossible. In the words of an army colonel, Jorge Muzzio, at a military ceremony in 1975: "When the time for speeches has passed, there are many compatriots that either ignore or are impervious to the fact that in an inhospitable jungle and in the intricate cities there are valuable Argentines to defend what is everybody's patrimony."[40] At times like the 1970s, evading reality, as the regime conceived of it, was clearly at odds with the conviction that ignorance and indifference to the political circumstances implies positive consent to subversion.[41] Positive principles are what is needed in a world in which the rulers are haunted by active resistance (active negation). The 1976–83 regime felt that only by instilling certain convictions among the populace could they claim actually to be defeating subversion. The regime was not concerned simply with averting and alleviating the citizens' misery and suffering; a world of allies and foes required positive principles to change—and eliminate—the "bad" and the "mad." Thus, the principles championed by the regime were positive—goals that were usually expressed as "meeting the Fatherland's fate," "recovering society's genuine values," "rescuing Argentinity," or similar lofty-sounding words (whatever their meaning. Only positive action to impose an entire way of life upon the citizenry could fulfill the demands derived from these principles. And once the ruler assigns to himself the right—and the burden—to effect change, the notion of an impartial and detached authority becomes hopeless.

Barrington Moore has an interesting way of posing the dilemma created by the demand for positive support on the part of political regimes that pursue goals that transcend the rather humble reduction of misery and suffering.[42] When these goals are rejected as too timid,

> there is no external authority to which one can effectively appeal in order to make that person, group or state desist from dangerous acts. Neither God, nor the alleged forces of history nor some presumably rational structure of the universe can serve as effective arguments or sanctions. Even if it were possible to demonstrate with mathematical certainty that a certain form of predatory morality and society would lead to the

extermination of all humanity, a cruel and romantic egoist could still snap his fingers in disdain and lead the march on to Armageddon, firmly believing that humanity deserved no better than destruction.[43]

After all, ultimate beliefs are inconsistent with the admission that some authority (exterior to the ultimate beliefs) can validly pass judgment on acts performed in the name of paramount ideals. If it did, we would have to conclude that there is more to the world than foes and allies.

When, as in Argentina, the situation is one of "if you are not with us you are against us," criticism is inevitably viewed as complicitous with—or potentially allied to—insurgency. As the National Commission on the Disappearance of People termed it:

> The epithet "subversive" had such a vast and unpredictable reach, the struggle against the "subversive" had turned into a demential generalized repression with the drift that characterizes the hunting of witches and the possessed.[44]

Nothing could come closer to the witch-hunt approach to reality than the Argentine military and civilian ultra-right. A good example was *Cabildo,* the publication widely read by the military. This anti-Semitic, pro-Nazi periodical stated that the abuses committed by the army were "the inevitable result of the war against guerrillas." Anyone who failed to acknowledge this fact "belonged to the 'vast, and subtle faction of the international left.'"[45]

The adoption of positive principles and the consequent need to teach the populace the "true values" has created millions of victims around the world. A regime's discomfort with the citizens' inadmissible passivity is impeccably illustrated by Kay Warren in her discussion of the Guatemalan army's refusal to accept the neutrality of the peasantry. After an insurgent attack on a village, the soldiers would show up and pursue the Mayan peasants living in the area. Their reasoning was simple: Why were the surviving peasants not the target of the subversive aggression? If the peasants were not the victims of the subversive attackers, it must have been because they were themselves subversives.[46] One may conclude that only positive support of the military would safeguard the peasants from assassination, torture, and incarceration.

In Argentina, what was termed subversion in this world of black and white, included criticism of the teaching of "moral formation," a subject that the regime's education authorities introduced into high-school curricula.[47] Subversion also included rehearsing the works of Chilean poet Pablo Neruda.[48] Most importantly, being indifferent to or unappreciative of the role of the military in the dirty war was itself treachery. "There are no ignorants," said Buenos Aires governor General Iberico Saint Jean, "there are only accomplices."[49] "Naivete and indifference are also complicitous, added another high-ranking officer.[50] Saint Jean publicly claimed that the country was full of traitors. In 1978, he made this point crystal clear by explaining a new variety of betrayal: "Only God and History are entitled to pass judgment on us. We must, as Christians, be ready to forgive, but to forget the responsibilities of each and every one of us would be treason to the Fatherland."[51] Saint-Jean was certainly not alone: many officials saw themselves pronouncing words similar to those of Colonel Hugo Pascariello, who on the occasion of paying homage to army predecessors solemnly declared (in a harangue delivered before Videla) that "not seeing or not wanting to see are the greatest offenses against God and the Fatherland."[52]

De facto President Jorge Videla illustrated the far-reaching implications of bipolar logic and the way in which it goes hand in hand with the notion of positive principles. Perplexed about being brought to trial on charges of human rights violations, the general conveyed his confusion in a written presentation to the court. He expressed his conviction that it was a logical impossibility to believe that one could do evil when fighting evil itself. In a written presentation to the court Videla said:

> Morally equating the Armed Forces that acted in the repression with the subversives who unleashed the war is morally, legally, militarily and politically unacceptable. This equation steals from us the reality of the history lived by our Country. It is immoral to equate violence exercised from both sides. First, because it is well known that there is a just and necessary repression; and second, because condemning the violator for the same reasons, and with the same intensity as the Marxist subversive terrorist implies equalizing defense with aggression, legality with illegality, a system of values with one of "disvalues." In condemning the military in the same way, they [the subversives] are justified in the same way. . . . Because of this distortion the image of the guerrilla has been safeguarded while the image of those who defended the nation is deteriorated.[53]

The notion that suppressing an evil may have been an evil in itself was inconceivable for an obdurate believer in bipolar logic. The world operates like a seesaw. You cannot make one end go down without lifting the other: praise of the military is condemnation of subversion; finding generals criminally responsible is enhancing the image of the subversives.

The view of subversion described above allows us to uncover several characteristics of the dirty war. The dirty war was waged against an undeterminate category— "subversives." This elusive enemy included progressive intellectuals, ideologues, sympathizers, the indifferent, and the shy. In taking for granted that credulous or ignorant people would fall into the clutches of subversives, the military waged war against so many citizens that in the warriors' minds, and subsequently in their actions, the campaign was comparable in size to the one waged by the French against the Algerians. Also with a French parallel, the use of the expression *subversive* to define the enemy had a decisive impact on the scope of repression. In fact, from the point of view of the military and the wider ultraright, it wound up reproducing in Argentina the same situation the French army confronted in North Africa. In a way, the very use of the word *subversion* became a self-fulfilling prophecy.

When an enemy is so equivocally defined as to include critics, the neutral, and the shy, a conspiratorial version of politics becomes inevitable. In the military's concocted reality, the world was an immense threat to their cherished institutions and values; one could not be too careful in a threatened world. Such a fear also becomes endless, as demonstrated by many military men and their civilian sympathizers after the 1985 human rights trials: if only the evil can condemn the good then, behind the trials, the Alfonsin administration's purpose must have been to destroy the army.[54] This antiinstitutionalism was, of course, in itself "subversive."

For the conspiratorial mind, the defense of supreme values and institutions justified massive violence, even at the cost of sacrificing innocent people. This ability to justify their actions generated a sanctimonious character, contemptuous toward their critics. When international organizations and foreign governments protested large-scale human rights violations, the military called this reaction the Anti-Argentine Campaign. Those who believed that something had to be done about the routine violation of human rights were understood to be playing into the hands of subversion. Human rights activists, domestic and foreign journalists, and politicians who protested against the regime were disdainfully labeled "the useful idiots."

BIPOLAR LOGIC AND
THE GAME WITHOUT END

By insulating themselves from criticism voiced by foreign and domestic organizations, the Argentine military made its view self-confirming. There was a plot, and parties to this plot were newspeople, politicians, and human rights organizations from all over the world. This conspiratorial worldview operated like a game that the players cannot bring to an end. When persons play a game in which no rules have been agreed upon for its termination, every attempt to terminate the game will inevitably become a part of the game, because it cannot refer to the game itself. Once the game has started, every rule the parties agree on to end or change the game will be part of the game itself; both agreement and rule are therefore unqualified to modify or terminate the game. If the parties have not previously agreed on how to express their desire "really" to end the game, the game becomes unending. The assessment of the effectiveness, validity, and morality of the system can be obtained only by attaching value to events external to the system. To make such an assessment entails that those involved are paying heed to evidence stemming from (outside) experience and a neutral authority.[55] In short, only opinions and data obtained from outside the system can supply valid information about the system itself.

SELF-SEALING PROOFS:
HOW THEY WORK

As just noted, the confusion of antagonism with indifference, of enmity with ignorance, and of resistance with shyness necessarily leads to a conspiratorial conception of the world; when such a numerous enemy is protected by anonymity, the world becomes a huge conspiracy. Conspiratorial suspicions usually lead to the closing of the mind as it looks for the smallest hints to strip the enemy of his disguise. Moreover, the mind becomes especially closed when the campaign is waged in the name of God and Christianity. This condition necessarily results in adopting "self-sealing proofs." A self-sealing proof consists of posing an allegation in such way that the one being questioned cannot help but confirm it. To secure confirmation, the denouncer interprets denial of his denunciation as precisely the behavior the denunciation is addressing. The inescapability of the "truth" of the accusation rests with interpreting rebuttals as a sign that the interlocutor is in some way an ally of the conspirators. "Witches exist and only a witch can deny their existence" is an example of this approach. Although our interlocutor is given the option of disagreeing, this option is illusory because only witches, plotters, and subversives would dare contradict the speaker.

Self-sealing proofs often result from a particular way of looking at reality. They are based on taking for granted the correctness of a judgment as one deduced from an ultimate belief, the validity of which lies beyond discussion. Most dirty warriors privately claim, for instance, that their motives sanctified the brutality they resorted to. In consequence, disapproval of the dirty war can be the consequence only of a negligent mistake or bad will. Only turpitude, indifference, or malice could explain opposition to the dirty war. When we hold that ultimate truths justify our actions, we are caught in a game without end. As in games without end, the postulates espoused by the dirty warriors makes them impervious to experience and therefore beyond the possibility of rectification and correction.

For the logic of "friends and foes," there is simply no room for authoritative judgments stemming from emotionally detached and impartial people and institutions. Or worse still, it becomes impossible to conceive that the consequence of implementing a certain conceptual system or a doctrine could be wrong. The dogma becomes self sealed[56] and the players will admit to having been wrong only in that they may not have applied the doctrine radically enough; only "more of the same" could improve their performance. Compound this with the win-or-lose proposition implied in the war rhetoric derived from the doctrine of national security, and Argentina is ripe for bloodshed. To use the words of the gendarmerie's commander, Agustin Feced: "We will not engage in dialogue only with them [the subversives] because we have arrived at a synthesis: no more words! just defeat and annihilation."[57]

History provides us with many examples of self-sealing proofs. Persecutions and purges performed in the name of ultimate political or religious beliefs have usually been the consequence of seeing the world this way. The witch-hunters described by Tomas Szasz are the epitome of the deleterious effects of "self-sealing proofs".

As the Argentinean military of the 1970s demonstrated, "conspiracies" are often conceived in ways such that discussing the existence of a plot itself confirms the conspiracy. The dirty war soldiers did not content themselves with pursuing a concrete, tangible goal, such as protecting the citizenry from bomb blasts or abduction; in the name of God, they endeavored to eradicate evil. Thus, the conception that only a strong religious formation could save the army from contamination in the dirty war led the military into a perverse situation—one in which experience did not offer the possibility of change. There was no external, impartial authority. "Our mission was to fight against evil," an army officer explained to me in 1993.[58] If dissent, apathy, ignorance, and indifference constitute "evil," as military officials repeatedly emphasized in the 1970s, they were thus trapped in a self-contained system of belief—in the game-without-end dilemma. Like the players who cannot end the game for lack of an external rule, antisubversive warriors could find no limit to their crusade. Argentine authoritarianism was in many ways indistinguishable from totalitarianism.[59]

Many religious zealots are unable to admit dissent and criticism without weakening their perception of the consistency of their belief. In his account of the persecution of witches, Thomas S. Szasz exposes the deductive tack adopted by the fifteen-century inquisitors to reject criticism. Quoting the Dominicans Kraemer and Sprenger, Szasz says: "The belief that there are such beings as witches is so essential a part of the Catholic faith that to obstinately maintain the opposite opinion manifestly savors of heresy."[60] In brief: "To question the existence of witches is itself heretical [thus witchlike].[61] Thus, only one conclusion is acceptable: Witches exist. Either one may agree that there are witches, or one may attempt to deny their existence, thus proving oneself to be a witch. By this token, in the Argentine context only the agreement that the regime was (positively) saving the nation—the position of ultraright-wing groups—would secure immunity.

It now follows that fanaticism can be characterized as being generated by systems of belief closed to experience and to impartial authority. The concept is thus applicable to a range of spheres of social life—from the scientist who refuses to recognize contrary evidence to improve his research to the burning of witches during the Spanish Inquisition, and to most forms of totalitarianism. Fanaticism and the conspiratorial conception of the world that accompanies it can be identified at all levels of analysis.

For the Argentine right, the dirty war was a just war, one in which gaining victory was worthwhile even at the expense of the lives of thousands. Videla made this point clear at the Eleventh Conference of American Armies, held in 1975 in Montevideo. "We will achieve the security of the country regardless of how many die in this pursuit,"[62] he asserted. An even more sadly memorable speech came from General Saint Jean, governor of Buenos Aires, who said: "We will first kill all the subversives; later, we will kill those who collaborate with them; then we will kill those who remain indifferent and, finally, we will kill the shy."[63]

To elaborate further, conceptions of the world that are closed to the influence of external reality are usually removed from discussion because, once the belief is adopted, the basic premises become self-evident. Differing views necessarily disqualify the disbeliever altogether.[64] Self-righteousness becomes inevitable, as shown by the Timerman case, in which the courts (including the military tribunals and the country's military-appointed supreme court) could not induce high-ranking military officers to release Timerman, a journalist and owner of the Buenos Aires newspaper *La Opinion.*

In spite of Timerman's advocacy of the military regime, he too, had become a target of the dirty war. He had claimed that the regime had been unjustly targeted by human rights organizations and the foreign press,[65] but this did not exempt him from becoming an enemy of the dirty warriors. Timerman's ordeal was unleashed by accusations by the pro-Nazi publication *Cabildo.* Timerman, it said, had had financial dealings with the Montoneros. *Cabildo* also claimed that *La Opinion* was modeled after *Le Monde,* "the daily bible of our intellectual bolcheviques in Paris";[66] the *Washington Post* was equally pernicious, according to *Cabildo.* However, the lunacy of the allegations did not save Timerman.

In early 1977, in consequence of *Cabildo's* accusations,

an army commando team abducted Timerman from his home in the middle of the night. Unlike many abductees, Timerman was not assassinated, perhaps because of a fear of a major international scandal: the journalist had personal connections in Israel and the United States. He was sent to trial before civilian and military tribunals, which acquitted him of all the charges. Thus, with no legal reason for holding him in captivity, General Videla declared Timerman a threat to the country's security under the terms of the state of siege.

What followed is perhaps the best example of the military's self-righteous obduracy. The suspicion remained that, beyond the courts' "formalities," Timerman was guilty of subversion, even though a judicial bureaucracy would not have him convicted. When Genaro Carrio, Timerman's lawyer, filed a plea of habeas corpus and the supreme court requested the president to explain the reasons for the journalist's captivity, the response left the court with no option but to order the prisoner be set free. As the executive explained, Timerman's captivity was based on counts identical to those on which his acquittals were pronounced.[67] Neither the evident reasons supporting the supreme court's decision nor the international clamor that the case provoked in the United States and Western Europe[68] affected the generals' persistence; at a meeting held to decide Timerman's fate, most of the generals voted against his release. Only after threat of international sanctions against the regime compelled Videla to order his release was Timerman freed—still against the opinion of the majority of the generals. Timerman was not to be allowed to leave the country without further chastisement, however: he was stripped of his adoptive Argentine citizenship.

The release had been the culmination of a furious battle between Videla and an enraged generalship. Only when Videla and the entire supreme court threatened to resign, did Timerman's wardens, Generals Suarez Mason and Camps, agree to comply with the order of release.[69] Still more stubborn, Third Army Corps commander General Benjamin Menendez attempted a coup against his own comrades.[70] Although Menendez's coup failed for want of support, the case illustrates the total rejection of a moral and legal authority that consisted, in this case, of judges that the de facto regime had itself appointed. The Timerman case was among the clearest examples of fanaticism.

Authoritarian regimes are likely to generate self-sealing proofs. They tend to operate on the assumption that any criticism, however moderate, represents a blanket opposition to everything they stand for. International criticism, regardless of the authoritativeness of the source, was considered to be an intentional plot; at best, it was an inadvertent alliance with subversion. Subversion was now using its power to entice foreign governments and organizations into destroying the military regime and its supporters. In 1979, Guillermo Suarez-Mason, then a general and army chief of staff, declared to the press that it was international Marxism that was raising protests against Argentina, although worldwide "some useful idiots" were playing into the Marxists' hands.[71] Enumerating the environments in which subversion was still present, the general included religious, political, educational, economic, cultural, and labor areas.

When in 1977 Amnesty International dispatched a three-member commission, it was treated as a prosubversive interloper. An obsequious Argentine press highlighted the fact that Lord Averbury, one of the three envoys, wore a red tie, calling it a symbol of unconfessed Marxist convictions.[72] Averbury and his colleagues Patricia Feeney and Robert Drinan were persistently queried about their "selectiveness" in singling out Argentina: why weren't they investigating abuses in the Soviet Union or Cuba? Robert Cox, the *Buenos Aires Herald*'s valiant editor, noted that

Amnesty had drawn not only animosity from the official sphere (which could have been counted on) but also bitterness from the population at large.[73]

Amnesty's report about human rights violations met with an angry reaction from the authorities. From the regime's standpoint, Amnesty had been infected by international Marxism. The commission was being used by the subversive anti-Argentina campaign. A foreign ministry communique declared that "we have finished with trying to get Amnesty to understand our situation." Army General Fermin Ochoa published a "revelation" of the real nature of human rights organizations: "Amnesty International," he said, "was carrying out on a global scale the incarnation of a Marxist campaign that seeks to hinder relations between the Old and New Worlds."[74]

Similar negative reactions came with the September 1979 visit by the Inter-American Commission on Human Rights (IACHR). At the prospect of the commission's visit, one of the army heads exhibited how deeply ingrained self-sealing proofs had become among the military top brass. Guillermo Suarez-Mason, the army chief of staff, thought that for the commission to make a loyal, negative report was a logical impossibility. Only those who had nothing to hide would agree to inspection by members of human rights organizations. That members of the IACHR were being allowed to visit Argentina was the best evidence of the government's integrity and peace of mind. It was a "demonstration of what the country is and that the outcome [of the inspection] should be positive. I am not sure that it will work out that way, but that is the way it should be."[75] Thus, for the regime's logic, the commission was left with the choice of drafting a "positive" report or betraying its host's goodwill. This reasoning resembles the logic of the rabbi who claimed he had talked to God. When somebody accused him of lying, the rabbi responded: "Would God talk to a liar?"[76]

Local newspaper headlines asked of the IACHR visit: "What are they looking for?" Most cars and trucks in Argentina's main cities bore stickers (distributed by the police) that mocked the issue of human rights. The stickers displayed an Argentine flag and the words, "We Argentines are Right and Humane."

In this climate, the IACHR team conducted numerous interviews; notably, Tom Farer visited several prisons.[77] The answer to the team's report might have been anticipated: the world had many "useful idiots" instrumental to left-wing subversion.[78] This kind of allegation appealed to nationalism and managed to distract public attention from the recognition that the reports issued by Amnesty and IACHR were, in fact, true.

The fiction that an anti-Argentine campaign was poisoning world opinion against Argentina sank deeply into the national mind. "Denunciation" had become a dangerous new political tool. Conveying the official view, the May issue of *Siete Dias*, one of the most popular Argentine magazines, observed: "Using denunciation as one of its main political tools, Argentine terrorist organizations have invested their efforts in the creation of institutions to serve them in attaining their main goals: to accuse the ruling government, whatever it may be, of being repressive and of violating human rights."[79] A list of names was affixed to the article. They were the members of a vast organization that the military labeled as the "Anti-Argentine Network." Among members of the organization were François Mitterand, Willy Brandt, and Felipe Gonzalez.

As perhaps could be expected, this aversion to criticism spilled over to all areas of political life. After the Falklands/Malvinas fiasco, the armed forces appointed a Commission of Analysis and Evaluation. Its purpose, according to the founding executive decree, was to establish what had happened—"The aggrieved national sovereignty and the dignity of Argentina so demanded." To give the commission maximum authority in the armed forces, the decree named as head of the commission Lieutenant General Benjamin Rattembach, probably the most prestigious officer in the army.[80] Interestingly, the commission's report mentions Argentina's diplomatic blunders—in particular, the regime's reluctance to abide by UN Security Council resolution 502, in which Argentine forces were ordered to withdraw from the islands while Britain and Argentina sought a peaceful solution to the conflict.[81] Foreseeing that the Rattembach Commission would judge those involved with severity, the military regime ordered the members of the commission to keep their findings top secret. The report was indeed stringent: on September 16, 1983, the commission recommended that the commanders of the army and the navy, Admiral Jorge Isaac Anaya and General Galtieri, be executed. The commission found that the military junta had led the country into a war without adequate preparation, thus "placing the country and its armed forces in a critical situation." In 1986, the supreme council sentenced the two commanders to prison terms, and in October 1988 a federal court upheld the convictions. The commanders were eventually pardoned in a 1989 decree by Carlos Menem.

The story of the Rattembach Report is in itself interesting. In 1984, a naval officer sued Rattembach in connection with the document. The general recovered his copy (to present it as evidence at court) and subsequently refused to turn it in. The "secret" report was later published by a civilian group, which managed to lay hands on it. After General Rattembach's death, and in accordance with his wishes, his wife refused to return the report to the government, despite ceaseless requests, first by telephone and later during visits made by military officers. A few weeks later, the widow's house was furtively searched; her telephone began to ring in the middle of the night, haunting her with death threats.[82]

In fact, the report would have improved whatever prestige the post-Falklands/Malvinas army may have had left, because it singled out those responsible for the catastrophe, with its human suffering and national embarrassment. The report's official version, however, was never made public.

CHAPTER 3

TERROR

After the regime's leaders concluded that the enemy was "subversion," winning the war became an overwhelming task. Not only were the rival forces extremely difficult to identify and detect, given their many faces, they also possessed the ability to expand and regenerate. Except for the few citizens who stood beyond suspicion, all members of society were seen as vulnerable to the inviting advances of this enemy with infinite shapes. All were therefore potential subversives. "Utilitarians," "contractualists," "positivists," and "Freudians" were named as kinds of subversives by 1976–83 officials. In impassioned speeches they defined threats to Argentina's traditions. And terror became the regime's principal political tool.

WHY TERROR?

Once it is established that the survival of basic national values depends on destroying the opponent, terror becomes the only feasible solution. The use of extreme and random violence is an economically expedient approach to controlling the population. Terror does not demand the collaboration of a large number of loyal civilians, as would resorting to the judiciary to enforce explicit rules. In fact, the new judiciary, whose members had been appointed by the regime, may well have been, like members of other institutions, contaminated by subversion. Unpredictable brutality isolates individuals; it destroys people's communications networks. It eliminates individuals' capacity to organize themselves, thus making concerted opposition impossible. Given the premises on which the military assessed their mission, terror was the logical mechanism to use.

I have briefly explained how violence pervaded Argentine politics in the early 1970s and the way in which, after the March 1976 takeover, the military regime intensified violence by increasing abductions and assassinations and by systematically using torture. I have also described how this violence targeted the most varied sectors of society, affecting most significantly those segments that could mobilize resistance: labor unions, factories, high schools, universities, professional organizations, and the mass media. This method effectively disarticulated society.

The terrorism, being anonymous, also furthered the provision of formal camouflage for state violence.[1] However well grounded the accusations against the junta, the regime could always disclaim responsibility for brutality, giving room for diplomats to try to convince international bureaucracies and foreign administrations that they should ignore the truth.[2]

In a conversation I held with a former Venezuelan president, Carlos Andres Perez, he described to me his frustration when he attempted to protect Venezuelans who had been clandestinely abducted by Argentine death squads. Perez recalled how he called de facto President Jorge Videla to protect his compatriots from torture and assassination. An apparently embarrassed Videla revealed that, in spite of unofficially knowing about the abductions of the Venezuelans, there was nothing he could do. There was no way of knowing who had performed the abductions, nor the victims' whereabouts.[3] Videla made it clear that officially he did not even know about the disappearances.[4]

It was not only the clandestine nature of the military operations themselves that kept them secret; there was a parallel necessity to control the press. At a meeting held at the government house press office shortly after the coup, the regime's officials instructed editors and media owners about the dangers of an "irresponsible press." At this brief and somber meeting, they warned the media not to assist the cause of subversion: not to provide untimely accounts; and not to disfigure reality with partial versions of events that could weaken the antisubversive campaign.[5] The public, they said, should not be informed on sensitive topics, such as "information or comments on subversive episodes, the finding of bodies, kidnappings, disappearances, the death of seditious elements and the assassination of military personnel."[6] The regime wanted a "responsible press," a subdued press. To prove how serious they were, in April 1976 they killed several journalists, among them a photographer for the prominent (pro-regime) magazine, *Gente*. In May, Zelmar Michelini, a former Uruguayan minister of education working as a journalist in Buenos Aires, was abducted and murdered.[7] Maximo Gainza, who at that time was owner of the conservative Buenos Aires newspaper *La Prensa*, recalls a meeting with the navy's commander, Emilio Massera, in which the latter reminded

him of the importance of discretion. With the obvious purpose of intimidating Gainza, Massera said he had killed
several people "with his own hands."[8]

As a consequence of the regime's threats, a press that
had been formerly cautious fell into deep silence over-
night. Only the English-language *Buenos Aires Herald,* supported by the British and U.S. communities, dauntlessly
provided information (and even then it was a minimum).
After a while, *Herald* columnist Robert Cox became a victim of state abuse: a barrage of threats against his life and
that of his wife Maud compelled him to leave the country.

One might believe that silencing the press was a means
to keep the population unaware of the dirty war. But no;
stealth and terror are incompatible. Terror requires that
the populace be paralyzed by the evidence of brutality.
Thus, people learned about the ongoing violence with a
sense of unreality, as in a dream.[9] The presence of violence was exposed for everyone to see: unmarked cars
prowling major cities, with men brandishing shotguns
and Uzis, were a clear enough message. By 1977, there
was barely a citizen who had not either witnessed men in
plainclothes dumping a bloodied victim into the trunk of
a car or heard firsthand stories from a relative, close
friend, or neighbor about someone who had been taken
away.

State-sponsored violence was deliberately too obvious
to allow for ignorance. The army frequently set up road
blocks and few people felt beyond suspicion when all the
occupants of a car were ordered to get out, targeted by
three or four shotguns while an officer quizzed the trav-
elers. It seemed that there was something about us that
the interrogator would inevitably discover.

There was also needless, but ominous, deployment of
military forces. When the army went to detain Roberto
Bergalli, three trucks loaded with soldiers surrounded the
block in the suburban Buenos Aires residential area where

he lived with his wife and daughter. It was known to all that Bergalli had never possessed a firearm in the few months he had been in Argentina after a two-year sojourn at the German university of Cologne.

In a subliminal way, everyone knew that the Naval School of Mechanics, a monumental complex that sits on one of the main Buenos Aires thoroughfares, was a vast concentration camp where hundreds of prisoners were tortured. Not even apologists for the regime would have contested that the role of Army Intelligence Battalion 601 was to hunt down suspected political activists. The battalion is headquartered in one of the most visible areas of downtown Buenos Aires and the steel doors and shuttered windows of the unit's building awaken the curiosity of the most indifferent passersby. A sense of the violence that was happening was conveyed in many ways and stories of torture and disappearances inevitably came up in intimate conversation. The atmosphere of terror pervaded most sectors of society.

The regime dispensed measured access to the brutality. The tamed press would sometimes disclose gory events to remind society that unchecked violence was ever present. On August 21, 1976, the pro-official Buenos Aires newspaper *La Nacion,* for instance, revealed that workers in the suburbs of Buenos Aires had heard an explosion and subsequently discovered thirty corpses, mutilated to the point of unrecognizability, lying by the railways tracks.[10] The newspaper reported:

> It was established that twenty of the bodies belonged to men and eight to women. Not every victim's sex could be established because the bodies had been completely torn apart. It is presumed that, prior to the explosion, they had had their hands tied and had been exterminated with heavy gunfire. . . . The Ministry of the Interior has issued a communique confirming the discovery of the thirty corpses.[11]

Similarly, on July 3, 1976, another obeisant newspaper, *La Razon*, reported that a man had been driven to the Obelisk, in the middle of Buenos Aires, and there shot down. "The perpetrators," *La Razon* continued, "fled in the same car."[12] It is clear that these disclosures were ordered by the regime; neither *La Razon* nor *La Nacion* would have otherwise dared defy the government's injunction not to reveal insurgent activities or the deaths of "seditious elements or military personnel." Brutality had to be ever present, and to be seen to be ever present.

One of Argentina's most prominent human rights activists, Emilio Mignone, recalls a conversation in 1978 with Colonel Roberto Roualdes, the executive head of the repression campaign in the Buenos Aires zone, in which the officer flatly admitted that thousands of innocent people would be mercilessly killed: "I will consider the procedure successful if five terrorists fall for every hundred that we kill", the colonel unflinchingly admitted. After all, he continued, "Truman made no distinctions when he ordered his forces to drop the bomb in Hiroshima." To which Mignone replied: "But Truman signed a written order."[13]

Living with Terror

During this period (1976–80), people were linked in bizarre ways: the most remote connections could have a tragic bearing on people's lives. As if it were a tragicomedy, there were often ironic overtones. In 1975, during the Isabel Peron administration, a political detainee I visited in prison told me that one of his cell companions was a painter formally held as a threat to public security because he happened to be working at the house of a suspect when the police arrived. Cases like this became more frequent after 1976, by which time there was a general sense that few people were safe from random repression. For most citizens, there was no way to know who would be targeted next: decisions were made in the utmost secrecy and the variety of targeted persons was so great that there was no discernable pattern.

Clandestine action and secrecy in a terrorist state split the world into two: there is a realm peopled by the very few who are in power, who can make life and death decisions, with the addition of those close to them; and there is a second realm, in which people are left to guess how and when brutal force will be administered. In a world in which disinformation and confusion run rife, this second group inevitably holds widely varying versions of reality, because these versions are based on the array of assumptions individuals make in their quest to make sense of what is happening around them. The mind cannot operate in a vacuum.[14] It strives to assign meaning to events; to establish an order that will enable it to plan ahead by anticipating what might happen. On the one hand, the mind needs to discover the "rules" on which life and death decisions are made. On the other, it has to select information in order to make life tenable. In a terror state, these two aspects of the mind's functioning are given a unique task.

In a state with secret death squads, there are few clues on which to build a mental order and the few there are are ambiguous. To build a mental order, individuals depend on signals to which they can attach value. Some Argentines found these clues by reading between the lines of official speeches; others relied on the constant flow of gossip, the truth of which they sometimes took at face value; for others, it was photos of official events that revealed what was going on (for instance, one might obtain political information from the expression of some officials or from observing who was next to whom during a ceremony). The peculiar reality of a terrorized society is that it becomes difficult to distinguish genuine sources from those that people *want* to listen to. In 1982, everyone knew that the newspapers were lying about the developments of the Falkland/Malvinas Islands war—yet newspaper sales surpassed all previous records. Most people were attracted to what they wanted to be told; thus, the most sensationalist, mendacious sources of information sold widely, even among people who usually despised them for their poor ethical or critical standards.

In such a context, to attempt to penetrate the darkness in which the state apparatus operates we develop our own explanations of what goes on; we envisage a set of rules that, we believe, will help us avoid pain and death. In this anguished process, the hints we select are largely aimed at satisfying our hopes or confirming our fears. In establishing an order, our mood becomes an essential ingredient. Thus, we jump to conclusions on the bases of the first hint that will match our preconceptions, our desire to soothe our anguish.[15] In this process of making our reality, we sharpen our senses to grapple with what otherwise would be widely considered the most insignificant details.[16] Our own beliefs often become contradictory: we may repudiate someone (a police officer, for instance) for his justification of torture and yet accept his protection, even though this entails developing an affection for him. In cases like this, our contradictory feelings often serve the purpose of avoiding the shame of receiving favors from those we hate.[17] In the Argentine case, these contradictions often consisted of joining the oppressor at national rituals. These rituals included common expressions of rejection of human rights investigation to celebrating victories at soccer.

In the pursuit of order, the mind finds explanations in infinite minutiae, inferring causal connections that would never be seen as relevant in a less confusing situation. Paul Watzlawick illustrates this point with the example of the so-called multi-armed bandit. The subject of the experiment is left alone in a room, facing the "bandit," a circular dashboard with sixteen buttons. Without being given further information, the subject is instructed to find the "right" buttons and is told that an alarm will go off each time the right button is pressed. After a while, the subject of the experiment invariably comes up with an answer as to how the "system" operates. He has developed a set of rules that provide a solution. When told the system is a fabrication, because the alarm goes off randomly, at the experimenter's discretion, the uniform reaction of subjects is to deny this revelation and insist on the validity of their "discovery" of an underlying order.[18]

The similarity between the subject in Watzlawick's experiment and a community under terror is patent. Unable to bear the anguish of capricious brutality, we attempt to overcome our confusion and disinformation by formulating explanations; these themselves become new sources of confusion and disinformation. An adaptive reality replaces our internal chaos. This reality, however, little resembles the actual rules and criteria that guide state terrorism. Furthermore, because it is a largely personal fabrication, our reality cannot be shared with others. Interestingly, it was a common event in the Argentina of the early 1990s to find oneself among people who never admitted their lack of information about a given topic. Their usual reaction to their own ignorance was to concoct a convoluted theory. In the process, the most trivial issues became the center of complicated arguments.

In the terror period, those who, for whatever reason, felt they were likely targets of state violence, confronted a second quandary: did they or did they not truly want to *know* what was real? While, on the one hand, life becomes unbearable without minimal understanding of what is happening around us, our suspicions may at times become too painful to endure. Trying to deal with our confusion, we may be confronted by a dilemma—a situation in which the options are so dreaded as to make choice itself untenable. To surmount this quandary, we endeavor to create a livable order by believing what our selective information processing allows us to perceive. In this context, people cling to an array of hints—sometimes contradictory—that acquire meaning only in a context in which fear and confusion are paramount.[19] In 1992, a former left-wing militant told me how she managed to disengage herself from comrades who had been murdered or made to disappear. Although she had campaigned with them in factories, and sometimes shared the same hideouts, she also thought she had certain characteristics that were not common to the group; she would survive by using those elements. However flawed her reasoning, her strategy worked.

A Personal Story

In 1977, I learned through a very reticent acquaintance that I had been included on one of the army intelligence service's blacklists for petitioning the courts for the release of political prisoners Roberto Bergalli and Juan Bustos Ramirez. My informer, a state prosecutor, had learned about my situation through his links with the police. The fact that merely warning me could disgrace him before the regime made him extremely cautious. Reluctant to elaborate further, he suggested that I learn about my situation by immediately contacting somebody within the military. I refused to react.

A few months later, midnight telephone death threats began. It was an intriguing experience. I was thrown into a desperate mental search to discover not only who could want me dead, but also who I was in reality, because my imagined assassination could not fit into my own notion of my identity. Suspecting that a hint was waiting to be discovered, I began to search my past for clues. That search rapidly became an obsession that depleted me of energy and confidence.

In such situations, one is forced to confront a tormenting form of the dilemma outlined above. Remaining ignorant of the meaning of certain threats becomes untenable, but seeking information from those whom one assumes will know the answer has serious weaknesses. Indeed, to convey such fears to state officials may become—one speculates—a self-fulfilling prophecy: that for those trapped in a self-seeking-truth, fear will be viewed as an admission that we are politically involved and thus actually worthy of suspicion. A friend advised me to seek protection from General Juan Sassiain, the chief of the federal police, whom he knew. But I suspected, as many others did, too, that Sassiain himself was involved in the disappearances. I dismissed this alternative, since contemplation of its dangers only increased my anxiety. It brought back the image of *The 39 Steps,* the movie in which the hero discovers to his despair that the judge to whom he reveals the existence of the macabre plot is actually the mastermind behind the criminal intrigue.

I found a way to appease my fears by positioning my suspicions in a personal experience I concocted. This ploy—which involved believing that someone had tried to terrorize me on account of a personal grudge—allowed me to carry on with my life, although not without difficulty. It was a total fabrication. It seems quite obvious, now, that most likely the people who were threatening me were not just anybody: they knew too much about me. They were "officials"—well-trained operators who could have gathered the information only through wiretapping and constant surveillance. There was no other way that they could know so much about the smallest details of my everyday life. Today, the experience seems indeed instructive: these are the ways we cope with terror.

As my own story shows, the suspicion that, for the most whimsical reasons, we may become targets for torture and assassination is, as Kay Warren explains, an indescribable experience—one that leads to isolation.[20] Reluctant to bear our sense of complete impotence and to understand what we dread, we desperately strive to overcome the senselessness of terror by *discovering* explanations. As the Sabato commission points out in the prologue to *Nunca Mas,* many adapt by going about their lives as if terrible things were not happening.[21] As late as 1991, a friend reminded me that when Mexico suffered the 1985 earthquake, among the unearthed bodies were those of Argentine disappeared persons. The earthquake had taken place while the 1985 human rights trials of the military commanders were in progress and, to verify the identity of the victims, the court suspended the proceedings until any possible correspondence between the Mexican victims and the Argentine disappeared had been ascertained (whether established or disproven). This measure was aimed at dispelling any reasonable belief that the disappeared had voluntarily left the country, as many still believed. The outcome did in fact demonstrate that none of those listed as disappeared in Argentina in the 1970s were among those killed in the earthquake. Today, however, the Mexican earthquake myth still thrives in Argentina.

The repression in Argentina distressed the large majority of the population. To limit the category of victims to the disappeared, the tortured, and the jailed is to fail to apprehend the social repercussions of state terrorism. Protracted repression caused pain and anguish not only to those who were related to or associated with the killed and the disappeared, or even those who received death threats. The *prospect* of possibly being brutalized or assassinated created an environment of anguish that required adaptive strategies. Vast sectors of society applied extremely individualistic avoidance strategies. To make this possible, the reception of information became extremely selective, so as to permit the deliberate evasion of critical thinking and leave room for vagueness.[22] A clear example of this vagueness is the use of the term *paramilitary squads,* when referring to ultraright-wing gangs of different sorts—military, police, for example, and vigilante groups.[23]

Because it compels individuals to construct their own explanation for the violence, terror is extremely isolating. It is individuals removed from social networks who actually deal with terror. Many people simply decided to look the other way, as if pretending that nothing was going on would erase the violence and the pain. Acting as if everything continued to operate normally became customary for many Argentines. Lita, a working-class, middle-aged woman, recalls noticing six or seven Ford Falcons surrounding her block and hearing screams coming from her next-door neighbor's house. Yet to date she has never in her own mind acknowledged that violence had actually taken place. People stripped scary events of their meaning. In 1977, Mercedes Martinez, an upper-middle-class, well-educated and intelligent woman, attempted to visit her two daughters in a poor suburban neighborhood to which they had allegedly moved, only to find that the address did not exist. She had not connected this mystery with her daughters' shocking disclosure a few months earlier that they had joined the radical left-wing PRT (*Partido Revolucionario de los Trabajadores*). Only when four men in plainclothes, claiming to be policemen, showed up at her apartment inquiring about her daughters' whereabouts did she suspect that they could be in trouble. Her daughters in fact left the country and only returned to visit her after 1983. The three often discuss family history and events—but they never mention the daughters' activities in the 1970s.

A very clear example of the suppression of meaning in order to avoid direct confrontation with terrifying situations is provided by the case of the undertakers' union in the province of Cordoba. When I moved into the Casa Rosada, the government house, in December 1983, I came across a file chronicling these events. When the Alfonsin administration moved into the building, it had become clear that the military officials we were succeeding had destroyed every document they thought could incriminate them. There was little or nothing left inside the drawers and closets except formal mail; a few files, of little relevance, remained. Among the papers left intact we found a file labeled Petition by the Cordoba Undertakers. The former officials had obviously not attached importance to it. This file, however, was most illuminating.

In 1977, the union of undertakers in Cordoba had submitted a formal request to the military president, Jorge Videla. Since the military had taken over in March 1976, the number of bodies unloaded from army trucks to be buried had multiplied their work ten- to twentyfold and environmental contamination had rendered their work hazardous. No matter how hard they labored, the undertakers could not prevent the daily dumped corpses from piling up and decomposing. As the working conditions had deteriorated they demanded that, like the chemical and mining industries, the hazardous nature of their labor be officially recognized; once so designated by the bureaucracy, members of the union would receive extended holidays, reduced work schedules, and early retirement. In response to this plea, and on behalf of the president, an army colonel had rebuffed the petition. The rejection was not based on the inadmissibility of the request itself, but on the basis that it had been submitted to the wrong office: the petition should have been addressed to the commander of the Third Army Corps in Cordoba, General Luciano Benjamin Menendez; only he had the legal capacity to decide the case.

Not only did this file reveal that massive assassinations were routine for the military, but also that civilian sectors of the population themselves regarded these massive killings as normal events. There was no mention of the horror of the situation; the undertakers' concern was to obtain better working conditions, more holidays, and a wage increase. Running parallel with the regime's strategy of denying involvement in brutal practices, and also with the citizens' avoidance strategy, was this purely bureaucratic dialogue. Both parties, generals and undertakers, were acting as if nothing worthy of concern was actually happening. The federal government in Buenos Aires limited itself to issuing a formal response to an equally formal labor request.

THE NATIONALIST SPIRIT

The lack of trust that people felt was another cause of the avoidance strategies: people avoided sensitive issues unless they were certain of the loyalty of the audience. Careless disclosures were as dangerous as deliberate reports. Vast portions of society sequestered themselves in their own family circle, restricting non-kin relationships to old friends. This tactic proved to be extremely isolating; in some ways, it paralleled the official policy of dismissing foreign criticism on the grounds that no one is entitled to meddle in other's family affairs. For parents, fear of strangers and the constant effort to keep their children away from politics and trouble fostered family authoritarianism: children's activities were monitored. "Macro-authoritarianism" thus turned into microauthoritarianism.[24] This process of mental closure could be detected in the increasing nationalism, xenophobia, and tribalist exaltation of the family and fatherland.

Extreme caution led people to silence their worries. Conversation usually centered on trivial issues. The performance of the national soccer team and the campaign of Argentine tennis star Guillermo Vilas became national obsessions—obsessions the regime fostered. Each triumph at international soccer was a national victory, an achievement of the Argentine "breed." "*En casa mando yo*" ("At home, I am in command") was the type of headline after every victory Vilas achieved in Argentina. Ironically, the silence about the real Argentina could be read into an enormous sign located on Avenida 9 de Julio, the widest in Buenos Aires. The sign was supposedly aimed at honking drivers: *El Silencio es salud* (silence is health).

The importance of international sports can be seen in Argentina's staging of the 1978 soccer World Cup. This was a consequence of the regime's program to improve its image in the outside world. Nationalist sentiments were easily kindled and, once set in motion, provided a strong incentive to overlook domestic brutality. Grounded in such nationalistic feeling, in 1978 an overwhelming number of Argentines felt that the country was under unwarranted attack over the issue of human rights. The same year as the World Cup, a number of foreign governments, international human rights organizations, and European newspapers protested the numerous human rights violations in Argentina. Although they explicitly accused the military regime of complicity with the abductors and torturers of thousands of people, the populace, an easy prey to manipulation, confused criticism of the military regime with criticism of Argentina itself.

When regime officials complained about attempts to sabotage the World Cup, the population at large sided with the regime. In an open message to Videla, Tomas de Anchorena, the Argentine ambassador in France, gave his reasons as to why foreign groups were lobbying against people attending international events in Argentina (notably, the World Cup). "This campaign against Argentina," Anchorena said, "must be felt by every Argentine as an aggression against his country. It would be of great help to confront this campaign if, through private and public organizations, everybody established a permanent dialogue with their counterparts in Europe to express the reality of daily life in Argentina."[25] A sympathetic middle class reacted by writing thousands of outraged letters to the newspapers "to bare the treacherous subversive campaign" behind the stories of torture and death circulating around the world.

The nationalistic wave brought dismay to the Madres de Plaza de Mayo, who recall how, during that period, almost everybody forgot the disappeared. Rear Admiral Alberto Lacoste, head of organizing for the World Cup, was quoted asking himself: "Why do the Europeans continue to come to a cultured and civilized country like ours? What have they got against Argentines?"[26] At such a time, when people felt the duty to mobilize in defense of the country's honor, there was even less room than usual for criticism of human rights violations.[27] The "mad mummies," as the Madres were called, to a large majority had now become unpatriotic zealots.[28] I recall a letter published by the *Buenos Aires Herald* in early August 1978. The writer expressed surprise that the disappeared should cause so much international unrest while Europeans remained impervious to numerous young couples eloping in Europe. The press campaign fanned the nationalist flame and a large portion of the population reacted against what they now viewed as an orchestrated international campaign against the country. People were caught up in the trap of make-believe that Argentina was being targeted by an international conspiracy; the country was being defamed by the ERP and Montoneros' international allies, "useful idiots" from abroad operating as the new instrument of subversion. It was, in fact, given official credence, being labeled: "The anti-Argentina campaign." *Siete Dias,* one of the country's most popular magazines, published a list of personalities and institutions that lent themselves to the slanderous enterprise that Marxist terrorism was said to have orchestrated: "Using denunciation as one of its main political tools, Argentine terrorist organizations have invested their efforts in the creation of institutions to serve them to attain their main goals: to accuse the ruling government, whichever it may be, of being repressive and of violating human rights."[29]

When the World Cup matches were in progress, the country came to a standstill each time the national team was scheduled to compete. When Argentina's team won the cup, the entire population went out to celebrate; people by the million got together to share their joy. Throngs of celebrants, including many staunch human rights advocates who were risking their lives, forgot the country's real drama. In a fragmented society, an event like the World Cup victory was one of the few occasions when citizens could express their solidarity. It was a tribal response and it pervaded both the private and public spheres.

As mentioned in chapter 2, a similar tribalism set the country's mood against the international human rights campaigns. During the 1979 Inter-American Commission on Human Rights visit to the country, many citizens supported the official thesis that only the "Argentine Family" had the authority to deal with Argentine's problems.[30] A similarly chauvinistic reaction followed the decision by U.S. President Jimmy Carter to cut back on military aid as an expression of strong disapproval of the military regime's abuses.[31] Nationalism has an excellent explanation for suffering: it is caused by outsiders.[32] When blame is thus focused, we have a pretext to make common cause with those we fear—the actual opressors. For the terrorized, national sharing of emotions at times like this affords momentary alleviation of anxiety. There were many ways to obtain relief.

A sizeable number of citizens coped with terror by identifying with the terrorizers. Many of them had learned to view the world through the bipolar logic "If you are not with us you are against us." The alternatives, for these citizens, were "order" or "chaos." In the view of many in middle class, the Campora and Isabel Peron administrations had not only been violent and corrupt but had also left the country in an unbearably chaotic state. The influence of this background was so strong that it is worth going into in some detail: that period created the bi-polar mindset. During Campora's three-month interregnum, the ERP and the Montoneros had flaunted their banners, parading ceaselessly. On university campuses, members of left-wing groups demanded positive support from passers-by—people who just happened to be around during their demonstrations. Threatening bystanders, the radical activists would jump up and down, menacingly chanting: *"El que no salta es un gorilon"* (Those who do not jump with us are big gorillas, i.e., right-wingers). Fearing reprisals, many onlookers decided to jump. The atmosphere in the universities was indeed tense. Activists ceaselessly interrupted classes to harangue students and lecturers. A Montonero activist once threatened me with a gun during class when I opposed his attempt to circulate a political manifesto; intimidated students were expected to sign it. Fortunately, the two youths who had come into the classroom with him ushered him out. Left-wing radicals glued photos of Che Guevara on the walls of buildings throughout the country, and the Triple A and other right-wing groups responded with threats against "Bolshies," painting their slogans everywhere. Violence erupted in even the smallest towns. Left- and right-wing factions engaged in feuds in which relatives were sometimes opposed in warring factions.

Hence, as far back as the early 1970s, inhabitants of Argentina's cities had become increasingly accustomed to political violence. After 1974, when Isabel Peron took office, it was a commonplace to see parties of five or six cars, sirens wailing, drive at full speed through Buenos Aires or Cordoba, filled with heavily armed men in plainclothes. Waving shotguns and Uzis out of the windows of their Ford Falcons, the thugs in these motorcades drove through the busiest sectors of downtown, thumping on the hoods of other cars with the butts of their guns so that they could get right of way. Without police interference, these gangs would sometimes hunt their prey on malls, speeding over sidewalks, forcing pedestrians to scramble. Circulating news about assassinations made it clear that political violence had taken over the streets, but few complaints could be heard about the violence and the impunity with which right-wing gangs operated. People took it for granted that the men in the Ford Falcons belonged to Lopez Rega's Ministry of Social Welfare or to a right-wing labor union, probably Lorenzo Miguel's Metal Workers. Few people would mention the subject openly. The police, beyond their reluctance to interfere with the action of right-wing gangs, contributed to the state of uncertainty with their deliberate passivity. Their inaction fostered a greater sense of impotence. When left-wing activists held in prison were released in 1973 (congress having enacted Campora's amnesty for all politically motivated offences) police officers protested the measure, refusing to enforce the law. They also refused to take down formal complaints from citizens on even private matters such as theft and rape.

It is thus easy to understand how many people believed that in March 1976 their anguish had come to an end. The renewed and increased violence was seen as the price of order.[33] If an individual exposed his worries about state violence, a customary reply was: "This is the time to support them."

THE ISOLATING
EFFECTS OF TERROR

In this chapter, I have attempted to describe how terror can be mobilized as a political tool. *Terror* means more than the fear of violence on the streets; it has much deeper implications. Terror affects the perception of events; it fragments the vision of social reality, thus breaking down social communication. In a state of terror, isolation becomes patent: individuals break "dangerous" social ties and throw away possibly "incriminating evidence," such as books, that could render them "punishable." Juan Corradi describes the general adaptive behavior of the population under the military rule in Argentina: people abandoned, first, their political activities; second, they abandoned their political beliefs. They reduced associational activities and denied any evidence that inhumane practices were being carried out. Members of groups that were potential targets of state terror cultivated deliberate ignorance about what was going on. People adopted selfish strategies of survival; for example, competition and speculation.[34]

When terror reigns, citizens begin to act in a way sometimes attributed to patients in a mental institution. Take, for example, the wards for the severely ill patients as they appear in *One Flew Over the Cuckoo's Nest*. Ignoring the existence of other individuals, every inmate on the ward is absorbed by activities that do not relate to the rest of the patients. While one is building a toy wooden castle, the person next to him kicks a balloon around; a third patient is silently staring at a column; a fourth recites verses. Group coordination becomes impossible. If the building were on fire, the staff would have to save each patient individually because, even in an emergency, it would be impossible to organize cooperative action. This isolation is much like that in which Argentines learned to live.[35] Individuals built their own personal realities that could not be shared with others because each was immersed in a world of his own. In such a social environment, minds seldom meet.[36] Where meaningful communication is nonexistent (as with the mental patients) social actors cannot be expected to experience respect for one another: no cooperative scheme to improve their collective existence is possible. Not even the imminence of common catastrophe will generate belief in an authority capable of coordinating action to save those who lack, among themselves, a common perception of the world. The rise of an authority depends on the existence of such a common perception. The only goal terrorized people can be expected to share is the tribe's—the nation's victory at whatever: the 1978 World Cup or the Falklands/Malvinas Islands adventure. These effects of terror jeopardize the citizenry's ability to believe in others' rights and to respect institutions basic to democratic life.

State terror leads to general disbelief. Consequently, it leads to the impossibility of the existence of a moral authority. Such an authority depends on our perception of our own—and other people's—worth. Terror annihilates this perception; it kills our ideals, our self-respect. In a state of terror, feelings of shame and guilt are ever present: once our goals are compromised, our principles and loyalties deserted, inevitably there is instilled in us a sense of worthlessness.

CHAPTER 4

POWER AND TERROR

In mid-June 1982, in the wake of Argentina's surrender to the British forces on the Falkland/Malvinas Islands, de facto President General Fortunato Galtieri convoked the populace in the Plaza de Mayo, the square in front of the government house. Although the attendance had not been as it was to celebrate the April 2 invasion of the islands, the throng of people that congregated was large enough to fill the square. A sizeable segment of the population expected an explanation of elementary factors about the war that were far from evident. Inaccurate official reports about the military campaign had misled people. Until a few days before the conflict was over, the populace thought Argentina's armed forces were accomplishing victory after victory.

THE POSTWAR CONFUSION

There was indeed no concurrence between the government's convocation of the citizenry and the reasons that moved people to the square. Although the issue was never expressly elucidated, it is obvious that the government's purpose for the convocation was to muster support from the population at a time of crisis. The populace, instead, demanded an explanation for the twofold humiliation: that their country had lost a war allegedly waged to defend its sovereignty; and that they had been deceived about the accomplishments of the armed forces. Frustration and anger soared in the crowd when no account of what had happened in the South Atlantic was forthcoming. As tempers flared, the gathering was disbanded by police using tear gas and a barrage of rubber bullets. At the cost of three dead and dozens wounded, order was restored.

Less than an hour after these events, I got on a subway train at a station a few blocks from the plaza. The passengers had gathered in small groups and were vehemently protesting the war. There was seeming agreement among the participants—but what in fact was shared was bewilderment sufficient to conceal underlying lack of consensus. Some were arguing against military mismanagement of the war; others found that the conflict was untimely or that Argentine diplomacy had failed to prevent the United States from siding with the British. Only a few maintained that the April 2 invasion of the Falklands/Malvinas by the Argentine armed forces had been unwarranted; and even fewer contended that it had been an irresponsible, groundless, and immoral enterprise—an adventure that cost the lives of nearly one and a half thousand young conscripts.

The events at Plaza de Mayo were revealing in more than one way about the nature of the regime's power. The gathering in front of the government house over the surprising military defeat exposed the populace's extreme ignorance about the country's management in general. It also revealed that, in calling the citizenry to the gathering, the military rulers had not expected the popular reaction that followed. It showed that the generals knew little if anything about the sentiments and purposes that mobilized the citizenry to the square. It also became clear that this lack of a shared understanding of the meaning of political events had led to what today still seems a senseless use of violence.

The postwar events were also telling about the degree to which the perception of events varied among the populace. The loudness of the individuals expressing irrepressible wrath camouflaged their deeply discrepant versions of reality, but the differences were only apparent. The near-uniformity of the loudness with which these views were expressed said something about the existence of widely discordant belief systems.

POWER AND
DISCREPANT VERSIONS OF REALITY

The postwar gathering and violent culmination well illustrate the nature of political power under a terrorist regime. This model of power stems from the country's state of generalized confusion and disinformation. The main circumstances that shape the exercise of power in a terrorist state are a lack of basic communication links between the populace and the regime, and the fragmentation of reality among the citizens.

The notion of political power is complex and elusive. It encompasses both the conscious will of rulers and the unconscious processes that shape everyday life. It is both formal and informal: political power includes formal directives issued by individuals in certain roles and offices; it also includes persuasion and enticement by individuals acting behind the scenes—the "power behind the throne." Most students of political phenomena have defined power in a limited and exclusionary way. Liberals tend to view power as a deliberate phenomenon by which certain people induce other individuals to act in accordance with their desires. Marxists have largely focused on how prevailing material interests shape the ideology and practices of a given society. Although these different interpretations of the nature of political power have been instrumental in gaining an understanding of segments of political reality, they have not been able independently to explain the link between social reality and the full spectrum of power. In this chapter, I will attempt to show that understanding Argentina's state of terror requires that three different conceptions of power be seen as interrelated. These three conceptions are frequently considered to be irreconcilable. I will call them *articulating, disarticulating,* and *structural* power.

Articulating power is democratic power par excellence. Largely based on consensus, this notion of power addresses the political issue of social cooperation.[1] Organizing citizens' activities to achieve common purposes requires that a government be able to induce individuals to perform specific voluntary actions. Intentional power requires that specific goals be achieved in ways that require the citizens' intent. Actions that demand coordination range from defense-related activities to street traffic. I will examine how this articulating power operates in a state of terror and explain why such a state is incompatible with the primordial political mission of social coordination. In a terrorist state, it is *disarticulating* power that reigns, not *articulating* power.

In chapter 3, I explained the way in which terror fragments society's beliefs: how it diversifies the perception of social reality. It is the ability to attain this effect that I call disarticulating power. Instead of building consensus, disarticulating power is aimed at preventing coordinated opposition. It lies in the capacity to obtain and retain political control over a section of society by the frustration of coordination. By drastically limiting people's everyday language and causing general confusion, disarticulating power splits individuals' perception of reality.

Student survivors of detention centers recall their panic when they were routinely detained by Argentine military and antimutiny police units for identification and interrogation. Captors terrified them by lecturing them on the boundless liberty of army officers to torture and kill at will. With this practice, officers derived more than simple sadistic pleasure. They preempted any possible coordination between the detainees by effectively isolating each and every suspect. Each detainee built a different "theory" about their captors' pursuit and they were all distressed by the danger of being associated with the rest of the "suspects." By these means the police also guaranteed the impotence of the detainees to protest their harsh treatment, let alone escape. Deliberately or not, the military regime and its acolytes (and to a lesser extent the administration that preceded it) used terror as a general form of political power. They exercised the violence Simone Weil describes as the ability to turn persons into "corpses even before anybody or anything touches them."[2]

Although disarticulating power stands diametrically opposed to articulating power, to an extent the former is resorted to in all kinds of political arrangements. Mostly in face to face situations, and with minimal expression, disarticulating power is occasionally utilized even in the most democratic systems. Controlled violence enables a small police force to quell frays among street gangs and to disperse violent rioters. When urgency makes persuasion infeasible, it may sometimes be proper, even in rights-based democratic setting, to cause fear and confusion. Controlled, though random, baton blows often enable a comparatively small police force to disband throngs of angry protesters. In a democracy, however, these tactics are circumscribed and relatively seldom required. They are expected not to exceed minimal harm to individuals. In contrast with this restricted use of coercive power, a state of terror turns this violence into a political style. In Argentina, brutality became a general strategy to attain and retain political control. This tack strongly conditioned *structural* power.

Structural power is the way in which a society defines and resolves its conflicts. It was often said that, during Alfredo Stroessner's dictatorship in Paraguay, Roman Catholic priests used to preach to the poor on the value of being thankful for the small mercies that the landowners were willing to disburse for their toil. Rebellion was not only unfair, it was immoral; it was sinful and it was silly. In most cases, this pontification was not the churchmen's conscious effort to protect the landowners from the peasants' demands, but rather the consequence of their unwitting and sincere aspiration to reaffirm social peace at the expense of the workers' misery. Behind the priests' beliefs and their consequent manipulation of the peasants' minds to acquiesce to the status quo lay the strategies by which individuals or groups advance their interests.

The experience of power thus conceived is to be found in the system of meaning and values that we call culture.[3] The church in Paraguay adapted its definition of the conflict of interest between peasants and landowners to the fact that its own survival depended on the landowners' financial contributions. This adaptation generated the notion that, to improve the plight of the country's rural workers would jeopardize everybody's interests. In the priests' view, the workers themselves would suffer if decreased contributions deprived the workers of spiritual guidance. From this perspective, power adopts an essential role in configuring the people's conceptions of reality in a culture of terror.

In chapter 6, I will tackle the issue of structural power in connection with the dirty war—"blaming the victim" for terror, as was customary in the Argentina of the 1970s. When terror reigns, the power to coordinate social activities (intentional power) inevitably flounders, giving way to increased coercive violence (coercive power). Social habits and assumptions are thus modified (structural power).

AUTHORITY, POWER,
AND MEANING

In *On Violence*, Hannah Arendt defines power as the capacity of one person to elicit compliance from another. For Arendt, articulating power includes this other's (say, a second person's—the "doer's") performing a particular action out of compliance with the first person's (the "emitter's) moral standing, beyond merely the ability to use threats of physical harm to induce the doer to perform a particular action.[4] The goal of political power, Arendt explains, is to achieve a concerted action for a collective purpose.[5]

Power, according to this version, ought not be confused with violence. Violence is a one-sided process. When violence is present, the volition of the doer is rendered insignificant, because the doer is reduced entirely to being an object of the emitter's agency. Unlike as is the case with violence, power, according to this conception, is a complex collective process that cannot be located solely in the emitter or the doer; rather, it is in the relationship between the two: it is a form or process of interaction between individuals or groups.[6] Although, in Arendt's conception, articulating power cannot exist without the capacity effectively to resort to violence, it is essentially a relational category, in which certain individuals or groups are in a position deliberately to induce other people (intentionally) to undertake particular actions or achieve certain states of affairs.[7] In *On Violence* Arendt conflates the notions of articulating power and authority,[8] but both collapse when state terror reigns.

More recent writers have established a sharp distinction between power and authority. They couch the concept of authority in the idea of respect for the will of some persons or groups of persons. A person complies with the injunctions of someone (authoritative person or institution) on finding that doing so is morally compelling.[9] In this view, an agent does not obey an authority to obtain a benefit or avert a harm, but rather from the belief in the moral correctness of compliance in a specific case. The moral property attached to the concept of authority renders the promised benefits or threatened evils irrelevant. A morally motivated agent is indifferent to the personal benefits or harms that the chosen action may entail.

Power, on the other hand, induces individuals to obey because complying with injunctions is advantageous. Essential to power relations is the avoidance of evils (e.g., punishment) or the attainment of advantages (dangled as bait). Yet, as Flathman (and others) point out, authority and articulating power overlap in many ways. Threats and offers lie at the core of the notion of articulating power.[10] "In the most general and basic terms," Flathman writes, "power is the feature of interaction between—or among— two or more agents or groups of agents each of whom are capable of and are in fact acting intentionally."[11]

The nature of the exercise of articulating political power is *collective* in two relevant ways. First, the exercise of power depends to a large extent on the community's values and beliefs, to the extent that these values and beliefs encourage, accept, or reject the very exercise of power. Societies in which unbounded individualism is highly regarded will be more reluctant to accept the idea of fostering cooperative schemes through coercion than will those more supportive of collective endeavors. U.S. law professors of my acquaintance find the German *Anmeldung* intolerable. The German tradition, in which citizens report each change of residence to the local police, would probably be staunchly resisted in communities recently founded by pioneers. In pioneer country, traditions are built in the relative absence of state agents. The inhabitants of the vast Western United States are assumed to resist rules that the citizens of densely populated Europe find acceptable or even desirable. In most Western U.S. states, for instance, an individualist conception of self-defense has prevailed over the more restrained Eastern conception of self-help.[12] The expression of this displacement lies in that, in the Western U.S. legal tradition, individuals facing physical aggression are not expected to retreat before resorting to lethal means of defense, as they are in most Eastern U.S. states: it is not only our physical integrity that we are entitled to protect, but, insofar as they are important to us, also our self-esteem and image.

As with authority, power implies the existence of values and beliefs shared between those who issue orders and those who obey them. Power is based on the generation of incentives to perform (or not perform) certain actions.[13] To be able to exercise power, the person issuing orders must adapt the means of utilization, making them meaningful to those obeying in three ways. First, the threats and offers made must be meaningful to those whose actions the emitter intends to direct: it is not enough that utterances only reach the audience. Coordination becomes unattainable to a ruler ignorant of the doers' values.[14] Those receiving the commands may consider, for instance, that achieving a particular goal implies too high a cost; may deem that their dignity is too valuable to jeopardize in exchange for being spared a designated evil (punishment).

Second, threats and offers are effective insofar as they cover a limited area. A drive to broaden control over the population by vaguely describing punishable actions is self-defeating. The vaguer the definition (the more the number of offences) the less will people know what is expected of them. (Thus, ignorance among Argentines as to what was expected brought about only fear and confusion, thus neutralizing articulating power.)

Third, since political power is exercised on behalf of the community, by people occupying offices and roles, recognition by society of such offices and roles is essential.[15] Penalties sanctioned by a person or body that the community considers representative of its interests will have a more dissuasive effect than those enacted by persons or institutions considered to be acting independently of the community's will. In this area, articulating power and authority concur.

The exercise of articulating power also requires at least a minimum of precision in communication. To achieve social coordination by inducing certain actions presupposes (a) a fluent exchange of information between the government and the citizens and (b) such an exchange among the citizens themselves. To achieve their purposes, those in power require cooperative schemes based on groups and individuals easily and consistently exchanging messages to make their contributions fit common endeavors. Essential to the exercise of power thus conceived is the existence of a common normative reality. In the execution of standard practices, individuals are expected to coordinate their actions by observing common rules and practices: activities such as driving a car would be impossible if it were not performed on the basis of common assumptions; in the example cited, that other drivers conform to identical rules and practices.[16]

The Communication Breakdown in Argentina

Terror makes coordinated practices unattainable. In broad terms, political disengagement (fear of group activity) isolates individuals and, as some authors have mentioned, competition and self-help take the place of assistance and cooperation.[17] State terrorism hampers coordination and frustrates the exercise of articulating power. Is it a platitude to point out that when terror reigns all communication is substantially impaired? As mentioned earlier, anguish drives citizens to build their reality on personally selected bits and pieces of social events: the resulting variety of beliefs on a given topic make meaningful communication infeasible. The vast diversity of perceptions—with no consistent way of getting confirmation—generates a communication gap, between individual and individual, and between sectors of society. In a state of terror, the gaps between people result not only from different perceptions of reality but also from a conscious reluctance to communicate. When ominous, vague threats haunt us, only exceptionally do we feel safe enough to expose ourselves to others. We become chronically afraid that, by being overheard or carelessly quoted, our opinions will reach those who are watching.

In Buenos Aires, everybody "knew" their conversations were being monitored. Although the Argentine regime must have had some capacity to eavesdrop, the extent of the suspected supervision would have required thousands of communications/intelligence experts to tap even half the telephones whose owners thought they were under surveillance. In the face of "certainty" that their telephones were tapped, almost everyone I knew "communicated" only in improvised coded language, which increased confusion still further. This "coded language" consisted of utterances that evoked certain persons or situations: we expected our associations to be matched by the person we were talking to. This improvised system led, of course, to perplexing misunderstandings. Thus, terror created an insurmountable barrier to the exchange of even the most ordinary messages. There was also a comparable obstacle to necessary communications between state and citizens.

Communication between government and citizenry is by definition impeded when an individual has no idea of what acts, utterances, or gestures other than sheer, active obsequiousness may turn him, or her, into an enemy of the regime. For most of the population, official secrecy and the randomness of state-sponsored violence left little room for safety. Citizens had no rights; they were constantly reminded that respect did not exist. Only force existed.

In a world of secrecy and arbitrariness, even subaltern state officials are inevitably thrown into confusion. Not necessarily privy to their superiors' whims, in Argentina lower-level security personnel found themselves confronting a world of danger and hostility. Until the mid-1970s often targeted by left-wing insurgency, police personnel knew little about the nature of the violence, and even less, of course, about the overall strategy they were to implement. Direct participants in the repression campaign, policemen were nevertheless ignorant of the design behind the dirty war. This was for them a disorienting experience. Reluctant to give up a facade of control over the situation, officers became extremely hostile to the population at large. Immediately after the March military coup, the mother of a deaf girl, living in a heavily patrolled area, took her daughter to the police officer in command of the precinct to explain why the girl's problem would make it impossible for her to follow verbal instructions issued by the police. The officer replied that everything would be all right as long as the girl—a ten-year-old—did not do anything dubious. Officers acted

with extreme suspicion, seeking to replace their own dis-
orientation by assuming an artificial self-assurance.

The police soon developed a strong enmity with the
public, whom they treated with the distant and persecutory style usually confined to criminal suspects. People
pursuing the most trivial purposes, such as obtaining police certificates,[18] found that visiting a police precinct was
a frightful experience. Officials invariably ignored those
waiting at the precinct's counter. Acting as though obliv-
ious to the public's presence, an officer would from time
to time gaze through those waiting for assistance. After
an indefinite period, the officer would inquisitorially address somebody in the queue, and usually send them
away, whatever the explanation. People waiting to report
an offense were invariably informed they were at the
wrong precinct: at the precinct in the neighborhood where
the offense had been committed the victims were sent off
to their own neighborhood's station; those who went to
their neighborhood police station were dispatched to the
precinct where the violation had occurred. Finally, the
visitor would be told to come back later. But leaving the
police station was not without obstacles, because a bell
had to be rung to inform the sentries outside the precinct
gate that someone was entitled to leave. Even lawyers
(like myself) felt an indescribable sense of relief on getting
back to the street. The effect of these tortuous and often
contradictory procedures had a maddening effect on
those who experienced them. Ordinary citizens felt that
state agents were never protective but rather a source of
one's bewilderment and fear.

The similarities between the Argentine bureaucracy at
this time and mental institutions are salient. David L.
Rosenhan describes the "process of depersonalization" in
a hospital as being itself a cause of insanity. Assuming a
patient's incoherence and inability to assert himself, the
staff avoids engaging in meaningful communication with

patients; lack of credibility they take as a given.[19] The staff's indifference toward the patients' individuality, demonstrated through meaningless verbal exchanges, is itself a reason for insanity. A number of medical researchers have posed as patients to expose this dynamic. Rosenhan relates how a nurse unbuttoned her shirt in front of a group of patients as if they did not exist.[20] Unable to establish significant connections with the staff, the patients' experience is that their "mental disease" renders them unworthy of interaction. Rosenhan's researchers were so disturbed by this process of depersonalization that they asked to leave the institution much earlier than scheduled.[21] The institutional pattern of interaction fosters insanity; it becomes an independent cause for noncommunication between and among patients. The parallel with a terror state is easy to see.

But the resemblance between this mental institution and Argentina's experience goes further. After a number of attacks on military garrisons and police precincts by left-wing activists, the units imposed such tight security measures that ordinary citizens were dissuaded from approaching police stations for any reason. The police had dug themselves into self-protective trenches. Expecting to be treated as subversive suspects, the public refrained from turning to the police for protection or to report criminal activities. Shortly before the military coup, an investigative judge, Carlos Arigos, appeared at a precinct to conduct a probe in the middle of the night and was held against a wall for more than five minutes by policemen pointing automatic weapons at him. Security was such that one often wondered if the police confined their purpose to one of protecting themselves.

Frequently, the government issued orders that could not possibly be obeyed. In April 1976, for instance, gun owners were threatened with stiff punishments if found in possession of guns they failed to declare before a given date. Each gun had to be meticulously identified on specially designed and extremely detailed forms. The forms, however, were issued only a few hours before the deadline and most gun owners found it impossible to turn their weapons in to the police even if they had stood in line all night long. Citizens were also required to report the loss of personal documents. Having reported the loss of identification documents was the best protection against state repression, should those documents turn up at the scene of an insurgent action. But a certificate of reported loss would not be issued unless the police were shown the applicant's personal identification document. This of course was impossible: the purpose of the procedure was to report the loss of that very same piece of paper.

Bearing personal identity cards was mandatory. Cards could be obtained only at the police headquarters, where the line of applicants snaked from the third floor to the street. At the police station, men were forbidden to appear with beards and women had to wear skirts. After being fingerprinted, the applicant filled out the forms and was directed to return several days later. When one went back, one knew the file had gone through every possible intelligence office. The feeling was that there was always something there that could reveal we were suspected of something.

This official world of intermixed indifference, contempt, and suspicion kept individuals as far away from the police as possible. Working-class citizens would not seek police protection for any reason, not even to report a serious crime. Anselmo, who cleaned the changing room at a tennis club, told me how his twenty-year-old son had been murdered by a neighborhood gang. Although everybody in the vicinity knew who had done it, Anselmo would not go to the police: he was afraid of himself getting into trouble. No one trusted the police. Corruption in high places spilled over into different levels of social life:

stories circulated connecting the police, for example, with common crimes such as car theft. A well-known Argentine graphics designer, Ronald Shakespear, once came to my office because he had been deceived at an exchange house where he had sought to buy U.S. dollars. The cashier took his pesos and gave him a slip to collect his dollars, but when he submitted it to the teller who dispensed the dollars he was told he had already received them. When he threatened to go the police, a man came out from behind the counter and, opening his jacket to display his armpit holster, said: "I am the police." Together, Shakespear and I went to the police precinct in the financial district of downtown Buenos Aires, where I exhibited my lawyer's credentials. I asked to see a senior officer. After a few minutes, we were led to the comisario's (chief's) office. The comisario, expressionless, listened to us, and when Shakespear's account reached the point at which the police officer intervened, the comisario inquired: "Was it this man." Shakespear went pallid as a man emerged from behind a screen. Indeed, it was the same man, and he had obviously been listening to the entire story. I began to believe we were both in trouble. There was a moment of deep, endless silence, which the comisario interrupted by asking me if he had not seen me before. I made up a story of a dinner party, given by a chief of the police while I worked with former Minister of the Interior Laureano Landaburu. Name-dropping had a magical effect, and Shakespear was instructed to go back to the exchange office. He finally got his dollars. The story had a fortunate ending, but it spoke volumes about the degree of fear the police inspired in the citizenry.

Unless one had connections with the police, it was safer to settle disputes privately or, to forget the grievance altogether. Many people had no hope that their cases would ever be investigated; for them, there was no official justice system.

The distant, hostile attitude adopted by the security forces sometimes erupted in inexplicably violent ways. One day I overlooked a traffic signal that had set a 10 mph. speed limit near the Buenos Aires airport: we were stopped and instructed to pull over for a one-hour penalty. It was summer, and as the sun began to heat up the car we got out and waited for the time to pass. An air force officer came right at us and ordered us back into the car. When I told him that there was no reason to inflict bodily chastisement upon us, he pulled out his pistol and pointed it at my head. We got back into the car.

Official ruthlessness was not restricted to the security forces but became standard bureaucratic practice. In 1978, a former U.S. resident was petulantly sent away after offering to teach without salary in the history department of the University of Buenos Aires. He was told: "Your doctorate may well be from the University of Chicago or wherever you want; it is not an academic title issued by this university."

The use of state terror made the existence of articulating power relations extremely difficult at best. As already mentioned, violence dislocates social communication both horizontally—among the citizenry—and vertically—between the government and the populace. Caught in a vicious circle, the terrorist regime attempted to escalate violence to gain more control. As the system of threats and offers on which articulating power is built began to crumble, direct coercion replaced mere threats of punishment. Lack of spontaneous compliance based on respect for authority and the ineffectiveness of increasingly ambiguous threats, were replaced by the use of direct violence. Evidence of this trend in Argentina can be seen in that it was not until long after the proclaimed defeat of armed insurgency in 1978 that the military regime lifted the state of siege decreed by Isabel Peron in November 1974. This was when the October 1983 elections were held. Disarticulating power had little to do with the need to curb insurgency; it had become the prevailing form of political power.

A terrorist state has little room for articulating power. The exercise of articulating power is largely confined to contexts in which direct and specific orders override general rules. The effect of terror transforms power into the ability to destroy connections among citizens, thwarting all possible coordinated opposition. The whole notion of power as an intentional process is largely narrowed down to disarticulating power—to "the ability to talk and not to listen."[22] This self-renewing need to resort to force, with its accompanying torture and disappearing of thousands of people, instilled the notion, implicit or explicit, that, in Argentina, enforced suffering was a fact of life. As perceived by the population at large, the inescapability of pain provided the explanation for the acquired practice of blaming the victims of state brutality—the form that structural power adopts in a terrorist state.

THE ROLE OF BLAME
AND BLAMING

Blame plays an important role in the social life of a rights-based community. In such a community individuals value their own—and other people's—plans for their lives and are confident that institutions will protect their pursuit of personal ideals from the interference of third parties,[23] including the state. If an individual breaks the rules of such a society and causes harm to others, outrage at these deeds is converted into blaming. By blaming transgressors, we foster a sense of moral responsibility, both in the perpetrator and among society at large. Blaming also strengthens solidarity among individuals.[24] As a vehicle of control, blame conveys moral disapproval for harmful actions and converts into persuasion the indignation that these actions arouse. By blaming those who infringe our rights, we issue a message to society that such actions ought not to be repeated; at the same time, we provide reasons for wrongdoers to realize they have betrayed society's values.[25] Thus, this ideal form of blame is entrenched in our moral practices in two ways: first, by denouncing those who break society's rules; second, by convincing those who have wronged others that they deserve our condemnation. Although blaming is based on past events, it is thus also forward-looking, in that it creates an incentive for fostering respect for social values and practices.[26] In its ideal version, blame bolsters the authoritativeness of legal rules and practices. This notion of blame, however, is only a moral ideal.

Attaching lofty moral overtones to blame and blaming assumes that we can squarely identify those actions that bring about harm. This process of identification of those morally responsible for harming others is typically the case in "guilty" transgressions of the criminal law. Based on the duality of *guilty* and *innocent*, criminal legislation purports to provide clear parameters that will establish which actions are relevant in bringing about certain harms.

Beyond the realm of criminal legal practice, however, the issue of moral responsibility is, by and large, subject to disagreement, negotiation, and constant change. In the 1940s and 1950s, few people in the United States would have blamed automobile manufacturers for road accidents. The locus of blame fell generally on drivers, for possible negligence. To cite another example, this was true also in the case of people swimming in waters contaminated by industrial waste. The swimmers were blamed for the diseases they contracted.[27] While retaining its claim to moral authoritativeness, the practice of blaming has shifted from time to time, as did our notions of causation and moral responsibility. Outside the context of the criminal law, single-factor explanations (those that attach blame to a single party) are usually the consequence of an over-simplification of events.[28] As a general principle, the more we reflect on the origins of suffering, the less we view this suffering as the result of a single cause, and the more we see it as the outcome of a complex set of circumstances. In defining reality as one of friends and enemies, the authoritarian mind is prone to make the single-factor kind of oversimplification.

Blaming Turned on its Head

This process, involving a changing and often concurrent understanding of causes of harm and the resulting shifts of blame, does not detract from the original assumption, made above, that, as currently practiced, blaming has strong moral overtones. It expresses moral disapproval and indignation and seeks to transform the future behavior of those we blame. But a terrorist state drastically modifies the connections between blame, morality, and the transgression of explicit rules. The silencing of our outrage at brutality becomes a structural feature of society, because conscious indignation against state violence becomes both too painful and too dangerous. People live in constant fear that their condemnation will become perceptible and thus draw the violence upon themselves. Moreover, the sense of inevitability strips the practice of blaming of its mission of inhibiting future harmful actions. Blaming ceases to be a morally based mechanism of social control; at least, in the sense of compelling citizens to abide by explicitly agreed on principles and values.

As a consequence of this process, Argentine society developed the habit of looking at the victims of repression as the object of blame. The system of terror had, in Barrington Moore's words, "expropriated" the citizens' moral outrage.[29] In consequence, people shifted the focus of their anguish from the perpetrators to the victims.

An example from my personal experience: In October 1982, a man named Marcelo Dupont was abducted and found murdered in an empty lot in Buenos Aires. There were signs that he had been brutally tortured. The general assumption was, and still is, that Dupont had been murdered in retaliation for efforts made by his brother (Argentine diplomat Gregorio Dupont) to investigate the 1978 abduction and assassination of diplomat Elena Holmberg by military intelligence personnel.[30] A few days after the discovery of Marcelo Dupont's corpse, I mentioned the case to a colleague I ran into in the street. His reply was simple and usual in Argentina: *"Quien lo manda meterse"* ("Who pressed him into getting into trouble?").[31] He meant, of course, that by sticking his nose where he shouldn't have, Gregorio Dupont had caused his brother's assassination. Gregorio—who, in losing a brother, was in a sense a victim himself—was responsible for the assassination.

This seemingly strange practice of displacing the blame onto the victim (in this case, onto the victim's brother) is impeccably described in the prologue of the *Nunca Mas* report:

> In the society, the idea of un-protection became increasingly entrenched, the dark fear that anybody, no matter how innocent, could fall victim to that infinite witch hunt. Some were absorbed by overwhelming fear, while others were controlled by the conscious or unconscious proclivity to justify horror: "It must be something s/he must have done," was the whisper, as wanting to favor inscrutable Gods, looking at the children or parents of the disappeared as if they were pest-ridden. These sentiments were vacillating, because it was known that so many had been swallowed up by that bottomless abyss without being guilty of anything; because the struggle against the "subversive," with the drift that characterizes the hunting of witches and the possessed, had turned

into a dementedly generalized repression. Because the epithet "subversive" had such a vast and unpredictable reach.[32]

Many Argentines remember how in 1976 society developed this generalized practice of understanding violence by looking at the victim rather than the perpetrator.[33] The standard practice of blaming the victim for some unspecified conjectural involvement in "something" is comparable to the chauvinistic male's description of rape as a process in which the woman's actions in making herself look attractive are essential to her plight. A raped woman may be suspected of "causing" the incident for wearing "provocative" clothing or by otherwise seeming to express sexual desire.

In a state of terror, blaming serves several psychic functions that have little to do with the standard, explicit moral sentiments I have described. In three ways, blaming constitutes a way to distance ourselves from those who suffer. First, in "establishing" that the victim did something that we did not, we diminish our fear that we will be the next to suffer. We are not exactly like them; after all, they belong to a social category different from our own. Second, by assuming that those who undergo torture or who are made to disappear did something worthy of reproach, we feel less impotent before injustice. By blaming, we attempt to modify people's conduct. Thus, blaming is aimed at neutralizing our sense of impotence. If others join us in expressing such condemnation, we may change the course of events, and thus we would feel less helpless. Third, in attaching blame to the victim's actions, we suppress our own responsibility for the occurrence (just as parents sometimes blame small children for things they could not actually have done differently). Unable to accept unwarranted punishment, people often approach blame as establishing a system of "cosmic justice."[34] This can be seen in the way some people view

AIDS and cancer. For champions of "cosmic justice," cancer may be the consequence of (sometimes unexpressed) hostility; AIDS is said to be retribution for shameful lives.[35]

But in a state of inexplicable brutality there is yet a fourth effect: this one, we might say, places us as close to the repressor as our conscience will allow for. In Argentina, by censoring the victims we conveyed a perhaps subtle message (imperceptible even to ourselves) that we did not oppose the repressors' actions. Either because we simply took death and suffering as a given, or because we approved of the terror tactics, by blaming the tortured and the disappeared we sought to place ourselves beyond the suspicion that we sympathized with them.

I have explained how terrorist violence conducted by the state appears to us as inevitable pain.[36] This commonly perceived inevitability and the mechanism of turning our reproach toward the victims, on the unconscious expectation that "something will improve," became an outstanding feature of structural power in a state of terror. This innovative use of the practice of blame had an extremely negative impact on society's moral standards. Transformed into the expression of anguish, blaming the victim also became the language of our self-interests, waiving a possible claim to the impartiality required by moral authoritativeness. Consequently, in an indirect way, by giving up this moral authority to suppress violence, society learned to condone this violence. The answer to the suppression of the individual's moral worth and dignity was to acknowledge that in fact people had no rights, not even the most basic right not to be tortured and killed.

Thus, blaming fed into the rulers' self-sealing proof. Only those who sympathized with the subversive would be ready to condemn the regime, or, worse yet, lobby at foreign and international human rights fora against the military rule. After all, hadn't the Argentine community itself realized that only the ill-intentioned and the reckless were the objects of torture and assassination?

A RECAPITULATION

To summarize, in a terrorist state power adopts peculiar forms. Lacking a minimal moral authority, officials in such a state find that the absence of communication channels severely limits the exercise of articulating power. This deficiency in the capacity to coordinate actions is replaced by disarticulating power: the use of random violence.

A terrorist state deeply shapes structural power. One of the features of this power is the detaching of the practice of blaming from its usual moral connotations. Instead of focusing on those who bring about pain, blaming turns on the victim. This is a mechanism minimally to control future events and avoid anguish: we think of the victims as members of a separate community.

CHAPTER 5

LEARNING
TO LEARN

In the chapter 4, I dealt with the way in which power was shaped in Argentina during the years of the reign of relentless terror. I sought to demonstrate the regime's inability to exercise articulating power and how people learned to blame the victims in their efforts to deal with terror, with the inevitable consequence of detaching blame from standard versions of morality. The present chapter will show that Argentina's pattern of power today is basically unchanged from that era: there are strong indications that terror once again is gradually saturating Argentina's political life. I will try to show how certain learning processes lead to the rejuvenation of violence, thus rendering the establishment of democracy extremely difficult. First, I describe how the community now accepts the new forms of terror that are becoming ever more visible in Argentina. Second, through Gregory Bateson's theory of learning, I explain the social mechanisms that causes violence to recur. Third, I describe these mechanisms. I will provide examples of institutional disregard for basic individual rights.

IS TERROR BACK?

In 1993, ten years after the formal restoration of constitutional rule, general respect for individual liberties was neither visible nor evident in Argentina's life. For advocates of individual rights, the Argentine situation in the mid-1990s is bleak. By and large, the citizenry is apathetic in the face of renewed police brutality. Since the late 1980s, abuse has once more become widespread.

In 1992, in what may be considered another upsurge of institutional violence, political journalists, and commentators became the target of a campaign of threats, harassment, bomb scares, and battery. In spite of a sharp rise in belligerence against what the administration deems to be a hostile press, no one has thus far been arrested, let alone brought to trial. Violence is thus granted immunity.

But this condoning of violence is by no means the only evidence of renewed authoritarian practice. Dictatorial figures again are exerting electoral appeal. Military candidates for office were very popular in the 1991 provincial governors' elections they decided to contest. Some of the officers up for office have extensive records of human rights abuse, yet this well-known fact apparently had little negative impact on the voting population.

Reports of national and international human rights organizations indicated an increasing number of victims of police abuse in the early 1990s.[1] To a legal scholar writing in 1990, this new version of brutality looked like a token resurgence of the state of terror that reigned in the Argentina of the 1970s, particularly during the 1976–83 military dictatorship.[2] A number of political observers attribute the recent upsurge of violence to the impunity of military officers who were involved in the campaign of state terrorism during the dictatorship. They claim that the two laws that shrank the scope of legal responsibility of military and police personnel for actions between 1976 and 1983 had undermined people's confidence in the rule of law and, consequently, their respect for individual rights.[3] By the same reasoning, they attribute to President Carlos Menem's October 1989 and December 1990 pardons of convicted and indicted military officers an even stronger motive for skepticism about the democratization of the country. However, I contend that the new violence is merely a continuation of the practices and beliefs acquired during the stages of state terror; the small minority that opposed brutality in the 1970–80 period seems not to have grown any larger.

In 1991, an attorney complained to me that senior officers of the federal police merely shrugged when he protested that a youth had been badly beaten for no known reason at a precinct in the city of Buenos Aires.[4] These officers conveyed the impression that events of this kind were too frequent to permit a thorough investigation. Torture was becoming more and more common. An autopsy carried out in August 1993 on the body of a seventeen-year-old revealed signs of torture by electric shock and that the youth had died from heart failure at the precinct where he was held in the suburbs of Buenos Aires.[5] Violent police events have escalated since 1991. In 1993, hardly a day elapsed without news of a minor getting shot for activites such as kicking a ball into a neighbor's yard or splashing a former policeman's store with Coca-Cola.[6]

Widespread acceptance of brutality in Argentina is revealed not only by reports of brutal police procedures. With street criminality on the rise, a large portion of the citizenry accepts the inhumane treatment of suspects when it is allegedly dished out to protect the security and property of "decent" citizens. Police officer Luis Patti offers a clear example. Patti came to public notice in 1990 when a crowd staged a demonstration in the suburbs of Buenos Aires to support him when a provincial judge, Raul Borrino, ordered his arrest for torturing two detainees.[7] Such attitudes toward police strong arm tactics are of course not unknown in rights-based democracies; what makes these cases stand out is the popular reaction they caused. In response to Patti's arrest, a sizeable number of people from the community where Patti served stood up in his defense, claiming he had done the right thing to protect them. Further support came from forensic experts. Some detainees, they said, would harm themselves—"even with electrified wires"—to place blame on their captors. Torturing oneself with an electric prod is of course unthinkable—and would be especially difficult for suspects under arrest; hence, it is clear that not only did the physicians support Patti but they were willing enthusiastically and manifestly to perjure themselves to protect him. By overtly manipulating the facts, the experts were placing the blame on the victims of torture. Later, an appellate court had the case remanded to a new court on the grounds that, by indicting officer Patti, Judge Borrino had prejudiced himself. The new judge immediately had the charges of torture dropped and Patti did not even stand trial.[8]

A Buenos Aires newspaper reported that the country's public opinion was split between those who considered Patti a torturer and those who considered him a defender of security.[9] In districts where he had served, Patti's reputation for brutality had earned him the blessings of a majority of the population. Transformed into a public figure, the policeman became a frequent guest at social and public events, including a popular television show where he danced the tango before millions of spectators.[10] Patti facetiously declared that he "not only makes people dance but also dances himself" (in Argentine military jargon, to "dance" means to suffer inflicted pain).[11]

Civil liberties activists and observers from abroad found that Patti's brutal methods had made an extremely good impression among Argentina's highest officials. In contrast with the opinion of decent policemen who condemned Patti's methods,[12] Argentina's vice president, Eduardo Duhalde, said that in his opinion the officer was a "model for policemen."[13] Patti's reputation became so inflated that President Menem himself chose him for a special assignment; namely, to investigate a case of rape and murder of a young woman, Maria Soledad Morales, in the northern province of Catamarca.[14] The case had become the focus of nationwide public attention because of the personalities indicted for Morales's death. Among them were high police personnel, members of the inner circle of Catamarca's governor, and Guillermo Luque, the son of a national congressman.[15] A huge majority of Catamarca's population enthusiastically welcomed Patti's arrival. For those who skeptically viewed him as an officer who sought to ingratiate himself with the politically and economically powerful, his performance was foreseeable: Patti muddled the case by delaying the arrest of the suspects.[16] Reliable sources claim that he even helped some suspects evade arrest. Patti returned to Buenos Aires having botched the entire investigation.[17] As an epilogue to Patti's story, it should be noted that in September 1993 President Menem appointed him as the acting administrator of the Mercado Central, at that time the main food supply center for Buenos Aires.[18]

In 1991 there was another example of Argentine society's inclination to approve brutality: the Santos case. A respectable engineer from Buenos Aires, Horacio Santos, killed two young men for stealing his car stereo. The cause of distress is not the existence of a Santos; there are Santoses everywhere. It is the popular reaction to the episode that renders it worrisome. The victim of previous attacks on his property, Santos engaged in a wild car chase that ended in the death of both robbers. Santos literally executed the thieves—shooting the youngsters in the head at point-blank range after they had stepped out of their car and offered to return the stolen stereo. Journalists, politicians, and a vast sector of Buenos Aires public opinion declared that Santos had done the right thing.

The case—as with the Patti affair—incited heated arguments. Santos's supporters were astonishingly numerous. Well-known television journalists stood up to justify the assassination, blatantly claiming they would have acted in the same way had they been in his shoes. Santos's neighbors praised his action before the TV cameras, claiming he had contributed to cleansing the neighborhood. Lawyer Antonio Troccoli, one of President Alfonsin's closest advisers and a man with a long record in support of democracy, stopped short of applauding Santos, blaming the occurrence on the state's inability to curb street crime. If ordinary citizens were forced to bear arms from want of security in the streets, Troccoli reasoned, such episodes were likely to occur.

One of the alarming features of the Santos case was the slackness of the parties involved in its investigation, including those charged with prosecuting the case. Police investigators had received testimony from eyewitnesses who revealed that Santos intended to hunt down the teenagers when the chase started. These witnesses testified that someone else was driving the car, enabling Santos to shoot as they approached the victims. This should have been evidence that Santos had acted in cold blood. Instead, with the prosecution's consent, these witnesses did not appear before the court. The incident was interpreted as one in which Santos had acted alone and in a state of emotional disturbance.

More Examples: International Ripple

Argentina's renewed contempt for basic individual rights has had international repercussions. Recent violations of these rights were brought to the attention of the Spanish public when, in 1990, a Spanish police officer was convicted of torture after the tribunal rebuffed his claim that he had acted under his superiors' directives. A journalist commenting on the case facetiously wrote that it was unfortunate for the policeman that he had performed torture in Spain instead of Argentina, the "kingdom of impunity."[19]

The indifference of Argentines to human suffering in the 1990s is not confined to the police section of the news. In his account of police abuse, Paul Chevigny, a U.S. law professor, notes that the population responds to brutality with extreme apathy.[20] And a U.S. priest who spent 1990 in Argentina was appalled by the inhumanity displayed by the police. Another American, a social worker, remembers that one of his neighbors in Buenos Aires declared she would refrain from reporting having had a wheelbarrow and other humdrum utensils stolen from her yard from the well-grounded fear that, if the suspects were found to be minors, the police were especially likely to execute them. Argentine researcher Laura Gingold has noted that, in numerous cases of police assassination of lower-class adolescents, most members of the community are undisturbed.[21] Gingold also notes that, for many neighbors and acquaintances of the victims of brutality, the dictatorship is still in force; for others, "there is something the victim must have done."[22] The conclusion to be drawn from Laura Gingold's research as well as from the episodes I give here is that structural power—a particular kind of power that terror has created—remains the same in this period following the dirty war's constant infringement of rights. Blame is still placed upon the victims.

One may assume that acquiescence to violent practices at least demonstrates that lower-class citizens are being victimized by a badly trained police force. Regular violence is now mostly directed against the poor, many of whom are shantytown dwellers. But there are also victims in other sectors. Since 1992, there have been constant reports of death threats to, and harassment of, journalists who, the government claims, are agents of a monopolized and antagonistic mass media. The threateners proved to have the kind of detailed information that only the state intelligence apparatus can provide, such as the victim's and the family's daily schedules. Meanwhile, the Consejo de Seguridad (National Security Council)[23] clings to the worst of Argentine traditions by instructing the provincial police to keep an individualized record of their local population's political beliefs and affiliation. Gustavo Veliz, in 1993 the minister of the interior and the highest official with direct authority over the police, admitted that in ordering the record-keeping the government had exhibited "extreme turpitude."[24] It seems ironic that one of the strongest complaints against such "ideological espionage" (as it was widely known in September 1993) should have risen in the northern province of Tucuman by political followers of General Domingo Bussi, who had served as the 1976 dictatorship's delegate to that province (Bussi was accused of regularly using massive violence).[25]

Events at the 1993 Argentine Rural Exposition demonstrated that brutality was at least condoned, if not directly encouraged, by the highest official clique. This annual show is the showcase for the largest and most powerful association of ranchowners in Argentina. On August 14, violence erupted as an organized gang assailed spectators who jeered at Menem after his inaugural speech. The spectators were protesting the administration's economic policies. Ignoring the police covering the area, the gang went on to attack protesters outside the compound. Journalists covering the events were also victims of the violence. Some had their cameras destroyed. For voicing her dissent, Norma Pla, a delegate of Argentina's extremely poorly paid pensioners, was also attacked, having her wig yanked off.

Reminiscent of the military dictatorship's dirty war techniques, the area seemed to have become a "free zone." Mobsters enjoyed immunity similar to that of the anti-subversive gangs in the 1970s. Not a single assailant was arrested, in spite of the abundant security personnel deployed in the exposition's area for the visit by the president and members of his cabinet.[26] Conjecture about where the attackers had come from varied considerably. For some researchers, they had been recruited at a soccer club, the president of which, a man named Barrionuevo, is in Menem's closest circle. Others presumed that, like many other bands, the gang had been hired by Menem's supporters at the Mercado Central (the central market— soon to be put under Patti's direction). Others believe that some members of these gangs had operated with the army gangs (*patotas*) and task forces during the military dictatorship.[27] A journalist, Hernan Lopez Echagüe, was attacked on August 19 after publishing a note in *Pagina 12*[28] describing the recruitment of toughs at the Mercado Central. A week later, Echagüe suffered a second and almost fatal assault. He was taken to a hospital by a samaritan taxi driver who found him lying unconscious in the street. In what was clearly a warning to reporters not to interfere, a second journalist had his face slashed. President Menem and Eduardo Duhalde, his former vice-president who was by now governor of Buenos Aires province, showed not the slightest alarm. They nonchalantly attributed the violence to passing partisan political passions that, like cold weather, will soon wither away.[29]

To public amazement, government officials remained undisturbed by the episode at the rural exposition. Secretary of Agriculture Felipe Sola candidly explained to the press that the attacks "were caused" by those who had attended the inauguration "to insult the President."[30] Menem's former ambassador to Honduras, Alberto Brito Lima, who had witnessed the beating of journalists, said the violence was a "logical reaction to the press's unfair reports."[31] Brito—reportedly a salient partaker at the Ezeiza massacre in June 1973[32]—explained: "There was something they must have done to bring the beating upon themselves." This was indeed a foreseeable reaction by Brito.

Information surfaced that right-wing, authoritarian, corporatist Peronistas were present at the exposition. Experienced bullyboy Jorge Cesarsky had also attended the rural's inauguration. Cesarsky had built himself a reputation as henchman for ultraright-wing Peronista Lieutenant Colonel Jorge Osinde, who allegedly commanded the killing and torturing of left-wing militants near the Ezeiza airport on Peron's return from Spain in 1973.[33] An admirer of Jose Primo de Rivera,[34] Generalissimo Franco's fascistic ideologue in the 1930s, Cesarsky bluntly justified the aggression.[35] With the very same words with which Peron dispatched the left-wing activists to their fate in the square in 1973, Cesarsky explained that those who had suffered the violence at the exposition were "infiltrators."[36] The "real aggressors," he said, were those who suffered the blows: the "subversive of the 1970s."[37]

This example of the pervasive appeal to violence that Argentina's society exhibits exposes the degree of the country's authoritarian contempt for individual rights. Such contempt may surprise many observers who in 1985 noted the support for the human rights trials. In the next section I set out to explain the recurrence of violence and the adaptation that will be required of Argentine society for its eradication.

CONDITIONED BY
A THEORY OF TERROR

In spite of the widespread support that individual rights groups enjoyed in the early and middle 1980s, especially in 1985 at the time of the trials of military officers, it seems that in the 1990s individual rights have lost their appeal in Argentina. Except for a very small group of political and human rights activists and a similarly small number of students, the role that basic rights can play is now unimportant for the population at large. Indeed, the populace seems well adapted to violence.

In the 1970s, the constant experience of random brutality gradually began to shape Argentines' perceptions, not only of the country's reality but of the world in general. Once terror became a way to understand social reality, it also became the general theory through which political events acquire significance. By *theory* I am not referring to the ordinary notions of a consistent set of postulates or an elaborate conception of knowledge: I allude to the ideology, the beliefs, that condition any kind of inquiry.[38] This theory—established among the general (terrorized) population of the 1970s—will tend to lag, long after the terror machine begins to quiet down. Many students of ideology use the word *worldview*. I use *epistemology* instead, and narrowly define it: I want to stress that state terror produces a limited set of basic principles and values upon which or through which all other experience is understood. Terror provides a lens through which all else is seen.[39]

It is well known that, in Argentina, particularly between 1974 and 1980, right-wing groups, including the army and its ultraright-wing allies, waged a widespread campaign of disappearances, torture, and assassinations. Encompassing loftier goals than merely quashing left-wing insurgency, the campaigners aspired to instill in the population their ultimate goals, which they termed as "cherishing the country's Hispanic Catholic heritage" and "restoring the traditions of the Fatherland" to "encounter Argentina's fate," whatever these interpretations of history and the army mean.[40] The principles that shaped state action were "active principles": They went beyond those things people were expected to refrain from doing; they stretched to positive actions that individuals were required to perform.[41] The population was to meet expectations such as pledging allegiance to national symbols. Citizens were criminally convicted, for instance, for remaining seated while the national anthem was being played at a national festivity.[42] Amendments to legislation made such "contempt" punishable. Students were not merely expected to refrain from being disrespectful toward the teaching of the country's traditions; they had to demonstrate their positive feelings for such teaching. As already mentioned, short hair and a tie for men and long, dark skirts for women were the uniforms on campuses. Women were barred from wearing slacks (not to mention shorts, even in summer). To put it once more in the words of General Acdel Vilas: "Naivete and indifference imply subversive complicity."[43]

The absoluteness of these principles (as explained earlier) made the existence of an authority external to the campaigners themselves logically impossible. Definitive principles are, by definition, worth all possible sacrifices: humanity should not survive if it does not deserve to survive. If chosen by the tyrant, one would inevitably have to suffer torture and death. There was simply no escape. That the victim should bear the blame for what happened was a part of the ideology that both groups, the terrorizers and the terrorized, held in common; the former because the (collective) values they stood for were too precious to give way to individualistic principles (Videla[44] and Roualdes made illustrative statements to this effect).

Hence—again as mentioned earlier—the secrecy and ruthlessness employed by the state apparatus split the polity into two ideological camps. There were those who controlled disarticulating power and there were those who could be controlled by it.* Thus, adaptation to state terror had a direct impact on people's understanding of the world, on their all encompassing ideology. It profoundly informed their theory of reality.[45] Individuals in both groups experienced idiosyncratic adjustments as they increasingly incorporated the violence into their pattern of normalcy. Many children learned this normalcy in a curiously quick way. A two-year-old girl, sitting at dinner with her father and mother in their Buenos Aires apartment in 1974 when a deafening explosion sounded, acted as if nothing unusual had happened. The girl told her startled parents with total calm: "It was a bomb."[46]

Thus, the state of terror produced two—and only two—reactions to it. It also produced a single underlying value system or epistemology—one lens through which the world was understood. It is in this that its genius and its power lies: its ability to limit ideological options to two—to bipolar, dialectically related views of the state, of terror, of self, and of the world.

For those holding the first ideological position, the *conspiratorial* (i.e., those directly or indirectly behind the state terrorist campaign to quell ubiquitous legions of subversives) the world was one in which no room was left for

---

*Although I treat them with different terminology, the "fatalism" I deal with in this chapter is but one face of the notion of "structural power" and its effects on the practice of blaming that I tackle in chapter 2.

optimistic trust. The world "out there" was filled with furtive enemies whose destructive purposes could be neutralized only by indiscriminate violence. This conspiratorial conception was bolstered by the Roman Catholic army chaplains and the bishopric, which gave almost unanimous, enthusiastic support to the dirty war. Those holding the other ideological option (the terrorized) developed a fatalistic outlook. Like the salivating Pavlovian dog that has no expectations of changing the course of events, this sector, battered by repeated experiences, came to view any attempt to avoid chastisement as a futile enterprise. Terror had instilled an adaptive weltanschauung among members of both groups. People had built their experience of terror into their epistemology—their philosophies or theories about the world, and the attendant insights.[47]

Our perception of events is conditioned by a set of premises that shapes our theory of the world and determines our interaction with reality.[48] If, for example, we repeatedly experience persecution, our adaptive mechanisms will teach us that the world is not one that we should trust and, consequently, we will punctuate events in such a way that will confirm the theory. By his own distrustful behavior, the paranoid will generate in others the hostility and suspicion that confirms that the world is indeed persecutory.[49] Conversely, If we have learned to be optimistic and trustful of other people, we will find that there is always a facet of other people's conduct that reinforces our trust and optimism.[50] Although distrust and optimism have been learned in a specific context, they become the ideologies through which we contemplate the world; we act as if this original context were ever present. The premises on which we build our notion of reality create our epistemologies. These epistemologies have more to do with specific historical and social contexts than with the particular events that we perceive within these contexts. Adjustment to a state of terror causes individuals to adopt a set of premises about the world in general that will continue to be present even when there is no direct threat of harm.

Adaptive changes of this sort are a part of the process of learning. Such learning, or relearning, about the nature of the world one lives in takes place at a higher, more abstract plane than the simple learning of facts. While in a state of terror, the "facts" refer to particular events (such as a bomb blast, or the scene of a roped man being thrown into the trunk of a car); the new set of premises, the adaptive theory, involves a perception of a broader set of circumstances: a construction of the general context in which these events are perceived.[51]

In the Argentina of the 1970s, this general context consisted of an ongoing dialogue between the *conspiratorials* and the *fatalists*. These two groups emerged from the unfolding process of one's dialogue about conspiracy, Fatherland, subversion, and silence. Through the distinct punctuation of social relations, individuals (drawing on either ideology) developed complementary theories of the country's political environment.[52] Refusal to render positive support enhanced suspicions among the conspiritorials that the enemy was everywhere. The logical response was random terror against the "unfriendly," the "shy," the "forgetful,"—the raw material for recruitment by the "anti-Argentine" campaigners.[53] The fatalists' answer to unpredictable, random violence was increased skepticism—the apathy that scholars refer to when the victims' relatives take suffering as inevitable.[54] Both parties to this dialogue confirmed their theories about the political scenario. For the conspiratorials it was clear that more of the same was the necessary course of action. For the fatalists, shyness, apathy, and detachment were the only options left. Meanwhile, the number of victims of brutality grew larger.

Acquired in the context of state terror, these views became genuine "insights." Transcending their historical framework, these enclosed theories of reality developed into full-blown, universal theories of social life. Consistent with the worldviews adopted by a large portion of the Argentine community, both theories constructed a world of extreme hostility. And these theories persisted, even when the determining circumstances in which they originated were no longer present (or at least had ameliorated).

For the conspiratorial outlook, the 1985 human rights trials and the media's criticism of the dirty war were part of the subversive conspiracy. Every officer who testified at the mutiny trials of the December 1990 plotters explained the issue almost identically: the human rights trials were instrumental to the subversives' ends; the prosecutors and judges were tools of the conspiracy, if not actual accomplices.[55] They claimed that the chiefs of staff (whom those on trial had sought to depose) had not done enough either to stop the human rights trials or to prevent a defamatory press from negatively affecting the minds of the Argentine population.[56] They felt that the exposure of children, by the media, to a "deformed" reality had turned children against their military parents.

On the other side, as Gingold reports, the fatalists find that the continued perpetration of abuses by the police and widespread support of these abuses by sectors of the middle class demonstrate that the dictatorship has not ended.[57] In some sense, although attenuated, the dirty war is still present. This continues to render democracy extremely difficult of attainment.

Neither the conspiratorial nor the fatalist theory of reality are compatible with a rights-based democracy. The language of rights is one by which citizens make claims against one another and demand respect as responsible individuals. The acknowledgement of respect for the person that stems from this recognition is dependent on the value attached to notions such as free will, responsibility, and duty.[58] The theories that emerged from the state of terror produced their own discourse and this became a part of common parlance, reproducing those very theories of social reality and inhibiting the development of a language of freedom and respect.

Indeed, the dialogue between the two theories of conspiratorials and fatalists reinforced each other. In their unmitigated demand for positive support and the perception of a permanent and ubiquitous enemy, sectors in control of the violence in the 1990s have no room in which to concede rights to their rivals. The values and principles they set out to protect are too vital—too vital to anyone in their right mind—to compromise in the name of rights. Defense of individual rights is the work of either accomplices or idiots. Blame the victim. "There is something he must have done."[59] Concomitantly, the fatalist theory of the world is also incompatible with the basic notions of freedom, responsibility, and respect. The lack of self-respect and esteem that a fatalistic conception of history implies necessarily translates into lack of respect for human worth in general. Thus, the dialogue goes on. There is no sign that individual rights and responsibility will play a relevant—let alone essential—role in the popular Argentine mind.

Indeed, in the 1990s, with new symptoms of state terror accelerating, judges clearly support police brutality, and large sectors of the middle class acquiesce, to the detriment of articulating power. In the post-military era, the courts have circumscribed the already limited role of individual rights. In 1993, the federal appellate court in the city of La Plata sentenced a noncommissioned marine officer to three years in prison for abducting a high school principal with the help of the patrol under his command. The supreme court overturned the conviction on the grounds that violence had not been duly demonstrated. Commenting on this decision, a journalist sensibly inquired whether the abduction of the principal by an armed army patrol was not in itself sufficient evidence that coercion had been employed.[60]

Where interests collide, the judiciary has allotted declining weight to individual rights. When relatives of the victims of the dirty war requested authorization to unearth bodies discovered in secret mass graves, judges either denied such authorizations or granted them unenthusiastically. In a 1993 decision, the supreme court decided against the identification of an adolescent whom the claimants had recognized as a close relative. The youth had allegedly been stolen as a baby from his mother before her execution at a clandestine detention center. Refusing a petition that the boy be given a blood test to prove his identity, the court grounded its pronouncement on the premise that extracting blood implies unjustifiable pain.[61] Thus, in the two cases mentioned here, the court adopted contradictory standards: an extremely narrow definition of violence to acquit the marine officer, and a broad standard to deny the family its petition for a blood test. The courts have almost unanimously dragged their feet in ordering the measures necessary to establish the identity of children of disappeared persons. Indeed, the judiciary seems unwilling to acknowledge the claimants' rights to identify a relative in spite of the simplicity of the procedure.

The executive branch, by refusing to supply any help to the data banks, has rendered the identification of the corpses of presumed victims of repression extremely difficult.[62] President Menem vetoed a law of congress that would have exempted relatives of the victims of repression from compulsory military service, saying such exemptions would be a "privilege." The government has also been reluctant to seek the extradition of putative parents of children of the disappeared, thus making it impossible for the original families to recover their children.

There is a narrow relationship between popular support for brutality and institutional obliviousness to the rights of victims of repression. The estranged children of the disappeared are but one example. As did the military of the 1970s, many Argentines in the 1990s, including judges and public officials, have decided that there is no room for rights in a war against evil. As Gingold reports, the police dehumanize possible suspects to the extent that they commonly refer to them as "bulks" and "targets."[63] They understand the new evil as whomever threatens society's basic values: in the main, this means "property." In the same indiscriminate way that subversion was earlier defined, offenders are now lumped together: the cassette recorder burglars in the Santos case, the children of subversive suspects, a depraved teenager Soledad Morales . . . all, in the name of "decency," to blame for the violent loss of their own lives. For commentators who followed the Soledad case, the girl's virginity became the main issue in the investigation of her death. The teenager's sexual life was more important than the actions of the suspected rapists and killers.[64]

The old bipolar logic, "If you are not with us you are against us," is back in force. In denying the victim's right not to be tortured by Luis Patti, in granting respectable citizens the power to kill minors for property offenses, killings and torture again become the price Argentines pay for order. Argentines justify assaults on dissenters and journalists for unsettling this social order. Rogelio Garcia Lupo, one of the most prominent political commentators in the country, claims that there are qualitative similarities between the "private" hired gangs acting in the 1990s against journalists and the "public" gangs operating in the 1970s against suspected subversives. By raping their victims and plundering their belongings, the latter actually blurred in the Argentine mind the boundaries between the private and the public.[65]

The middle class, having supported the dictatorship

that shaped their "understanding" (extreme violence has to be condoned if not encouraged) now finds that rights are nonessential. Their adopted philosophy teaches them that human life and suffering have little intrinsic value. In the same way, an even larger segment of the community has learned not to challenge the conspiritorial view, because violence is, after all, a fact of life that has to be endured. Legal rules that outlaw Patti's violence are impediments to the health of the Fatherland; thus, the rules have to be blatantly ignored. The credibility of media that report state-sponsored violence is undermined by accusations of being a "monopolized" and "partisan" press. Human rights activists pressing for accountability are increasingly losing their authority. In the 1990s, there is no recognizable authority to generate awareness that torture and assassinations are violations of rights of such magnitude that, perhaps with the exception of desperate circumstances, members of a rights-based community would want stopped without delay. The players are still engaged in the game without end."[66]

So much for commentary on mere approach to political conflict: there is more to the new system's similarities with the military dictatorship than this. The old, well-known faces of the top military of the 1970s are beginning to resurface, as are fascistic groups like the anti-Semitic Tacuara. Violence is increasing. The groups of rowdies may well end up killing dissenters, as the Triple A did under the Isabel Peron administration.[67] By threatening two hundred journalists, terror is likely to have begun to work its way among thousands of people. The use of the logic of terror becomes all the more evident in the president's rhetoric—when, for example, popular demands for a better education are met by Menem's unsubstantiated accusation that the demonstrators are being manipulated by subversive activists. Similarly, the president accused "left wing activists" of promoting the investigation of the killing of a conscript by his superiors in a military compound.[68] The president denounced a left-wing convocation as being organized to promote "hatred and a class struggle."[69]

In this chapter I have described how, in spite of the population's broad support of the 1985 human rights trials, the notion of rights is far from being a revered value in Argentina. Not only has the citizenry shown little interest in the protection of rights, but the courts have found a wide assortment of interests to override these rights. One need not be a pessimist seriously to suspect that the old terror is still alive and well and living in Argentina, ready to inflict a lot of suffering.

THE OUTCOME
OF THE
HUMAN RIGHTS TRIALS

In chapter 5, I attempted to explain the way in which some Argentines support violence while others fatalistically endure this violence. I also explained how the peculiarity of the dialogue between the two "factions," conspiratorials and fatalists, leaves no room for the notion of individual rights. In this chapter I address two interconnected issues. The first involves the seeming contradiction between the enthusiastic popular support of the human rights trials and the populace's present acquiescence in—if not direct support of—state-related brutality. The second issue deals with the reasons why, in spite of its central role in Argentina's "transition to democracy," the judiciary has failed to become authoritative: lack of consensus over the impartiality of judicial decisions, as I will explain, renders the judiciary ineffective in asserting individual rights.

SUPPORT FOR THE TRIALS
BUT A BLIND EYE FOR VIOLENCE

Official indifference to (and perhaps even support of) aggression against journalists and widespread police torture indicate what seems to be a contradiction between the vast popular support for the human rights trials and the country's lack of concern about everyday state-related violence. This general stance toward violence largely stems, I have suggested, from the adaptation to an atmosphere of persecution and terror that rendered individuals unconscious of their own, and others', rights. Argentina is still far from becoming the rights-based democracy that in 1983 many thought it would become. At that time, the fact that millions of people supported the human rights trials seemed to indicate that individual rights had acquired a central role in the country's political life.

Support for the trials and repeated mobilizations against the impunity with which military officers acted may have invited this conclusion—that the Argentine populace would strive to strengthen the country's institutions to prevent a relapse into the extreme violence of the 1970s and 1980s. Indeed, after 1983 the populace staged numerous rallies against measures that benefitted officers indicted or convicted for human rights violations. The most numerous and vociferous of these rallies were staged in 1986 and 1987, against the Alfonsin administration's proposed Full Stop and Due Obedience laws, and in 1989 and 1990 in opposition to Menem's blanket pardons of all military personnel (among the pardoned were human rights transgressors, officers responsible for the Falklands/Malvinas catastrophe, and mutineers during the Alfonsin administration). This support for having military officers punished, however, shows only one side of popular sentiments. The other became noticeable at the 1991 elections.

In these gubernatorial and congressional elections, candidates with extremely authoritarian views had astonishing appeal. Military officers running for provincial governorships and seats in the lower house captured a substantial portion of the electorate. The appeal of these officers seemed to be enhanced, rather that diminished, if—as was the case with some of them—they had been particularly tyrannical. Some of these candidates had either represented the military dictatorship (in the same jurisdictions where they were running in 1991) or had opposed the first postdictatorial administration for its efforts to have human rights abusers sent to trial. In fact, some of the candidates were paradigms of the dictatorial abuses the human rights trials were addressed to expose.

Despite his reputation for having run a ruthless campaign against dissenters as a military delegate in the province of Tucuman, General Domingo Bussi received 43 percent of the votes—in that very same province. He may have done even better than that. The winner was pop singer Ramon "Palito" Ortega, the Peronista Party candidate, whom President Menem personally backed: yet many observers agree that Ortega's win was the consequence of ballot manipulation by the federal government's supervisor.

Another example of the appeal of prototypes of the dictatorial era was that of retired Colonel David Ruiz Palacios, who commanded the federal police as the dictatorship's deputy minister of the interior. In 1991, Ruiz was favored by the polls to win the elections in Chaco Province by a landslide. When he was barred from running because he had not lived in the province long enough to qualify, Ruiz handpicked his own substitute—who won the election easily.[1]

Perhaps the most surprising event was the success of Aldo Rico, the former lieutenant colonel, who ran for governor of Buenos Aires, Argentina's largest province. Rico, cashiered and criminally prosecuted during the Alfonsin administration for leading military rebellions against his commanders in April 1987 and January 1988, was pardoned by Menem in 1989. In 1991, political analysts and journalists considered that he and his newly founded party, MODIM, might win a little over 2 percent of the electorate. Identified with a staunchly undemocratic faction of the army, Rico's party obtained three seats in the national congress; almost 11 percent of the province voted for his ticket.[2] This is particularly astonishing considering that Rico's revolts were aimed at removing the military commanders *for not stopping the trials of officers accused of violating human rights.* Like the large majority of his comrades, Rico believed that the generals' failure was jeopardizing the dignity and unity of the army. Going further than his colleagues, however, Rico had demonstrated himself to be a man of action, rising up in arms and threatening to cause a bloodbath.[3]

After the 1991 elections, most political observers conjectured that support for Rico and his party had come about because of a desperation vote by the Buenos Aires poor, especially shantytown dwellers. But polls reveal that Rico's voters were mostly middle class.[4] This episode makes it obvious: many middle-class voters find the promise of order irresistible, even if it means condoning torture and assassination.

Some observers feel that the electoral participation of military officers indicates an auspicious shift. They prefer to interpret the officers' electoral success as a democratization of military officers rather than the militarization of the country's partisan politics. Optimistic scholars claim that the officers' political campaigns demonstrate that formerly authoritarian, pro-coup individuals are now being drawn into the democratic game. I disagree. Considerably more skeptical, I believe that their participation in the electoral process does not show that these candidates attach worth to the democratic system; the reason for their participation is, rather, that these officers are fully aware that they could not succeed in installing a new military regime. A durable military takeover is probably not feasible, given enduring conflicts within the military (these conflicts include, among other things, blaming one another for the 1976 dictatorship's economic debacle, the 1982 Falklands/Malvinas fiasco, and numerous officers' involvement in the misappropriation of personal effects sent to the drafted combatants). It has become patent to all, even those who take prodemocratic, international rhetoric with a grain of salt, that a military government in Argentina would find it both economically and politically impossible to survive in isolation from the international community.

The participation of ultraright-wing military officers in partisan politics is also taking place in other Latin American countries. One example is the case of former Bolivian dictator General Hugo Banzer, who ran in the country's 1993 presidential elections. It is also clear that the discourse of these officers-turned-politician is often that of traditional corporatist nationalists, and thus hardly compatible with a rights-based democracy. Rico, for example, illustrated his contempt for democracy by publicly claiming that, had he been among the army's general staff, he would never have accepted that his subordinates be brought to trial.[5]

The Issue of Morality

What do we make of these contradictions? On the one hand we have the demonstrations in favor of punishment; on the other the outcome of the 1991 elections. What seems to be true is that, given the country's craving for tranquility and order, popular support for punishing state abuse may prove to be misleading. I have claimed that the spirit behind the popular support of punishing human rights abuses is intimately connected to the peculiarities of the social practice of blaming as shaped by the reign of terror. Derived from this practice, the issue of whom to try among the numerous military officers who, actively or passively, directly or indirectly, had been involved in its execution, aid, or support is indeed complex.

As late as mid-1992, few Argentines questioned the premise that perpetrators of human rights violations carried out during the 1976–83 dictatorship should be put on trial. Setting aside the views of ultraright-wing civilians and army officers, and the relatively small sector of the populace that suffered personal loss at the hands of left-wing terrorism, a large majority agrees that trying *some* human rights violators was appropriate. There is, however, no consensus as to why the trials were suitable (or necessary), and even less agreement as to what category of wrongdoers warranted criminal punishment.

The numerous interviews I held with officers in the early 1990s in Buenos Aires clearly showed that few of them thought that trying human rights abuses was in itself unjust. Among the latter stand those who believe that war criminals are not punishable if their side wins the war. A moral skeptic and firm believer in this principle is General Eduardo Viola, the second military president after General Videla. Viola blatantly attested that, had the Allies lost World War II against the Axis, the trials of war criminals would have been held in Virginia.[6] Other than that, opinions as to why and who varied considerably. Officers agreed almost unanimously that the Alfonsin administration's human rights policy had been disastrous; but there is no consensus as to what rendered the policy calamitous.

For some officers, the rigidity of military discipline renders prosecutions of junior personnel unwarranted. They felt that officers should not be blamed for what they do as long as they do it in the furtherance of superior orders, regardless of the orders' content.[7] The fact that some of these orders contravene a basic sense of compassion and decency does not detract from the fact that obedience is a soldierly virtue—and after a successful armed campaign against subversion, such obedience should be encouraged, not condemned.[8]

For other officers, the due-obedience defense that was resorted to by some indicted officers should not have exonerated anyone who could tell right from wrong; such officers should have resisted their seniors' immoral directives. The decisive ingredient of punishability should have been the quality of the motives underlying the violence. Punishment, claimed this group, should have been exacted only upon those comrades who had acted out of selfishness.[9] The due-obedience argument should carry little weight, because honorable soldiers, they maintained, should never follow orders that hurt their moral sensibility. There are times, they said, when military necessity demands that prisoners be tortured and even killed, because in war undesirable measures may be the lesser evil. This opinion illuminates a moral dilemma, a quandary that political and moral philosophers share with theorists of criminal law: when pressed to determine the culpability of transgressors of the positive law who find that conforming to the legal system violates their moral beliefs, these scholars are largely unable to come up with a straightforward answer. It is, in a broad sense, the case of the conscientious objector.[10] The issue of guilt becomes controversial when such persons break the law out of their moral convictions, whatever value we attach to them.

Many scholars believe, as I do, that punishment is warranted only if the perpetrator's legal guilt also implies moral blame. If transgressors of the law believe they are doing the morally correct thing, the justification of the criminal sanction becomes at least doubtful. This issue has a certain air of paradox, insofar as experience indicates that many of the most cruel and systematic transgressors of human rights are likely to have acted out of profound moral convictions. The basic claim, for those who entertain that these perpetrators ought to be excused, is that the fact of selflessness places those officers who tortured and killed for their country beyond criminal blame. It should be noted that philosophical concern about punishment has not simply addressed the issue of enforcing the law, but also the moral reasons that justify punishment. These moral bases deal perforce with moral guilt. For defenders of the "selfless soldier," military officers are not less guilty because they follow orders. Blind compliance does not fit the ideal of a moral officer. A moral officer is obligated to disobey his commanders and the law when he finds that compliance is morally wrong. It is, moreover, inconceivable that morality should give way to hierarchical formality: whether we refer to a young lieutenant or to a general, altruism ought be encouraged.[11]

For other officers, including Mohamed Ali Seineldin, the convicted colonel, the Alfonsin administration's greatest flaw was that of overlooking military and civilian groups who deliberately benefited from the dirty war—as was the case with many intelligence personnel. Most such agents who committed abuses did so to their own advantage. Officers such as Seineldin claim that these agents, many of them civilians, were the worst abusers and looters; they were the men in the ominous "green Ford Falcons,"[12] in the trunks of which thousands were taken away for good.[13] Entitled to kill and torture by the military services, intelligence personnel, by this account, committed rape and larceny for their own pleasure and benefit.

Intelligence agents also took full advantage of the confidential nature of their activities, escaping indictments. A case in point is civilian agent Raul Guglielminetti.[14] In spite of his gruesome personal record, this ruffian was able to take advantage of the lack of political interest in prosecuting civilians. Guglielminetti even managed to sneak into the Alfonsin administration, becoming a member of the president's security staff. Before fleeing the country in 1986, under suspicion of recent participation in the extortive abduction of a businessman, Guglielminetti occupied an office a few yards from the president's quarters in the Casa Rosada. As a member of the government house security staff, Guglielminetti was able to be present at presidential meetings.[15] For Seineldin and his followers, the lesson is that, unlike honest officers who were indicted outright, ruffians like Guglielminetti got off because punishing civilians was politically unattractive.[16] This reluctance to prosecute civilians made it obvious to Seineldin and his followers that the human rights trials were but a partisan political stratagem, leading directly to revenge.

Only a handful of steadfastly democratic officers who had overtly opposed their comrades' methods during the dictatorship did not believe that the trials, as conducted, were essentially "political." The rest were convinced such was the case. "Political trials," in this conception, meant compromising the impartiality of the courts to secure convictions for political, partisan, or personal convenience. Whether from personal hatred or simple demagoguery, the trials were a masquerade to conceal the design to damage the armed forces' reputation. As lawyer Roberto Durrieu, the military regime's deputy minister of justice, explained it to me, instead of enhancing the prestige of the judiciary, the human rights trials eroded the authority of the judges. For reasons entirely different to his, I believe there is more than some truth to Durrieu's conclusion.

As the military understood it, the persecution of offi-

cers for their part in the dirty war—young officers in particular—had intentionally, or at least recklessly, eroded the
cohesiveness of the armed forces, weakening the country's
defense system. The civilian government's "persecutions"
had fractured the armed forces' loyalty and discipline.[17]
One of the most prominent proponents of this opinion
was General Jorge Arguindegui, President Alfonsin's first
army chief of staff. On a 1991 TV talk show,[18] Arguindegui
explained that Argentina's military vulnerability was a
consequence of the pernicious influence of two of President Alfonsin's senior advisers; namely, Carlos Nino and
me. It is true that the trials eroded cohesiveness between
junior and senior officers—it was already weak—but for
reasons other than we had expected. Conflict between the
ranks was a consequence of the claim of younger officers
that, in facing the flurry of accusations of torture, murder,
and rape, their seniors did not rise to the occasion with
loyalty. Not only did the generals not exercise their force
to stop the trials, but, having agreed to allow the trials to
continue, the generals would not hold themselves accountable for, at least having consented to their subordinates' deeds. By and large, the Alfonsin administration's
human rights policy brought about an intense exchange
of accusations among military personnel.

Voicing their dissent about the trials, many officers of
middle rank maintained that the two-pronged strategy
(prosecuting only top planners and direct, junior, perpetrators) was untenable. This schema invited the absurd result that, while young lieutenants were being tried for
bloodying their hands, the bulk of the majors and colonels
under whose orders these young officers had served remained unpunished. These majors and colonels had now
been promoted to the ranks of colonels and generals, with
no legal responsibility for the crimes, because they had
neither designed the repressive campaign (as had the
generals) nor personally engaged in torture, murder, or

rape (as had younger officers and noncommissioned officers). The top-and-bottom-only strategy had disturbing
effects on the relationship between senior and junior officers. One may assume that this process had indeed negatively affected the loyalty that seniors owe their juniors,
and caused, in return, a widespread contempt in the juniors for their superiors.[19] This policy had encouraged
the generals to pass on their responsibility by erasing
their own names from the lists of suspects they submitted
to the civilian authorities.

Although the judicial process had exacerbated the already existing clashes among officers, the elected administration was not entirely responsible for the tension in
the armed forces. Serious dissent had broken out in the
late 1970s over each of the three branch's portion of power.
Before the civilian administration stepped in, in the early
1980s, the feud increased—a consequence of corruption
among the upper cadres and apportionment among the
three branches of responsibility for the Falklands/Malvi-
nas fiasco. The armed forces' officials chose to forget their
old quarrels, however, to claim unanimously that the government's human rights policy was the single cause of
their unrest. The trials, and a relentless press campaign
that packaged the information about newly discovered secret graves and clandestine detention centers, eroded the
army's prestige and morale. Many officers with children
claim to have been forced to confront their offsprings'
suspicion that they had been involved in the torture and
the rape of prisoners. An army major told me that, since
1984, he had to face the misgivings of his two boys about
his being a military officer. Returning from school, they
would often query him: "Are you, too, a murderer?"[20]

At first, military officialdom reacted to what was felt to
be government enmity by treating government officials,
including the president, with extreme coldness. Since late
1984, groups of officers, most of them probably from mil-

itary intelligence, have waged a campaign of bomb scares, followed by the abduction of young political activists and death threats to human rights advocates. Although nobody was seriously injured by the blasts and the kidnapped reappeared two or three days after their abduction, these events nourished a climate of anxiety. About a hundred young political activists left the country until the atmosphere eased. Perhaps the most serious of these incidents was the 1985 discovery of a bomb planted in the province of Cordoba, four hundred miles north of Buenos Aires, on the very spot where President Alfonsin was scheduled to speak a few hours later.

LACK OF

JUDICIAL AUTHORITY

It was not only the army and its sympathizers who held the human rights trials to be "political." After the Buenos Aires federal court handed down its verdict convicting only five out of nine commanders, most human rights activists claimed *they* were victims of political fraud. At one end of the spectrum of the human rights organizations, the Madres de Plaza de Mayo—the Mothers—firmly claimed that the government did whatever it could to limit the prosecutions to an insignificant number of culprits. Unlike most activists, who were exclusively concerned with military and police violators, the Mothers believed that a wide sector of the citizenry, including priests, lawyers, and physicians, should also have been tried and punished. Cruel, ideological repression, they claim, would never have been possible had it not been supported by thousands of civilian accomplices and instigators. These accomplices deserved to be punished. As one of the leading Mothers stated it: "We are talking about the crime of genocide. All three (branches) of the armed forces accompanied by many civilians organized this crime. The church was another accomplice. Testimonies have proved the extent of the complicity of the church, and these so-called priests cannot be allowed to walk free."[21] Were they to do so, said the Mothers, social institutions would convey that basic rights have no relevant place in Argentina's political system.

However, most civil rights organizations and their supporters did agree that the courts had been politically slanted. Attesting to the courts' arbitrariness was the sentencing of a former brigadier, Orlando Agosti, to only four and a half years for his responsibility as the air force's delegate to the 1976 junta. Who could otherwise explain that, convicted on three counts of theft and eight of torture, the former brigadier should have been given such a light sentence. It was clear that the Alfonsin government had done its best to shrink the number of convicted officers. Numerous measures unveiled the Alfonsin administration's urge to compromise with the genocides.[22] These ranged from the active role assigned to the supreme council of the armed forces as the trial court to the limitations imposed by the Full Stop and Due Obedience laws. Over time, even the most cautious civil liberties militants became critical of what they considered an overly compromising policy. What became evident was the great disparity between new versions of recent history and the violence itself.

A FRAGMENTED COMMUNITY

Wide disagreement about the country's recent history is not only a consequence of different conceptions of the legitimacy and role of criminal justice; it also reflects incompatible versions about basic facts. An outstanding feature about Argentina is the way in which lack of formal, authoritative institutions has contributed to a multiplicity of versions of recent history. Opinions concerning the dirty war vary dramatically. Among facts that are disputed are, the size of the left-wing terrorist organizations operating before and after the military takeover in 1976;[23] the number of victims of state terrorism;[24] whether or not junior and noncommissioned officers were independently able to torture and assassinate suspects; the existence or nonexistence, of civilian paramilitary gangs operating under direct control of the military command—or even beyond such control. Some unsubstantiated accounts circulated that the military had even held their own secret trials, dealing with larceny and other "excesses" such as torture, rape, and murder. This last account has been refuted.

Such disagreement reflects a society that is extremely fragmented at every social level. Even high officials in the Alfonsin administration held irreconcilable views on essential topics; for example, disagreement as to the very nature of the dirty war and the degree to which junior officers could refuse to torture and assassinate prisoners. Alfonsin's minister of education, Julio Rajneri—a newspaper owner—emphasized that the government's human rights strategy of convicting torturers and murderers was doomed to fail because junior officers had acted under constant threats from their comrades and superiors. Invoking first-hand information, Rajneri told me in 1987 that the military upper cadres did not tolerate resistance and threatened to execute those who disobeyed. Thus, Rajneri concluded, extreme intimidation excused junior officers for carrying out atrocities. This account suggests that the dirty war was waged by a disciplined army operating strictly under the initiatives of the generals. In contrast with Rajneri's account, other officials, myself included, maintained that young officers had had enough freedom to not participate in the abuse of prisoners. Ostracism by their comrades was probably the worst possible punishment. This version coincides with the notion that the dirty war was not designed and conducted entirely by the generals, as I have suggested. The dirty war was a combination of the generals' adoption of the doctrine of national security and the escalation of what were almost private scuffles, engaged in by young officers, with "subversion" As in many discussions on similar subjects, officials participating in forging a human rights policy could not agree on the facts—facts essential to assessing the responsibility of junior cadres. Four years after the president's indictment of the members of the ruling juntas, the administration's leaders had not been able to agree on the most basic issues concerning military responsibility.

Argentine society is torn by the split versions of the *who*, the *how*, and the *why* of the dirty war. The most perplexing feature about this fragmentation of public opinion is that hardly anybody, including lawyers, base their positions on the courts' decisions. The December 1985 Buenos Aires federal court's conviction of five members of the first three juntas seemed to carry no weight with people in their interpretation of what had happened. Similarly, the verdict of the supreme court late in 1986 upholding the convictions also seemed irrelevant to public opinion.[25] These are but examples of the fact that, in Argentina, judicial decisions lack authoritativeness, both in establishing the facts brought to trial and in evaluating these facts. Thus, controversies about what should have been done about past human rights violations continue unabated, with no hope that an authoritative arbiter will bring them to an end. True, spirits seem to have calmed down in the 1990s, but this is not because the judiciary is now mustering popular respect; it is the result of the fatalists' dwindling concern about state abuses.

Most of the disputes among the president's close aides—and it should be said that they were intense disputes—revolved first around the political convenience of holding the trials and, later, on the scope of the proceeding. The controversies involved two groups: well-articulated, principled defenders of the trials and those who based their arguments mostly on circumstantial considerations. The latter largely emphasized the case's negative bearing on the mood of the army and their propensity to stage a new coup. There was an assumption; stressed by the antitrials advocates, that these trials were riskier than those held at Nuremberg and Athens. The Nazi genocides and war criminals were convicted by an international tribunal set up by the World War II victors; and although the Greek colonels were convicted by a domestic court, this court was a military tribunal, acting with the support of the army generalship after the Cyprus fiasco.

In Argentina, however, the lack of precedent, added to the popular, pro-trial effervescence and a threatening military, blurred our perception of the genuine, systemic reasons weighing against the trials as they were conceived. In the Argentine case, the culprits were members of the same army that claimed—and still claims—to have won the armed war against subversion. Not only did the military find the charges incomprehensible; most of them also felt that the citizenry, instead of acknowledging the armed forces' triumph, was now turning its back on them. Emilio Massera, the murderous naval delegate to the first junta, seemed not only sincere but also right when he made his final statement at the trials. He referred to those who had supported him as now hoping that he be punished in "this fickle Fatherland."

Another aspect of the trials that the military objected to was that the federal courts would have the final say on offenses alleged to have been perpetrated by military personnel. The designated trial court was a military tribunal, but the federal courts had wide authority to review the military tribunal's decisions. Officers felt the trials disrupted an enduring Latin American tradition by which the military are tried solely by their own courts. This perceived intrusion of the judiciary had itself become a matter of resistance and concern—and the top legal counselors of the three services said as much to me. They worried that this initial interference would set the precedent for further meddling of the civilian courts in offenses committed in the barracks. They feared the precedent indicated that civilian prosecutors would end up sending police to the barracks to investigate cases of petty theft of detail among the military rank and file.

From a practical perspective, the trials were indeed a constant source of confrontation and pressure for all sectors, including, of course, the military. They proved to be extremely time consuming for officials, including the president. Army officers and politicians were apprehensive, and presidential military aides took every opportunity to convey their alarm. Under debate were the criminal nature of the dirty war, the extent to which loyalty and obedience played a special excusing role among the military, and the notions of self-defense and necessity as applied to the military's alleged defense of the country and of the Christian world. Once the trials were set up, the entire populace focused on the question of criminal responsibility; there was very little consideration of the institutional dimensions of the transition to democracy.

For many officers, the "legal" battle waged at the courts was a continuation of their perceived victorious "armed battle," but for the Alfonsin administration, the issue had a larger scope than competing for power with the armed forces. The undertaking symbolized a decision to approach the entire issue of democratizing the country in a certain manner. The trials, indeed, provided a particular way, a means, to come to terms with the past, to instill individual responsibility, to establish the scope and depth of the truth, and, most of all, to write the country's recent history in the language of moral responsibility.

However, the language of *guilt* and *innocence* limits the relevant facts to an extremely limited time frame. The language of criminal responsibility is based on limiting the facts to a very narrow time span. Guilt and innocence are couched in the language of individual actions, of specific processes that we ascribe to individuals to establish whether their actions fit the legal definition of a criminal offense. Thus, instead of there being a wide debate, attention turned merely to the question of guilt or innocence. There was no public consideration of the institutional dimensions of the transition to democracy.

THE COURTS
AS THE CENTER OF TRANSITION

Placing the courts at the center of the transitional process meant circumscribing what had been an all-encompassing political conflict. This history was to be viewed in the comparatively limited dimensions of the criminal trials. The tension behind the trials hinted that the project of "judicializing" the debate over the country's history could provide harder facts than any other source. Authoritative courts would furnish an official version of reality to which a majority would subscribe—a majority large enough to shrink the scope for speculation and rumor about what the country had gone through. It was considered in the Alfonsin administration that a sufficiently supported judicial decision over any aspect of the dirty war would be less likely to be challenged than a parliamentary investigation. It is normally assumed that pinning a charge of torture or assassination on an individual senior officer is more convincing to the public than for it to have the opinion of an investigative commission. The rigors of the criminal procedure and the principle that the accused are presumed innocent unless proven guilty leaves considerably less play for contestation by right-wing sectors than does a parliamentary probe.

In Argentina, the problem with the court solution was that the judges had little prestige among the populace. They were considered to be either inexperienced or undemocratic, or both. The new judges appointed by the Alfonsin administration were young and inexperienced; those originally appointed by the military regime and reappointed in 1983 were suspected of not having democratic convictions. A general lack of confidence conditioned support of the verdict. Various social sectors challenged judicial decisions that did not suit their particular passions. Convictions would never have been accepted by the military and their followers; acquittals would never have been accepted by pro-rights groups. Thus, whatever the outcome, the trials threatened to erode the frail authority of the courts, transforming the "judicialization" of politics into the "politicalization" of the judges.

During my tenure as an adviser to the president, a day did not pass when I did not receive numerous telephone calls or visitors with strong views on the issues debated at court. Largely they expressed concern, even alarm, about the upheaval the human rights trials were causing within the armed forces. Some spoke about the negative impact that trying certain officers would bring about among their comrades, others the "senselessness" of confronting the military—the most powerful political sector. High officials and an array of personal friends and political sympathizers with the military regime shared their concern about what the trials could bring about.

The decision to stage the trials necessarily entailed the exercise of discretion: to try all those responsible was plainly absurd. Directly or indirectly, thousands of officers were implicated in human rights abuse. In the streets, groups favoring the trials made their presence noticeable, organizing rallies and sit-ins and threatening to intensify this presence if the outcome of the trials were not minimally satisfactory. On the other side, military officers in uniform challenged the courts and the Alfonsin administration. They openly appeared in gropus to show their support for indicted comrades. It was thus foreseeable from the start that the intensity of the contention taking place outside the courtroom would void whatever decision was arrived at by an already weakened judiciary.

Central to the military's attitude was a feeling of being targeted. Although the president had publicly declared he would press charges against a few ERP and Montonero leaders, the public discussion about the trials enraged the officers: they felt they were being blamed for every act of violence that had taken place. Some impartial observers shared this opinion. In late 1991, one judge who had served on the panel that tried the military commanders confided to me that, although he was convinced of the criminal responsibility of the generals, the exclusive concentration on army officers left him unsettled. After all, he said, what had made the military terrorist campaign possible in the first place was that vast numbers of people had granted them a blank check to reinstate order.[26] Moreover, by focusing almost exclusively on military officers, prosecutors overlooked the fact that most torturers had been civilians acting with intelligence units. In fact, even military officers were killed for investigating abuses by civilians. Major Sosa Molina, for example, was assassinated for investigating the activities of the Triple A.

I have already quoted the former admiral, Massera, about the populace's fickleness. He was not alone in this view. Two of the judges from the federal criminal court that convicted him told me there were times they felt there were sides to the trials of the commanders that felt unjust. It was not that those convicted did not deserve their sentences; but some of the accusers, witnessing the trials to see the officers convicted, had supported them and their methods.

Regarding the Political Situation

In considering the trials and their impact on building a rights-based community, I have yet to deal with the issue of the weaknesses of the trials with reference to the political situation of Argentina in the 1980s. The central issue is not simply that tension was caused by a potentially resurgent military, nor the resulting circumscription of governmental action. Rather, the question is whether, or to what extent, criminal trials, given their inherent nature, are capable of bringing about a political setting in which individual rights and responsibility are central.[27] My contention is that, in Argentina, there are structural, systemic grounds that were not sufficiently weighed before deciding, as President Alfonsin did, to indict human rights abusers.

I earlier described how Argentine authoritarianism had been linked to the conception of a world in which little, if any, room was left for neutrality and dispassionate, critical distance. I have also explained how the dictatorial mind sets itself up to generate this split: allies versus foes, conspiratorial accounts of political reality that turn themselves into a cause for further authoritarianism. I have also described how, trapped by their beliefs, the military and their allies rendered themselves insensitive to experience, and how a terrorized population learned to view violence as fatalistically unchangeable, thus feeding the suspicion that subversives were everywhere. Both sides were trapped in a game without end. Here, I attempt to expose how, in a special way, the courts also contributed to the impossibility of effecting change.

By instilling among the citizenry a bipolar interpretation of the world—"the guilty" and "the innocent"—the criminal trials recreated a scheme akin to that of "If you are not with us you are against us." Society was divided once more by institutionalized blame: what had formerly been subversives versus crusaders in the mid-1980s became the guilty versus the innocent. Paradoxically, the most attractive feature about the trials—the establishingment of one common truth—was also their greatest weakness: the inevitable over-simplification of history: There was no middle ground between the innocent and the guilty.

Thus, while the ideal rights-based democrat conceives blaming as a means to achieve aspirations of solidarity that enhance liberty and equality,[28] the meaning of solidarity through blaming acquires an entirely different purpose in a terrorized community.[29] There are numerous examples of communities enhancing common values through punishing transgressors and waging retaliatory wars. There is a social solidarity that is devoid of self-respect (e.g., witch-burning in New England; the Spanish conquistadores impaling natives in South America). In Argentina, terrorized fatalists manipulated blame for reasons other than reinforcing the community's respect and dignity. So did conspiratorials. As, in the 1970s the fatalists believed that victims caused their own pain, in the 1990s there was nothing we could do if the violence originated in a milieu to which we were alien: that of the *milicos asesinos* (military murderers).

I have described how, within the Argentine context, the practice of blaming sprang from sentiments other than those by which we try to convince violators not to harm us again. Such use of blaming implies that we treat wrongdoers as moral persons. By placing the fault on the disappeared—a class different from our own—blame became a self-serving device. It became a way to limit the violence to a defined social sector. By an analogous interpretation, in the 1990s our blame befell a class segregated from our own community: the population shifted its focus to the military—a new single-factor explanation for our suffering.[30]

It now seems clear that the common desire to have the military punished expressed the qualified, though popularly felt, need to promote social solidarity. The current appeal of police violence and the electoral success of dictatorial personalities strengthens our belief that the pursuit of punishment is unrelated to promoting the dignity of individuals. The retributive emotions behind the rallies and public protests, one may conjecture, were aimed at achieving a kind of social solidarity—a solidarity the nation had experienced during the apogee of the military regime. It will be recalled that, in 1978, the Madres were scolded for damaging the country's international image during the World Cup. The 1980s campaign to punish military officers must be regarded in similar light.

But if the popular sentiments behind the trials did not stem from a sense of individual dignity, it may be suggested that holding these trials was preferable to passivity. Doing nothing confirms our impotence; here, the community was able to convey its power by bringing some military officers to trial. The community, one may assume, is more likely to learn about its rights from the process of reacting against those who humiliated them.[31] Although I cannot see objections to this logic, there still seem to be many drawbacks to the trials strategy: by zeroing in almost exclusively on a relatively small, and defined, number of human rights abusers, the trials threatened to become the formal instrument to thwart the basic logic on which we build the very notion of responsibility. As a direct consequence of the criminal trials, formalized blame implied absolution for many civilians who had supported the military dictatorship: instead of being among the blamed, they were among the accusers. The trials contributed to the widely shared conviction that those not indicted were innocent. The negative side of the trials included the impossibility of pressing charges against thousands of civilian and military instigators and accomplices of the dirty war. Indeed, those who supported the military regime until the 1979 economic debacle and the 1982 Falkland/Malvinas fiasco saw themselves as being entitled to become accusers. In turn, this perceived betrayal by their former allies confirmed the military's conspiratorial theory: they now viewed themselves threatened by an even larger number of conspirators. Indeed, the military felt that, having been encouraged by the citizenry to restore order, they had now been made responsible for all the violence in the country since the 1970s. This almost certainly is the situation that Videla, the former general, had in mind when in 1993 he repeated his long-held conviction that he was a scapegoat.[32]

With a few exceptions (such as the Madres, who insisted that numerous civilians should also be tried) most people pointed exclusively to the military and the military-controlled police for all the suffering in Argentina. In this context, the assassins of the Peronista Triple A, the hoodlums of the Metal Workers' Union, and other right-wing groups were largely forgotten. Also disregarded were bloody episodes such as the June 1973 massacre marking Peron's return from Spain.[33] The slaughter of the young left-wing Peronistas who tried to control the Peronista movement was never mentioned, let alone probed. There was some kind of understanding that these victims deserved death for having feigned to be Peronistas as a cover for their left-wing persuasion. Society's authoritarian single-cause explanation for the source of its distress consisted no longer in blaming the victims; the single cause was now the military.

In spite of President Alfonsin's instructions to prosecute some of the Montoneros and ERP heads, many of whom had been made to disappear or had fled the country, there was a general atmosphere of obliviousness toward civilians (both right wing and left wing) who had been directly or indirectly involved in violence. Top politicians, trade union leaders, and ultraright-wing civilians who had used extreme violence while operating with Peron's Jose Lopez Rega were among those overlooked.

The military, with all the brutality of recent times laid at their door, retreated into bitterness. Remorse, shame, and even simple reflection, were all swamped by this bitterness at being pinpointed, as they believed, only for being members of the armed forces. This sense of being burdened freed these officers from even a minimal sense of moral responsibility for what they had actually ordered and done. The perception of betrayal by former allies (now turned into accusers) overshadowed the civilian government's claim that the trials did not, in fact, address the military as such but only those responsible for the abhorrent crimes. Thus, as the means of instilling a basic sense of individual responsibility, the trials were impaired by the politics of retributive justice.

This persistence of the single-factor element suggests, that the populace will again support a dictatorial intervention if the country's background conditions deteriorate. The recent Patti and Santos cases support such a belief.[34] The electoral appeal of General Bussi and Colonel Ruiz-Palacios[35] suggest that the desire for a tough hand to reinstate social order may be as strong now as it was back in the 1970s. The support for Santos indicates that many armed citizens are ready to protect their stereos at any cost. The background of a single-cause approach invites the analogy between the 1970s subversives and the 1990s property offenders. The cases in which children and youngsters are killed for posing petty threats to private property, and the police and judicial reactions to these episodes, can only be explained by noticing that people are using the lens of a bipolar logic: "If you are not with us you are against us."

At least two reasons suggest themselves as explanations for this single-cause oversimplification and distortion of history. The first comes from the political opportunism when human rights activism was at its zenith. There was a mid-1980s official move toward prosecuting Peronista henchmen, and this may well have been interpreted as political revenge against members of the traditionally largest party. There is a theory that, if prosecuted, right-wing trade unions may have been tempted to concoct a new, destabilizing alliance with military groups. Indeed, such a scheme would only reproduce the civic-military coalition that terrorized the populace in the era before the military coup, thus posing a major threat to the democratic experiment.

The second reason is less obvious: it rests in the popularly shared wishful thinking that society's evils had ended with the military regime. James Neilson, an expert on Argentine politics, wrote:

> During the first years of democracy, politicians, union leaders, entrepreneurs and other citizens sought to convince themselves that the military dictatorship and everything that went with it had been a phenomenon isolated from the *real country;* something comparable to the occupation of the national territory by foreign forces. It was obviously not that way. The dictatorship was born from the entrails of Argentine society. It was the completion of a long standing national tradition and a large portion of the civilian ruling class acted as accomplices of the military dictatorship before turning their backs upon them when their time was running out. They later condemned the military.[36]

The expectation contains two practical and equally distorted implications. The first is that, of all the right-wing groups in Argentina, only the military resorted to brutality, and only the military still would. The second is that the massive suffering of the 1970s has taught civilian left- and right-wing factions that almost any political style is preferable to violence. Assigning blame exclusively to the military may well, since it was a fairly widely shared, familiar belief, have served the fatalists' purpose of self-appeasement. The magical attainment of an imagined peaceful society would rest on the collective desire to punish the military for their violence. Building a peaceful society would be as simple as putting a few officers away for their crimes, consequently deterring their comrades from again overturning a civilian government. However, things do not seem to be working out that way.

Present tolerance of violence indicates that the collective drive to punish military abusers did not sufficiently promote respect for persons—an indispensable ingredient of a rights-based democracy. By refusing to accept the painful fact that terror originated in the very entrails of the community, the populace—using the single-factor mechanism—was able to stifle its guilt and shame for passivity toward the suffering. It seems only too obvious that looking at the pain as the consequence of the activities of a well-defined sector means rewriting the recent history of Argentina. The fact that many military officers were guilty of terrorism does not gainsay the truth in their claim that they were scapegoated. Beside the shameful deeds of many officers stand the no less-shameful actions of many civilians.

To challenge the current interpretation of the country's recent past, by exposing the nature of *the cause* of brutality, involves questioning the very motives behind the massive support for the human rights trials. It seems clear that support for court action did not rest on any belief in the impartiality of the courts. Present lack of respect for the courts' verdicts stems from a general public view that leaves no room for judicial independence. It is difficult to imagine the popular reaction if Videla and Camps had been acquitted, for example as a consequence of the evidence that they had ignored what was happening under their noses. It seems that the authority of the courts did not rest on popular respect for their judgment; rather, it lay in their ability to formalize, in legal style, a previous political decision to put some officers away.

The authority of the courts presupposes a "general belief" that their decisions convincingly establish the facts and properly evaluate their normative relevance. The principal element contributing to general respect for the courts stems from a claim of impartiality. Impartiality is only possible, one assumes, because we expect the courts to be detached from personal loyalties, partisan interests, and the passions that surround conspicuous criminal cases. The attainment of impartiality, however, depends on preconditions. Impartial judgments seem possible only insofar as the courts are sufficiently insulated from the social and political events that light our most intense emotions.

In trying a case involving the torture of a political prisoner, for instance, the courts' impartiality is possible only insofar as the judges disengage themselves from attaching value to political ideals and values. Disregard of the rule that instructs the courts to restrain themselves to consider only those acts that cause the suffering as described by the criminal law makes impartial disengagement impossible. There is more to the credibility of the courts than simple independence from prejudice and current passions. If a dispassionate, unprejudiced judge were allowed to assess the intrinsic quality of the torturer's ultimate goals, such as the honest intent to thwart a threat against Argentina's Christian mores, for instance, impartiality would easily be foiled. It seems inevitable that the judge's consideration of the culprit's ultimate purposes would play an essential role in deciding the case.

The impartiality of the courts does not mean neutrality in the face of all values; it means that we believe in the court's neutrality to all extralegal values and rules. Thus, impartiality would often be impaired if the background conditions of a case were rendered relevant to the decision. If this should happen, convictions would be based not so much on what the defendant did but rather on who and what he, or she, is. The distinctive authoritativeness of the courts results from the satisfactory exercise of the freedom they enjoy to assess the evidence pertaining to a very limited range of facts. The personalization of responsibility through the prism of guilt and innocence become conceptually senseless if the courts were to consider a broad range of background factors that are present in our daily lives. To be convincing, the language of guilt and innocence must be couched in established facts and rules. Guilt and innocence are simply senseless if the relevant facts and values are as wide as the complex universe with which anthropologists, sociologists and historians deal.

Criminal trials resemble games in that, in each case, the "truth" about the facts presupposes correlating limited facts with a system of rules, the authority of which is an assumed given.[37] We don't care about conditions external to the game itself. Unlike the authority of the police, that of the courts stems from their ability to exercise good judgment. Unlike historians, anthropologists, and sociologists, the courts base their decisions on sets of rules that are assumed to be both valid and just. It seems platitudinous to state that conditions external to the rules that define the game are irrelevant to the scoring of points. In a way akin to the indifference of games to background conditions, "guilt" and "innocence" presuppose that, although facets of the criminal trials may lend themselves to debate, this debate is normally confined to discrepancies concerning the interpretation of rules and facts. To reach V (a verdict) the courts establish whether D (the deed) falls within L (a legal definition). The courts—unlike the police—do not merely enforce the rules but also (impartially) decide the case on the basis of weighting a specified action against the set of rules. Although the authority of the courts is assumed to involve the exercise of prudence, this prudence consists mostly of the populace's disposition to hold its conclusions revocable by the "better judgment" of the court. The courts' discretion (similar to that of a tennis umpires) results from keeping the trials sealed from political and social background circumstances. Indeed, the courts may consider only a limited number of legally accepted circumstances to aquit the culprit, or, if they convict, to temper the punishment. Torture is punishable even if performed to save Christianity from destruction, or to secure that "the Fatherland" adopts the right path. The authority of the courts largely rests on the conviction that the judges are in a better position to discern the appropriate rules and establish the facts as a consequence of applying the right procedures. The assumption that the courts will give in to background considerations based on social or political considerations implies weakening their authoritativeness, and turns a trial into a political trial.

In Argentina, given the conspiratorials' appeal to self-sealing proofs and their reluctance to accept external authority, convictions by the newly appointed democratic judges could never have been authoritative convictions. For the most part, it seems clear that the fatalists' feeling of helplessness is incompatible with the notion of having rights: of being entitled effectively to press claims against those in control of violence. For conspiratorials, the trials were a mild expression of that same subversion they had militarily vanquished. These are, I believe, the reasons that the 1985 human rights trials were not able to affirm people's dignity. Instead, they recreated a new expression of the old dialogue between conspiratorials and fatalists. This dialogue, of course, undermined what little authority the courts enjoyed before the trials.

Argentina's fragmented society did not, and still does not, regard the trials as a means of instilling a sense of personal responsibility essential to a rights-based democracy. The military at no time respected their comrades' indictments and convictions. Since punishment depends on a degree of authoritativeness, they understood the courts' decision as a demonstration of the administration's control over the judges; the judges were the instrument of revenge.

Roberto Durrieu, the military regime's deputy secretary of justice and later legal adviser to Videla complained to me about President Alfonsin's December 1983 decree ordering the prosecutors to file criminal charges against the members of the first three military juntas. In a conversation we held in 1991, Durrieu interpreted the decree's *grounds for prosecution* as being intended to influence the courts' decisions; i.e., that they were a visible breach of basic republican principles. Durrieu's assumption that the courts were submissive includes a suggestion that Alfonsin would have secretly "instructed" the judges, rather than expose the courts, and himself, to worldwide criticism.

The Mothers and their followers also considered the courts' decisions to be political. Alas! For the Mothers, only political reasons could have driven the courts to acquit some of the generals and admirals of the three first juntas. Only political reasons could have sentenced some of those found guilty with extreme lenience.[38] The judges, according to the Mothers, were serving what they conjectured was the purpose of the administration: to make peace with the army.[39]

And so: the attempt to end the contention between opposing political conceptions was forced into the very narrow construction of the court of justice. This judicial assessment, strictly through the prism of criminal justice, of the comprehensive recent history of Argentina offered two possible results. The first was the *judicialization of politics*. The dramatic social events would be turned into occurrences to be discussed, appraised, and established at the courts—if the courts were authoritative enough to muster consensus. The second possibility, if the courts proved not to be sufficiently authoritative to make their verdicts popularly credible, would be the opposite. Indeed, the average person's conception came to be based on the courts' rulings: what actually took place was the *politicization of the judiciary.* In prosecuting only one sector of society, important aspects of the country's reality were lost, in exchange for very limited legal options of guilt and innocence, wrapped in extreme procedural formalism. This formalism contributed to the lack of development of a sense of the citizens' individual responsibility. As a consequence, it is not difficult to foresee that Argentina's lack of political authority and articulating power will provide room for terror.

NOTES

INTRODUCTION

1. I slash-mark the name of the islands to quell two kinds of criticism: first, that of being impervious to reality, and second, that of deserting the traditional Argentinean claim to the archipelago. I thus acknowledge the legal fact (one shared by almost the entire world) and at the same time attempt to avert being considered callous, disloyal, or both.

2. I adopt the expression *corrective justice* from Ackerman, *Liberal Revolution*.

3. Menem succeeded Alfonsin in 1989 following a general election (the first president after the general's regime having been Alfonsin). Menem was retained in 1995 following a constitutional amendment that made his reelection possible.

4. Among the firsthand sources I was able to interview (in mid-1992) was a high National Gendarmerie (Gendarmeria Nacional) officer.

5. See the newspaper, *Buenos Aires Herald*, July 10, 1992.

6. See the Buenos Aires newspaper, *Clarin,* Apr. 30, 1994, p. 10.

7. Ibid.

8. See, for instance, Paul G. Chevigny's recent research on the relation between police brutality and popular consent to such violence, "Police Deadly Force," pp. 389–425.

9. Gregory Bateson provides a simple and striking definition of what I will call a "rights-based democracy": *the setting in which the worth and responsibility of individuals reigns supreme* See Bateson, "Social Planning and the Concept of Deutero-Learning," in *Steps,* p. 162.

10. See chap. 2 of this book.

11. See chap. 6 of this book.

12. Amartya Sen points out that subjugated people will abandon their belief in their own and other persons' rights in order to accommodate themselves to the attainment of "small mercies." Sen, *On Ethics.*

13. By *shame* I here refer to the sentiment that stems from our incapacity to act autonomously. Shame, thus, lies beyond making the wrong choices. It comprises our lack of autonomy (that is, of choice). See Williams, *Shame and Necessity,* chap. 4.

14. See Wechsler, *A Miracle,* p. 241.

15. A former political prisoner told me that the pardoning of the generals made him feel the same way that a raped woman in a chauvinistic society sees herself. If the rapist is not convicted, she is likely to feel guilty, a blameworthy participant in the wrongdoing. She needs an institutional response to the wrongdoing to support her dignity.

16. Though narrowly linked to power, punishment also reflects authority, particularly if we want to be able to discriminate between this institution and other forms of state coercion. See Flathman, *Political Authority,* p. 157.

17. This assertion is valid whatever version is taken of the role of the generals in deciding to stage a coup and appeal to terrorist violence. See chap. 1 of this volume.

18. Malamud-Goti, "Transitional Governments in the Breach."

19. Przeworski, *Democracy.*

20. Ibid.

21. An examination of fanaticism is made in chap. 2 of this book.

22. CEMIDA was a very small group of democratic officers, most of them retired, who opposed the military regime and, most of all, the violence it resorted to. These officers were a very special clique. One of them, Colonel Augusto Rattembach, is a musician and composer.

23. Colonel Jose Luis Garcia, one of the founders of the pro-rights military group CEMIDA (see note 22) confessed to me (July 1992) that he could not say how he would have acted had he been on active duty

during the worst years of repression. Military peer pressure is so strong that to act contrary to it entails the risk of being left entirely isolated.

24. Such a sanction, given the high esteem with which the uniform is regarded, carries strong moral connotations for officers. This type of punishment was never imposed on officers indicted for atrocities. Such officers later benefited from the Full Stop and the Due Obedience laws. Interview with General Ernesto Lopez-Meyer, at CEMIDA.

25. Neilson, *El fin,* p. 241.

26. Nozick, *Philosophical Explanations,* p. 370.

27. See claims of the Madres de Plaza de Mayo, supra note 3. See also note 40, below.

28. See Chapter 6 of this book.

29. As a former officer of the Third Army Corps claims, the corps commander, General Benjamin Menendez, had every officer under his orders assassinate a "subversive" suspect (July 1992 interview).

30. Hart, "Prolegomenon to the Principles of Punishment," in Hart, *Punishment.*

31. "All ethical doctrines worth our attention take consequences into account in judging rightness. One which did not would simply be irrational, crazy," Rawls, *Theory of Justice,* p. 30.

32. Braithwaite and Pettit, *Not Just Deserts.*

33. See John Mackie, *Morality and Retributive Emotions,* in 1 *Criminal Justice Ethics,* 3 nn. 1–4 (1982).

34. I explain this in "Punishment and a Rights Based Democracy," *Criminal Justice Ethics,* summer/fall 1991, pp. 3–13.

35. Utilitarians may adopt the view that deterrence and reformation of the criminal are but two aspects to consider in the pursuit of overall social utility. A broader view of such utility may demand computing the welfare of the direct and indirect victims of crime. This approach, however unusual, may have some appeal when, as in the case of Argentina's terrorist state, the victims were millions of people killed, tortured, and terrorized. The weakness of such an approach, lies in its limitation when the victims are only a few. In that case, their interest in regaining full membership in their community may not be as great as their interest in having their cases sealed.

35. Rawls, *Theory of Justice,* p. 446, n. 48.

36. The state in which some Native Americans live in the western United States may be a good example. Experts on the Cheyenne, for example, have argued that even in the 1990s members of the Cheyenne nation are not only deprived of the material means of existence but are also compelled to live against their own religious creed and ethos.

37. See chap. 6.

38. I wish to point out that my critique to the Federal Court of Buenos Aires is clearly an ex post facto appraisal. Scholarly discussions unleashed by the 1985 trials provide empirical and conceptual acumen that was not available at the time the trials took place.

39. See chap. 6.

40. The Madres de Plaza de Mayo are a group of mothers of youths made to disappear during the military dictatorship. Staunchly denouncing the human rights abuses perpetrated during the 1976–83 period, the Madres paraded wearing white scarfs around the square that sits across the street from Government House in Buenos Aires. This group became an important organization in the late 1970s. Though currently split, the group is still active today.

41. A good example of this interpretation is the work of journalists Grecco and Gonzalez, *Argentina*, p. 140. Despite the lack of empirical support for many of their assertions, the book was successful in that it was awarded first prize for 1990 Essays and Journalistic Investigations. This award is Argentina's most important for research journalism.

42. Triple A's name is taken from Argentine Anti-Communist Alliance.

43. See Comision, *Nunca Mas*, p. 254.

44. See Mignone, *Witness*. José-Maria Ghio, researcher on the Roman Catholic Church in Latin America, conveyed to me his conclusion that without the support of the Church, the Argentine military would not have dared to wage the campaign of terror between 1976 and 1980. Had their confessors turned their backs on them, the officers of the armed forces would have been left in total isolation.

45. Conversation with a member of the Buenos Aires Federal Criminal Appellate Court, Sept. 18, 1991.

46. See Henberg, *Retribution*, chap. 1.

47. See Feinberg, *On Doing*, chap. 8.

48. See Henberg, *Retribution*, chap. 3.

49. See Smiley, *Moral Responsibility*, p. 179.

50. I develop this notion in chap. 4.

51. See chap. 5.

CHAPTER 1

1. Other known groups were the Fuerzas Armadas Peronistas (FAP), the Fuerzas Armadas de Liberacion (FAL), and the Fuerzas Armadas Revolucionarias (FAR).

2. See Seoane, *Todo o nada*, p. 67.

3. See Page, *Peron,* p. 220.

4. See Sigal and Veron, *Peron o Muerte,* p. 123.

5. Ibid.

6. See Giussani, *Montoneros.*

7. Rock, *Authoritarian Argentina,* p. 215.

8. Naipul, "Argentina," pp. 13–18.

9. I here use the term *populism* as interchangeable with *personalimo,* the preeminence of a particular leader, rather than an identifiable ideology or program.

10. Rock, "Political Movements," p. 3.

11. See O'Donnell, *Y a mi que me importa?,* p. 23.

12. See Naipaul, "Argentina," pp. 13–18.

13. Seoane, *Todo o nada,* p. 64.

14. See Frontalini and Caiati, *El mito,* p. 58.

15. According to the CONADEP report, *Nunca Mas,* the first of these centers was La Escuelita (Little School) in the locality of Famaillá. See Comision, *Nunca Mas,* p. 213.

16. Tomas Eloy Martinez describes this pathetic scene in his *The Peron Novel,* chap. 20, p. 342.

17. See Martinez, *Peron* (note 16 above).

18. See Giussani, *Montoneros.*

19. See Hodges, *Argentina's "Dirty War,"* p. 175.

20. See Page, *Peron,* p. 488.

21. Ibid., p. 480.

22. Ibid., p. 493.

23. See Seoane, *Todo o nada,* p. 246.

24. I interviewed this army colonel in July 1992.

25. Page, *Peron,* p. 498.

26. See Barros and Coelho, "Military Intervention," pp. 437–43.

27. See O'Donnell, "Modernization," p. 96.

28. Ibid., p. 104.

29. Executive decree no. 158/83, Dec. 13, 1983.

30. The executive's message to congress to ground a draft project to restrain the scope of the human rights trials of military personnel (May 13, 1987).

31. This was the opinion of Colonel Mohamed Ali Seineldin and his men, a group that rebelled against the generals (see later in this chapter). They claimed the generals had acquiesced to the holding of human rights trials. They also claimed that in the 1970s the army did not accept its institutional responsibility for quelling insurgency. "Reality presented itself very differently than it did for older generations still attached to the model of World War II. Videla rejected the idea of reshap-

ing the army's training and structure to fight a war on subversion. Peron shared the idea that it was for the police to control subversion." Quote by Major Pedro Mercado, with the approval of Seineldin (interview in the military prison of Magdalena, July 20, 1992).

32. See Barros and Coelho, "Military Intervention," pp. 437–43.

33. Ibid.

34. Interview Aug. 3, 1992, at the military prison in Magdalena.

35. Seoane, *Todo o nada*, p. 249. I will later deal with the origin and influence of the expression *subversion*.

36. Support for the "horizontal" version in apportioning responsibility for the terrorism can be found in an account of the reasoning of the Buenos Aires Federal Court—the court that convicted five junta members ("Proceso a los Ex Integrantes de las Juntas Milikares," published by El Derecho, no date). In this account of the verdict, the court stated that, by and large, the situation generated by the military was not one of self-defense, as the generals claimed, but one of "collective revenge" (p. 18). Torturing of unarmed prisoners was an expression of the vindictive sentiment of the military (p. 22). In the court's view, such vindictiveness reflects the "private" nature of a conflict in which many officers acted out of their own initiative. This view echoes claims made by officers in interviews with the author.

37. See Corradi, "Culture of Fear," pp. 113–29. I deal with the notions of violence and power in chapter 4.

38. Andersen, *Dossier Secreto*, p. 165.

39. Comision, *Nunca Mas*, p. 224.

40. Ibid., p. 225.

41. Ibid.

42. One of the victims, Alejandro Diaz, rendered testimony at the 1985 human rights trials. Diaz was seventeen when he was taken away. He was able to guess the reason for his abduction when he ran into other students who had participated in a "special tickets" campaign. See Buenos Aires newspaper *Clarin*, May 10, 1985.

43. Andersen, *Dossier Secreto*, p. 202.

44. See Comision *Nunca Mas*, p. 357.

45. Luncheon at CEMIDA, July 1, 1992. Present were Colonels Jose Luis Garcia, Augusto Rattembach, Juan Jaime Cesio, and Horacio Ballester. CEMIDA, an association of military officers who had opposed the dirty war and favored the trials of human rights violators, was created at the end of the military dictatorship. Only a handful of officers joined CEMIDA.

46. *Nunca Mas*, p. 359.

47. See Fisher, *Mothers of the Disappeared*, p. 108.

48. Ibid., p. 111.

49. See Mignone, *Witness,* p. 66.

50. Floriani's testimony was described to me in detail by one of the members of the federal court in the 1985 trial (Interview, Buenos Aires, July 20, 1992).

51. *Nunca Mas,* the CONADEP report, was first published in 1984. See Comision, *Nunca Mas.*

52. Luncheon at CEMIDA, July 1, 1992.

53. See Andersen, *Dossier Secreto,* ch. 14, pp. 194–204.

54. See Rock, *Authoritarian Argentina,* p. 229.

55. Andersen, *Dossier Secreto,* p. 203.

56. I obtained this list of words from Argentine anthropologist Carmen Ferradás in New York, 1992.

57. See Monteon, "Can Argentina's Democracy Survive?" p. 26.

58. Quoted in Monteon, "Can Argentina's Democracy Survive?"

59. See Fisher, *Mothers of the Disappeared,* chap. 6.

60. Monteon, "Can Argentina's Democracy Survive?"

61. Asamblea Permanente por los Derechos Humanos.

62. See Garro and Dahl, "Legal Accountability," pp. 283–487.

63. See Americas Watch, *Truth and Partial Justice,* p. 18.

64. Before the supreme court invalidated the self-amnesty, congress had passed law no. 23.040. Although the legislature did not have the power thus to invalidate it, the act sought to make a strong statement against the amnesty.

65. Overcoming the obstacle of a self-amnesty de facto law was more complicated than meets the eye. It is a basic tenet of liberal criminal law that the culprit be tried according to the best legal conditions in force between the time of the alleged offense and the time of trial. When an amnesty is enacted, a subsequent derogation of this amnesty does not affect the normative status of the defendants. This derogation is to be considered ex post facto in relationship to the offense. The derogation that would make the crime punishable is tantamount to rendering the offender's act punishable by sanctioning a new legal prohibition. One may believe that the nullification of the amnesty, of rendering it nonexistent, would stem from the fact that it was sanctioned by decree, and not by congress. But there is a caveat about this tack: the argument is valid in relationship to most of the legal transactions done and undone during the dictatorship. It need not be said that this solution would have caused more damage than simply not trying human rights violations. See Nino, *La validez,* chap. 5.

66. Critics of the Alfonsin administration human rights policy underscore the fact that the clause referring to "atrocious and aberrant

acts" was added in the senate, making it possible to prosecute torturers regardless of whether or not they were following orders. See for instance Verbitsky, *Civiles y militares,* p. 73.

67. See Americas Watch, *Truth and Partial Justice.*

68. One can understand the inappropriateness of these defenses (self-defense and necessity) in acknowledging that the justification of such actions is that they frustrate an evil when, for some reason, the state is unable to prevent this evil. A citizen may shoot an assailant to save his neighbor from an armed robber when the police are not around; the difference is that the commanders were themselves the heads of state.

69. See Speck, "Trial."

70. See Neilson, "Parque jurasico."

71. Interview with Seineldin at the military prison, Magdalena, July 20, 1992.

72. General Heriberto Auel, at the hearing in the trial of Seineldin and his acolytes charged with rebelling against the heads of the army on Dec. 2, 1990. Transcript of the federal court, June 5, 1995: C.284-H1.

73. Interview at the Magdalena military prison where Seineldin is serving a life sentence for rebelling against the army's command, Aug. 1992.

74. See testimonies rendered at the Seineldin trial, 1991.

75. Transcript of testimony by Colonel Jorge Luis Toccalino at the Seineldin trials, Apr. 23, 1991: C47-H6.

76. Testimony of General Heriberto Auel, ibid.

77. Testimony of Colonel Florentino Diaz Loza, ibid.: C45-H2.

78. Testimony of Toccalino, ibid.: C47-H5.

CHAPTER 2

1. See *Buenos Aires Herald,* July 10, 1992.

2. The Madres de Plaza de Mayo, as noted earlier, is a group of women—mothers of youths made to disappear during the military dictatorship. Staunchly denouncing the human rights abuses perpetrated from 1976 to 1983, the Madres paraded, wearing white scarfs, around the square that sits across the street from the government house in Buenos Aires. The group became an important human rights organization in the late 1970s and 1980s.

3. Rock, *Authoritarian Argentina,* p. 194.

4. Interview with Rogelio Garcia Lupo, Argentine writer and Rosas's close friend (in Buenos Aires, Aug. 22, 1992).

5. It was unusual for officers on active duty to serve as diplomats.

6. See Andersen, *Dossier Secreto*, p. 63. I disagree with Andersen's description of Rosas as a plotter and even more with his idea that he was influenced by U.S. General Maxwell Taylor's version of the National Security doctrine. Within Argentina's context, Rosas seems to stand out as a democratic officer whose main sources of inspiration in envisaging the army's role were his colleagues in France. In the struggle between the ultrarightwing, Catholic officers of the Cité Catholique and more democratic, professional soldiers, Rosas seem to have been influenced by the latter.

7. Mignone identifies two of these officers as Lieut. Col. L. de Maurois and Lieut. Col. Francois Pierre Badie. See Mignone, *Derechos humanos*, p. 64.

8. See Rock, *Authoritarian Argentina*, p. 196.

9. Talk with Rattembach, June 24, 1992.

10. Description of Rosas by his friend Rogelio Garcia Lupo.

11. Rock, *Authoritarian Argentina*, p. 201.

12. Interview with Ballester at his apartment in downtown Buenos Aires, Aug. 23, 1991. Ballester is a founding member of CEMIDA.

13. Graziano views Ongania's "mysticism of redemption" as one of the roots of the conception of the "internal enemy." *Divine Violence*, p. 20.

14. Interview with Colonel Mohamed Ali Seineldin at the military prison of Magdalena, July 20, 1992.

15. Interview with Breide Obeid, a former captain convicted of mutiny for participating in the 1990 uprising, Magdalena, July 20, 1992.

16. Heer, *The Medieval World*, p. 110.

17. Ibid., p. 112.

18. See Popper, *The Open Society*, p. 88. (The italic type used for the words *subvert* and *subversion* is added by the author.)

19. Bateson, "Conventions."

20. I deal with the notion of reality and acquiring an epistemology in chap. 5.

21. See Bateson, "Conventions."

22. Editorial in *La Opinion*, Aug. 25, 1977.

23. *La Opinion*, Sept. 12, 1976.

24. *La Nacion*, 12 May, 1977.

25. *La Nacion*, Feb. 2, 1977.

26. Rear Admiral Ruben Chamorro, *La Nacion*, Mar. 4, 1978.

27. See Popper, *The Open Society*, chap. 1.

28. Watzlawick, *Muenchhausen' Pigtail*, p. 186.

29. Popper, "La sociedad abierta," p. 23.

30. See Sigal and Veron. *Peron o Muerte.*

31. See Rock, "Antecedents," pp. 1–35.

32. *La Nacion,* May 25, 1976.

33. *La Nacion,* 15 Feb., 1977.

34. Admiral Ruben Jacinto Chamorro, *La Nacion,* May 4, 1978; see Frontalini and Caiati, *El mito,* p. 23.

35. See Frontalini and Caiati, *El mito,* p. 21.

36. See Lewis, "The Right and the Military," pp. 147–80.

37. See Elster, "Active and Passive," p. 175.

38. Ibid.

39. Watzlawick, "Components," p. 231.

40. See Fraga, *Ejercito,* p. 235.

41. Watzlawick, "Components," pp. 206–248.

42. Moore, *Injustice,* p. 448.

43. Ibid., p. 449.

44. Comision, *Nunca Mas,* p. 9.

45. Quoted by Rock, *Authoritarian Argentina,* p. 226.

46. Warren, "Interpreting," p. 37.

47. Quoting the army's chief of staff at the time, General Guillermo Suarez-Mason; *Clarin,* July 7, 1979.

48. From an army report on lawyers Gustavo Adolfo Roca and Lucio Garzon Maceda, *La Nacion,* May 10, 1976.

49. *La Opinion,* May 29, 1978; Frontalini and Caiati, p. 24.

50. General Acdel Vilas, commander of the forces fighting the ERP in Tucuman in 1975.

51. Speech delivered in Apr. 1978 to the Chamber of Public Relations at the Plaza Hotel, Buenos Aires.

52. See Mignone, *Witness,* p. 106.

53. Videla, *Ante Los Jueces,* p. 17.

54. When former colonel Aldo Rico expressed this view on June 9, 1992, on the Tiempo Nuevo TV show (Telefe Channel), he was reiterating a sentiment ceaselessly expressed by most of his comrades.

55. See Watzlawick et al., *Teoria,* p. 21; also Stolzemberg, "Inquiry," pp. 257–309.

56. Watzlawick, "Components."

57. Frontalini and Caiati, *El mito,* p. 22; *La Prensa,* Aug. 16, 1978.

58. Colonel Oscar Vega, interview held in the military prison in Magdalena, July 20, 1993. Vega was one of the top officers in command of the Dec. 2, 1990 military revolt against the generals. The rebels were a group of devout Catholics who claimed that the generals had failed to defend the armed forces against constant aggression by the press. Although they conceded that the dirty war had been plagued with abuses, they also held that the human rights trials had damaged the army's dignity, scapegoating officers who had in fact defended the country's supreme values.

59. Unlike the Nazis and Soviet Communists, the Argentine regime did not articulate an explicit set of principles to make total ideologies. This fact, however, does not bespeak a similarity with Nazism and Stalinism. In appealing to an open definition of the enemy, the Argentine military attempted to control citizens' minds and bodies. The alleged duration of totalitarianism presents itself as contingent upon the efficiency of those in power to control the opposition—and it was not the Argentine military's beliefs that ended their domination but rather their lack of efficiency. One may characterize the military regime in Argentina as being particularly stupid. One can similarly claim that Nazism did not last as long as Hitler expected: it was the war that toppled the German Nazis, but the war was not alien to the ideology that drove Hitler. The Argentine dictatorship and the Nazi mind shared an inability to assess their own performances from outside their own values—the values from which they originated. This closed-mindedness and the lack of heed for experience are the features that, in this context, make the systems similar.

60. Szasz, *Manufacture of Madness*, p. 8.

61. Ibid.

62. *Clarin*, Oct. 24, 1975.

63. See Acuña and Smulovitz, "Ni Olvido ni Perdon."

64. See Stolzemberg, "Inquiry," p. 260.

65. Guest, *Behind the Disappearances*," p. 154.

66. Ibid.

67. See the court's decision in Fallos 300:816 and 301:771 of July 1978 and Sept. 1979.

68. See Guest, *Behind the Disappearances*, p. 289.

69. See paper by Andres D'Alessio, the former attorney general, "Las violaciones."

70. See Andersen, *Dossier Secreto*, p. 286.

71. *Clarin*, July 7, 1979.

72. Guest, *Behind the Disappearances*, p. 82.

73. Ibid., p. 84.

74. Ibid., p. 85.

75. Declaration by General Suarez-Mason to journalists, in *Clarin*, Sept. 23, 1979.

76. See Paul Watzlawick, "Components," p. 226.

77. See Guest, *Behind the Disappearances*, p. 177.

78. Speech by Suarez-Mason in Buenos Aires newspaper *Clarin*, July 7, 1979.

79. Buenos Aires magazine *Siete Dias*, May 18–24, 1978.

80. Other members of the commission were General Sanchez de Bus-

tamante, Admiral Alberto Vago, Vice Admiral Jorge Boffi, and Brigadier General Carlos Alberto Rey.

81. Rattembach, *Informe Rattembach: El Drama de Malvinas.*

82. Ibid. and an interview with Colonel Augusto Rattembach (son of General Rattembach) June 24, 1992.

CHAPTER 3

1. Heymann, "Should Prosecutors?" pp. 203–23.

2. Iain Guest, *Behind the Disappearances,* shows the extent to which this diplomatic tactic was actually used by the military regime.

3. I met President Perez at the presidential palace in Caracas, Venezuela, in Dec. 1992.

4. Conversation with Perez, Dec. 1992.

5. See interview with journalist and CONADEP member Magdalena Ruiz Guiñazú, in Moncalvillo et al., *Juicio a la impunidad,* p. 45.

6. See Andersen, *Dossier Secreto,* p. 216.

7. Ibid.

8. Ibid., p. 303.

9. See Graziano, *Divine Violence,* p. 73.

10. I have taken the quotes from Frontalini and Caiati, *El mito de la guerra sucia,* p. 88.

11. Ibid., p. 89.

12. Ibid.

13. Interview with Mignone at his apartment in downtown Buenos Aires, Aug. 5, 1991.

14. See Watzlawick, *How Real?* chap. 3.

15. Watzlawick, *How Real?* p. 28.

16. See Watzlawick, *How Real?* p. 29.

17. See Rorty, "Self Deception," pp. 115–33.

18. Watzlawick, *How Real?* p. 51.

19. See ibid., p. 45.

20. Warren, "Interpreting," p. 25–57.

21. See Comision report, *Nunca Mas* p. 7.

22. See Rorty, "Self Deception," pp. 115–33. Rorty claims that while some individuals form highly centralized and uniform habits, in other people these systems are more loosely connected. This latter strategy consists of an adaptive, "sanity-preserving" compartimentalization; however, this compartmentalization hinders the rectification of incompatible beliefs.

23. When, in the spring of 1992, a group of Colombian officials re-

sponsible for peace negotiations with guerrillas gave a talk at the School of International Affairs at Columbia University, they repeatedly referred to "the paramilitary." When queried about the nature of these paramilitary groups, they revealed the extent of the vagueness in the use of this expression. *Paramilitary*, they said, included groups formed by the police, the army, landowners, and drug traffickers.

24. Corradi, "Culture of Fear," pp. 147–59.

25. The April 23, 1978 issue of *Revista Esquiú* quotes Anchorena's report:

> Max Walter is the visible head of the campaign which has set up a committee called "Committee to Boycott the World Cup." This committee is attempting to make the Soccer Federation suspend the cup in Argentina on the grounds that human rights are not being respected. The same is happening with the World Congress on Cancer whose boycott has been implemented is a part of the same campaign. Mimeographed letters were sent to the physicians requesting that they should repudiate the Congress.

26. See Fisher, *Mothers of the Disappeared*, p. 72.

27. Ibid.

28. Ibid.

29. See *Siete Días,* May 18–24, 1978. The same article contains a list of members labeled as the Anti-Argentine Network. Among the names are France's former president, François Mitterand, former chancellor of Germany, Willy Brandt, and Spain's Felipe Gonzalez.

30. See chap. 2 on the bumper-sticker campaign. Stickers urged foreigners to leave the country.

31. See Guest, *Behind the Disappearances,* 1990 p. 164.

32. Moore, *Injustice*, p. 485.

33. See Corradi, "Culture of Fear," pp. 113–129.

34. Ibid., p. 113.

35. In chap. 5, I claim that once people learn to live by a certain conception of reality, a pattern sets in that remains even after the circumstances that contributed to its establishment have changed. See also Nino, *Un país,* chap. 4. By using theory-of-games models, Nino demonstrates how, unable to follow basic rules, Argentines found themselves in a situation in which cooperative action became impossible.

36. See Skolnik, "Bateson's Concept," p. 90.

CHAPTER 4

1. Flathman, *Practice of Political Authority,* p. 128.

2. Weil, "The Iliad."

3. See Nordstrom and Martin, "Culture of Conflict," p. 6.

4. In Arendt, *On Violence*, pp. 43, 46.

5. Although Arendt conflates the notion of authority with that of power, she acknowledges that only authority lies in the "unquestioned recognition" of a particular person or an office Ibid., p. 45.

6. Ibid., p. 37.

7. Ibid.

8. A distinction between the two is acknowledged by Arendt in other works, for example *Between Past and Future*, p. 122.

9. See Raz, *Morality of Freedom*, chap. 1; Flathman, *Practice of Political Authority*, chap. 7.

10. See Taylor, *Community, Anarchy and Liberty*, p. 10. To the concepts of threat and offers, Taylor adds the concept of a "throffer." A combination of punishment and reward, a throffer consists of O obtaining a benefit if he does X, and a punishment if he does not do X.

11. Flathman, *Practice of Political Authority*, p. 129.

12. See Fletcher, *Crime* chap. 2.

13. See Taylor, *Community, Anarchy and Liberty*, p. 13.

14. Ibid., p. 149.

15. Flathman, p. 150.

16. See for instance Piaget, *Les operations*.

17. Corradi, "Culture of Fear," pp. 113–31.

18. In Argentina, police certificates are required for many administrative purposes (e.g., insurance claims, proof of residence for driver's licence, etc.).

19. Rosenhan, "On Being Sane," pp. 117–45.

20. Ibid., p. 137.

21. Ibid.

22. See Deutsch, *Nerves of Government*, p. 111.

23. Braithwaite and Pettit, *Not Just Deserts*, chap. 7.

24. See Garland, *Punishment and Society*, chap. 3.

25. For instance, Duff, *Trials and Punishment*, p. 47.

26. See Smiley, *Moral Responsibility*, p. 177.

27. Ibid., p. 167.

28. Watzlawick, Weakland, and Fisch, *Change*, p. 45.

29. See Moore, *Injustice*, p. 500.

30. See Andersen, *Dossier Secreto*, pp. 283, 301. According to Andersen's information, the abduction and assassination of Dupont was carried out by 601 Army Intelligence Battalion personnel in an effort to discredit Emilio Massera, a naval service commander. Massera was the top suspect in Gregorio Dupont's investigation into the assassination of diplomat Helena Holmberg by Massera's thugs.

31. In this context, "nobody" means nobody with power, nobody with authority.

32. Prologue to the *Nunca Mas* report by the Comision Nacional, p. 9.

33. See, for instance, Suarez-Horozco, "Grammar of Terror," pp. 219–59.

34. See Henberg, *Retribution*, p. 22.

35. Ibid.

36. Moore, *Injustice*, p. 458.

CHAPTER 5

1. See Herrsher, "Police Torture Rises," p. 11.

2. See Chevigny, "Police Deadly Force," p. 389.

3. See chap. 1, where I refer to bill 23,492 of Dec. 1986, (the Full Stop Law) and 23,521 of June 1987 (the Due Obedience Law). These laws drastically limited the prosecution of military officers.

4. See Buenos Aires newspaper *Pagina 12*, Oct. 30, 1990.

5. Ibid., p. 4.

6. See *Pagina 12*, Aug. 5, 1993, p. 16. Journalist Sergio Resumil therein claims that in three days six minors lost their lives at the hands of the police: one minor was kicking a plastic bottle, another was mistaken for a thief (which he proved not to be), and a third was on his way to a party. See also the editorial comment in *La Nacion*, Aug. 12, 1993.

7. *Pagina 12*, Sept. 14, 1990, p. 7.

8. See Americas Watch, *Truth*, p. 81.

9. Buenos Aires newspaper *Ambito Financiero*, Oct. 19, 1990, p. 4.

10. Buenos Aires TV channel 9, Silvio Soldan's show.

11. Ibid.

12. Opinion stated to me by high-ranking federal police officers serving under the Alfonsin administration. They said they considered Patti simply to be a criminal.

13. *Buenos Aires Herald*, Aug. 8, 1991, p. 11. See also *Pagina 12*, Sept. 14, 1991, p. 7.

14. *Pagina 12*, Sept. 14, 1991, p. 7.

15. *Pagina 12*, Sept. 9, 1991, p. 7.

16. See Americas Watch, *Truth*, p. 82.

17. Ibid.

18. See Gonzalez, *Noticias*, pp. 78–81.

19. See Martinez, *Pagina 12*, p. 4.

20. See Chevigny, "Police Deadly Force." See also Americas Watch and Centro de Estudios Legales y Sociales, *Police Violence in Argentina: Torture and Police Killings in Buenos Aires*, 1991 report.

21. Gingold, "Justicia para todos."

22. Ibid.

23. The consejo was created by President Raul Alfonsin after a Jan. 1989 attempt by a left-wing group to take over the military barracks at La Tablada, on the outskirts of Buenos Aires.

24. See Buenos Aires newspapers *Clarin* and *La Nacion,* 28 July, 1993. Veliz resigned in Aug. 1993, claiming that the administration he was serving was way too dirty on many counts.

25. See Neilson, "Civilizacion y barbarie."

26. See *Pagina 12,* Aug. 14 and 15, 1993 and *La Nacion,* Aug. 19, 1993, p. 7.

27. See Termine et al., p. 72.

28. See *Pagina 12,* Aug. 22, 1993.

29. See Neilson, "La lucha es cruel."

30. TV news, Aug. 16.

31. *Pagina 12,* Aug. 18, 1993, p. 2.

32. See Mendez, *Confesiones,* p. 81.

33. See for example Page, *Peron,* p. 462.

34. Many right-wing Peronistas adopted Primo de Rivera as their hero. See Senkman, "The Right and Civilian Regimes."

35. See *Pagina 12,* Aug. 18, 1993.

36. Idem.

37. Ibid., p. 2.

38. See, for instance, Magee, *Popper.*

39. Lipsitz, *Lenses of Gender.*

40. See chap. 2 of this book.

41. Ibid.

42. See for instance Malamud-Goti, "Is there a Right to Disobey?" and Nino, *Etica y derechos humanos,* pp. 320 ff.

43. See chap. 2 of this book.

44. In a speech delivered at the 11th Conference of American Armies, held in 1975 in Montevideo, Videla stated: "We will achieve the security of the country regardless of how many die in this pursuit." See *Clarin,* Oct. 24 1975.

45. See Bateson, "Social Planning and the Concept of Deutero-Learning," in *Steps in the Ecology of Mind,* pp. 159 ff.; also Bateson, "Conventions," pp. 212 ff.

46. See magazine *Noticias,* Nov. 15, 1992, p. 84.

47. See Bateson, "Conventions," p. 218.

48. See Watzlawick, Beaven Bavelas, and Jackson, *Pragmatics,* p. 262.

49. See Bateson, *Steps,* p. 217.

50. As Bateson points out, this process is one in which validity ac-

tually depends on belief. "The more sharply the paradigms are defined, the more evident it becomes that the persons concerned in the interaction actually have a curious freedom to impose their own interpretation upon the sequences of interaction." Bateson, "Conventions." This means there is no objective interpretation of the world that will prove us to be wrong. Thus, in the relationship between a blind man and his guide boy, it may be the case that both believe they are in a position of dominance. While the blind man infers his own control from the fact that he feeds the boy, who has thus become dependant on him, the boy may believe that the blind man, without his aid, would not survive. Both interpretations derive from a different punctuation of their relationship. Both are valid provided that the parties believe in them.

51. Bateson, "Conventions," p. 216.

52. See the theory of systems of interactive processes in Paul Watzlawick, Beaven Bavelas, and Jackson, *Pragmatics,* chaps. 1 and 4; also Watzlawick, "Self Fulfilling Prophesies," pp. 95–117.

53. See chap. 2, "Self-Sealing Proofs."

54. See Gingold, "Justicia."

55. Three uprisings took place during the Alfonsin administration: two were led by Lieutenant Colonel Aldo Rico (Apr. 1987 and Jan. 1988), one by Colonel Mohamed Ali Seineldin (Jan. 1989). The Dec. 1990 Seineldin revolt against the generals came during the Menem administration.

56. The press's decision to disclose the abuses of the dirty war was labeled as a "campaign." When the 1989 rebellion against the generals broke out, one of the witnesses claimed that "the honor" of the army was at stake (see court session report for Apr. 25, 1991.)

57. Gingold, "Justicia para todos."

58. Bateson, "Social Planning and the Concept of Deutero Learning," in Steps.

59. See Gingold, "Justicia."

60. See Verbitsky, "Muros de silencio."

61. Ibid.

62. See Americas Watch and CELS report, *Verdad y Justicia,* p. 90.

63. See Gingold's research of a case in the Buenos Aires province, *Cronica de muertes anunciadas.*

64. See interview with Rogelio Garcia Lupo: "En este pais puede haber varias guerras al mismo tiempo," special report in Buenos Aires periodical *La Maga,* Sept. 15, 1993, pp. 2–5.

65. Ibid.

66. See chap. 2.

67. See Garcia Lupo report, *La Maga,* Sept. 15 1993.
68. See *Clarin,* Apr. 30, 1994, p. 10.
69. Ibid.

1. See *Pagina 12,* Aug. 16, 1991, p. 7.
2. In the province of Buenos Aires alone, 500,000 citizens voted for Rico. See *Pagina 12,* Sept. 10, 1991, p. 4; Kollman, "El Identikit de los Votantes."
3. Verbitsky, *Civiles y militares* and Guest, *Behind the Disappearances,* p. 555, n. 22.
4. Kollman, supra note 2; ibid, p. 3.
5. Statement at the Seineldin trials (June 17, 1991, records. C: 331 H. 1).
6. See Andersen, *Dossier Secreto.*
7. Article 514 of the military justice code exempts from punishment subordinate personnel acting under superior orders, except when the subordinates exceed themselves in the furtherance of such directives. When orders are manifestly illegal, the courts dismiss the defense on the ground that such directives are not binding on subordinate officers. This decision was reached in 1909 when a colonel who had barred a congressman from going into congress entered the defense that his commanding officer had ordered him to do so. See Fontan-Balestra, *Tratado de derecho penal.*
8. Among officers who held this view was General Raul Ramayo, legal adviser of the army during the early stages of the transition. He reminded me of his stance at a private encounter in early Aug. 1991.
9. Interview with Seineldin at the Magdalena military prison, Aug. 1992.
10. See my definition of conscientious objection in Malamud-Goti, "Is There the Right to Disobey?"
11. This opinion was given to me by Seineldin in the interview at Magdalena, July 1992.
12. Magdalena interview, July 1992.
13. Ibid.
14. In spite of being implicated in several gruesome cases of assassination and extortion, Guglielminetti served directly under Alfonsin until his participation in violent crimes became clearly evident. He fled to Spain in 1986. When I traveled Spain to visit the minister of the interior, seeking to secure Guglielminetti's extradition, we discovered that he had been under the protection of Spanish intelligence personnel.

15. See Verbitsky, *Civiles y militares*, p. 65.

16. Interview with Hector Romero Mundani, a former major, at the military prison in Magdalena, Aug. 3, 1992.

17. In the previously mentioned statements at the Seineldin trial, Aldo Rico (head of the mutinies staged against the Alfonsin administration in 1987 and 1988) said: "I would have never allowed my subordinate officers to stand trial." He continued: "The cornerstone of an army is not obedience but loyalty to one's own personnel. Command without leadership is clearly insufficient."

18. Buenos Aires channel 7, in the evening of Aug. 30, 1991.

19. In essence, this was the opinion of Seineldin and his group. Interviews at Magdalena, Aug. 1992.

20. Interviews at Magdalena, July 1992.

21. Fisher, *Mothers of the Disappeared*, p. 137, quoting Elsa de Becerra. The head of the Mothers, Hebe de Bonafini, declared:

> We're going to continue in the same way because we still haven't got justice. They've tried to convert us into the mothers of dead children and put an end to the problem of the disappeared. We will never accept they are dead until those responsible are punished. If we accepted that, we would be accepting that murderers and torturers can live freely in Argentina. They can't negotiate with the blood of our children. The Madres de Plaza de Mayo are never going to permit that.

Ibid., p. 158. See also Osiel, *Human Rights Policy*, pp. 135–78.

22. See Fisher, *Mothers of the Disappeared*, chap. 6.

23. One of the most reputable Argentine human rights activists, Emilio Mignone, claims that after the 1976 military coup there were virtually no left-wing combatants. Mignone, *Derechos Humanos*, p. 51 ff. Opposing this claim, former members of the ERP recalled in an interview with the author in July 1992 that, though considerably weakened, the ERP was still operating until late 1977 and even into 1978.

24. Comision Nacional, *Nunca Mas*. The *Commission* (CONADEP) registered about 8,960 disappearances, but some human rights activists maintain that the number should be increased to 20,000 and even 30,000.

25. Decision of 30 Dec., 1986, CSJN, Hum. Rts. L.J. 430 (1987) (Arg.).

26. It must be admitted, to the chagrin of many Argentines, that the bloodless Mar. 1976 military takeover enjoyed widespread popular support. See generally Fraga, *Ejercito*, p. 261 (1988). I agree with Fraga's view.

27. See, for instance, Gould, *Rethinking Democracy*, chap. 11.

28. See Garland, *Punishment*, p. 80.

29. See Malamud-Goti, "Punishment and a Rights Based Democracy," p. 3.

30. See chap. 6.

31. See Arendt, *Report on the Banality of Evil*, p. 226.

32. See Jorge Grecco in the *Clarin*, Nov. 11, 1993, quoting Videla's speech to young retired officers.

33. See chap. 2.

34. See chap. 5.

35. See chap. 3.

36. See Neilson, "Parque Jurasico."

37. This is similar to what Rawls calls "pure procedural justice." The system of allocation of burdens and benefits itself should be sufficient to elicit a just result. Rawls, *A Theory of Justice*, p. 85.

38. See Fisher, *Mothers of the Disappeared*, chap. 7.

39. Ibid.

BIBLIOGRAPHY

Ackerman, Bruce. *The Future of the Liberal Revolution*. New Haven, Conn.: Yale University Press, 1992.

Acuna, Carlos H., and Catalina Smulovitz. "Ni Olvido ni Perdon: Derechos humanos y tensiones civico-militares en la transicion argentina." Paper submitted at the XVIth International Congress of the Latin American Studies Association, Washington D.C., April 4–6, 1991. Buenos Aires: CEDES, 1991.

Andersen, Martin Edwin. *Dossier Secreto: Argentina's Desaparecidos and the Myth of the "Dirty War."* Boulder, Colo.: Westview Press, 1993.

Americas Watch, *Truth and Partial Justice in Argentina (An Update)*, report, April 1991.

Arendt, Hannah. *A Report on the Banality of Evil: Eichmann in Jerusalem* (revised and enlarged edn.). Aukland: Penguin, 1977.

——. *Between Past and Future: Eight Exercises in Political Thought.* Aukland: Penguin, 1968.

——. *On Violence*. San Diego: Harvest/HBJ, 1969.

Barros, Alexandre de S. C., and Edmundo C. Coelho. "Military Intervention and Withdrawal in South America," in *Armies and Politics in Latin America,* Abraham Lowenthal and J. Samuel Fitch, eds. New York: Holmes and Meier, 1986.

Bateson, Gregory. "Conventions and Communication: Where Validity Depends upon Belief," in *Communication: The Social Matrix of Psychiatry,* Jurgen Ruesch and Gregory Bateson, eds. New York: W. W. Norton, 1987.

———. *Steps in the Ecology of Mind.* New York: Ballantine, 1972.

Braithwaite, John and Philip Pettit. *Not Just Deserts: A Republican Theory of Criminal Justice.* New York: Oxford University Press, 1990.

Chevigny, Paul G. "Police Deadly Force as Social Control: Jamaica, Argentina and Brazil," in *Criminal Law Forum* 1, no. 3, spring 1990.

Comision Nacional Sobre la Desaparicion de Personas, *Nunca Mas,* Informe, 14th. edn. Buenos Aires: Editorial Universitaria de Buenos Aires, 1986. [Report of CONADEP, the National Commission the Disappearance of People.]

Corradi, Juan E. "The Culture of Fear in Civil Society," in *From Military Rule to Liberal Democracy in Argentina,* Monica Peralta-Ramos and Carlos H. Waisman, eds. Boulder, Colo.: Westview Press, 1987.

D'Alessio, Andres. "Las violaciones en general." Paper given at the Hebrew University of Jerusalem, Seminar on Violations of Human Rights in Argentina during the Military Regimes, 1982 (unpublished).

Deutsch, Karl W. *The Nerves of Government: Models of Political Communication and Control.* New York: Free Press, 1966.

Duff, R. A. *Trials and Punishment,* Cambridge, U.K.: Cambridge University Press, 1991.

Elster, Jon. "Active and Passive Negation: An Essay in Ibanskian Sociology," in *The Invented Reality: How do We Know What We Believe We Know (Contributions to Constructivism),* New York: W. W. Norton, 1981.

———, ed. *The Multiple Self.* Cambridge, U.K.: Cambridge University Press, 1987.

———. *Sour Grapes: Studies in the Subversion of Rationality.* New York: Cambridge University Press, 1991.

Feinberg, Joel. *On Doing and Deserving: Essays in the Theory of Responsibility.* Princeton, N.J.: Princeton University Press, 1970.

Fisher, Jo. *Mothers of the Disappeared,* London: Zed Press, and Boston: South End Press, 1989.

Flathman, Richard. *The Practice of Political Authority: Authority and the Authoritative.* Chicago: University of Chicago Press, 1980.

Fletcher, George P. *A Crime of Self Defense: Bernard Goetz and the Law on Trial.* New York: Free Press, and London: Macmillan, 1988.

Fontan-Balestra, Carlos. *Tratado de derecho penal,* 352, 2nd edn. Buenos Aires, Abeledo-Perrot, 1980.

Fraga, Rosendo, *Ejercito: Del escarnio al poder (1973–1976),* Buenos Aires: Editorial Planeta, 1988.

Frontalini, Daniel, and Maria Cristina Caiatti. *El mito de la guerra sucia,* with prologue by Emilio F. Mignone. Buenos Aires: Centro de Estudios Legales y Sociales (CELS), 1984.

Garland, David. *Punishment and Society: A Study in Social Theory,* Chicago: University of Chicago Press, 1990.

Garro, Alejandro, and Henry Dahl. "Legal Accountability for Human Rights Violations in Argentina: One Step Forward and Two Steps Backward," in *Human Rights Law Journal* 8, 1987.

Gingold, Laura. *Cronica de muertes anunciadas: El caso de Ingeniero Budge.* Buenos Aires: Documento CEDES/65, 1991.

———. "Justicia para todos." Paper submitted at seminar, "Derechos Humanos, Justicia, Politica y Sociedad," Centro de Estudios Legales y Sociales, Buenos Aires, September 20–21, 1991.

Giussani, Pablo. *Montoneros: La soberbia armada* 7th edn. Buenos Aires: Editorial Sudamericana-Planeta, 1986.

Gonzalez, Gustavo. Buenos Aires magazine *Noticias,* September 19, 1993, pp. 78–81 (no title).

Gould, Carol C. *Rethinking Democracy: Freedom and Social Cooperation in Politics.* Cambridge: Cambridge University Press, 1988.

Graziano, Frank. *Divine Violence,* Boulder, Colo.: Westview Press, 1992, p. 20.

Grecco, Jorge, and Gustavo Gonzalez. *Argentina: El ejercito que tenemos.* Buenos Aires: Editorial Sudamericana, 1990.

Guest, Iain. *Behind the Disappearances: Argentina's Dirty War against Human Rights and the United Nations.* Philadelphia: University of Pennsylvania Press, 1990.

Hart, H. L. A. *Punishment and Responsibility: Essays in the Philosophy of Law.* New York: Oxford University Press, 168.

Heer, Friedrich. *The Medieval World.* New York: Mentor, 1963.

Henberg, Marvin. *Retribution: Evil for Evil in Ethics, Law, and Literature.* Philadelphia: Temple University Press, 1990.

Herrsher, Roberto M. "Police Torture Rises," *Buenos Aires Herald,* July 9, 1991.

Heymann, Philip B. "Should the Prosecution Be Independant of the Executive in Prosecuting Government Abuses?" in *Transition to*

Democracy in Latin America, Irwin Stotzky, ed. Boulder, Colo.: Westview Press, 1993.

Hodges, Donald C. Argentina's "Dirty War": An Intellectual Biography. Austin: University of Texas Press, 1991, p. 175.

Kirkpatrick, Jeanne. Dictatorships and Double Standards: Rationalism and Reason in Politics, New York: Touchstone, Simon and Schuster, 1982.

Kollman, Raul. "El Identikit de los Votantes," in Pagina, 12 Sept. 15, 1991, p. 2.

Lewis, Paul. "The Right and the Military, 1955–1983," in The Argentine Right: Its History and Intellectual Origins, 1910 to the Present, Sandra McGee and Ronald H. Dolkart, eds. Wilmington, Del.: Scholarly Resources, 1993.

Lipsitz, Sandra. The Lenses of Gender: Transforming the Debate on Sexual Inequality. New Haven, Conn.: Yale University Press, 1993.

Magee, Bryan. Popper. London: Fontana and Collins, 1973.

Malamud-Goti, Jaime. "Is There a Right to Disobey the Law on Moral Grounds?" in Rechtstheorie 17:2, Berlin, Duncker & Humblot, 1986.

———. "La omision como el 'menosprecio punible' de los articulos 221 bis y 230 del codigo penal," in Nuevo Pensamiento Penal, no. 1, Buenos Aires, 1972, p. 235.

———. "Punishment and a Rights Based Democracy," in Criminal Justice Ethics 10, no. 2, summer/fall 1991, p. 3.

———. "Punishment and Human Dignity," in S'Vara: A Journal of Philosophy and Judaism 2, no. 1, Columbia University, Spring 1991.

———. "Punishing Human Rights Abuses in Fledgling Democracies: The Role of Discretion," in Transition to Democracy in Latin America: The Role of the Judiciary, Irwin Stotzky, ed. Boulder, Colo.: Westview Press, 1994.

———. "Transitional Governments in the Breach: Why Punish State Criminals," in Human Rights Quarterly 1, 1990.

Martinez, Juan Carlos. Pagina 12, Oct. 30, 1990, p. 4 (no title).

Martinez, Tomas Eloy. The Peron Novel, New York: Pantheon, 1988.

Mendez, Eugenio. Confesiones de un Montonero: La otra cara de la historia, 3rd edn. Buenos Aires: Sudamericana-Planeta, 1986.

Mignone, Emilio F. Derechos humanos y sociedad: El caso argentino. Buenos Aires: Centro de Estudios Legales y Sociales and Ediciones del Pensamiento Nacional, 1991.

———. Witness to the Truth: The Complicity of Church and Dictatorship in Argentina, 1976–1983, Phillip Berryman, trans. (from Spanish). Maryknoll, New York: Orbis, 1986.

Moncalvillo, Mona, et al. *Juicio a la impunidad*. Buenos Aires: Ediciones Tarso S.A., 1988.

Monteon, Michael. "Can Argentina's Democracy Survive Economic Disaster?" in *From Military Rule to Liberal Democracy*, Monica Peralta-Ramos and Carlos H. Waisman, eds. Boulder, Colo.: Westview Press, 1988.

Moore, Barrington Jr. *Injustice: The Social Bases of Obedience and Revolt*, New York: M. E. Sharpe, 1978.

Naipaul, V. S. "Argentina: Living with Cruelty," in *New York Review of Books*, January 20, 1992, pp. 13–18.

Neilson, James. "Civilizacion y barbarie," in *Noticias*, Buenos Aires, July 25, 1993.

———. *El fin de la quimera: Auge y ocaso de la Argentina populista*, Buenos Aires: Emece, 1991.

———. "La lucha es cruel," *Noticias*, Buenos Aires, September 12, 1993, p. 76.

———. "Parque jurasico," *Noticias*, July 18, 1993.

Nino, Carlos S. *Etica y derechos humanos: Un ensayo de fundamentacion*, 2nd. edn. Buenos Aires: Editorial Astrea, 1989.

———. *La validez del derecho*. Buenos Aires: Editorial Astrea, 1985.

———. *Un pais al margen de la ley: El estudio de la anomia como componente del subdesarrollo argentino*. Buenos Aires: Emece editores, 1992.

Nordstrom, Carolyn and JoAnn Martin. "The Culture of Conflict: Field Reality and Theory," in *The Paths of Domination, Resistance and Terror*, Carolyn Nordsstrom and JoAnn Martin, eds. Berkeley, Calif.: University of California Press, 1992.

Nozick, Robert. *Philosophical Explanations*. Oxford, U.K.: Clarendon Press, 1981.

O'Donnell, Guillermo A. "Modernization and Military Coups: Theory, Comparisons and the Argentine Case," in *Armies & Politics in Latin America*, Abraham F. Lowenthal and Samuel Fitch, eds. New York: Holmes and Meier, 1986.

——— *Y a mi que me importa? Notas sobre sociabilidad y politica en Argentina y Brasil*. Buenos Aires: Centro de Estudios de Estado y Sociedad, 1984.

Oksemberg Rorty, Amelie. "Self Deception, Akrasia and Rationality," in *The Multiple Self*, Jon Elster, ed. Cambridge, U.K.: Cambridge University Press, 1987.

Osiel, Mark. "The Making of Human Rights Policy in Argentina: The Impact of Ideas and Interests on a Legal Conflict," *Journal of Latin American Studies*, 18, 1987, pp. 135–78.

Page, Joseph A. *Peron: A Biography*. New York: Random House, 1983.

Piaget, Jean. *Les operations et la vie sociale*. Georg, Geneva: Publications des Sciences Economiques et Sociales de L'universite de Geneve, 1945.

Popper, Karl R. *La sociedad abierta y sus enemigos*, Eduardo Loedel, trans. Barcelona: Paidos, 1981, p. 23.

―――. *The Open Society and Its Enemies*, Vol. 1, Princeton, N.J.: Princeton University Press, 1962,

Przeworski, Adam. "Democracy as a Contingent Outcome of Conflicts," in *Constitutionalism and Democracy*, Jon Elster and Rune Slagstad, eds. New York: Cambridge Univ. Press, 1988.

Rattembach, Benjamin, et al. *Informe Rattembach: El Drama de Malvinas*, Buenos Aires: Ediciones Espartaco, 1988.

Raz, Joseph. *The Morality of Freedom*, Oxford, U.K.: Clarendon Press, 1988.

Rawls, John. *A Theory of Justice*. Cambridge, Mass.: Harvard University Press, 1971.

Rock, David. "Antecedents of the Argentine Right," in *The Argentine Right: Its History and Intellectual Origins, 1910 to the Present*, Sandra McGee Deutsch and Ronald H. Dolkart, eds. Wilmington, Del.: Scholarly Resources, 1993, pp. 1–35.

―――. *Authoritarian Argentina: The Nationalist Movement, Its History and Its Impact*. Berkeley, Calif.: University of California Press, 1993.

―――. "Political Movements in Argentina: A Sketch from Past to Present," in *From Military Rule to Liberal Democracy in Argentina*, Monica Peralta Ramos and Carlos H. Waisman, eds. Boulder, Colo.: Westview Press, 1987.

Rorty, Amelie Oksemberg. "Self Deception, Akrasia and Rationality," in *The Multiple Self*, Jon Elster, ed., Cambridge, U.K.: Cambridge University Press, 1987, pp. 115–33.

Rosenhan, David. "On Being Sane in Insane Places," in *The Invented Reality: How do We Know What We Believe We Know? (Contributions to Constructivism)*, Paul Watzlawick, ed. New York: W. W. Norton 1984, pp. 117–45.

Sen, Amartya K. *On Ethics and Economics*, Basil Blackwell, Oxford, 1990.

Senkman, Leonardo. "The Right and Civilian Regimes, 1955–1976," in *The Argentine Right: Its History and Intellectual Origins, 1910 to the Present*, Sandra McGee Deutsch and Ronald H. Dolkart, eds. Wilmington, Del.: Scholarly Resource, 1984, p. 131.

Seoane, Maria, *Todo o nada*, Buenos Aires: Editorial Planeta, 1991.

Sigal, S. and E. Veron. *Peron o Muerte*, Buenos Aires: Hispamerica, 1988.

Skolnik, Theodor. "Bateson's Concept of Mental Illness," in *The Individual, Communication and Society: Essays in the Memory of Gregory Bateson*, Robert W. Rieber, ed. Paris: Maison des Science del

Homme, and Cambridge, U.K.: Cambridge University Press, Studies in Emotion and Social Interaction, 1989, p. 90.

Smiley, Marion. *Moral Responsibility and the Boundaries of Community: Power and Accountability from a Moral Point of View.* Chicago: University of Chicago Press, 1992.

Speck, Paula K. "The Trial of the Argentine Junta: Responsibilities and Realities," in *Inter-American Law Review* 18, no. 3.

Stolzemberg, Gabriel. "Can Inquiry into the Foundations of Mathematics Tell Us Anything Interesting About the Mind?" in *The Invented Reality: How Do We Know What We Believe We Know? (Contributions to Constructivism)*, Paul Watzlawick, ed. New York: W. W. Norton, 1984.

Suarez-Horozco, Marcelo. "The Grammar of Terror: Psychocultural Responses to State Terrorism in Dirty War and Post-Dirty War Argentina," in *The Paths of Domination, Resistance and Terror,* Carolyn Nordstrom and JoAnn Martin, eds. Berkeley, Calif.: University of California Press, 1992.

Szasz, Thomas S. *The Manufacture of Madness: A Comparative Study of the Inquisition and the Mental Health Movement,"* New York: Harper Torchbooks, 1970.

Taylor, Michael. *Community, Anarchy and Liberty.* London: Cambridge University Press, 1982.

Termine, Laura et al. "Las jaulas abiertas", *Noticias,* September 5, Buenos Aires, 1993.

Verbitsky, Horacio. *Civiles y militares: memoria secreta de la transicion.* Buenos Aires: Editorial Contrapunto, 1987.

———. "Muros de silencio," in Buenos Aires newspaper *Pagina 12,* June 20, 1993, p. 14.

Videla, Jorge Rafael. *Ante Los Jueces.* Buenos Aires: Asociacion Juridica Argentina, 1984

Warren, Kay. "Interpreting *La Violencia* in Guatemala: Shapes of Mayan Silence & Resistance," in *The Violence Within: Cultural and Political Opposition in Divided Nations,* Kay Warren, ed. Boulder, Colo.: Westview Press, 1993.

Watzlawick, Paul, John H. Weakland, and Richard Fisch. *Change: Principles of Moral Formation and Problem Resolution.* New York: W. W. Norton, 1987.

Watzlawick, Paul. "Components of Ideological `Realities'" in *The Invented Realities: How Do We Know What We Believe We Know?* New York, W. W. Norton, 1984.

———. *How Real Is Real? Confusion, Disinformation, Communication,* New York: Vantage 1976.

————. *Muenchhausen's Pigtail*. New York: W. W. Norton, 1990.

————. "Self Fulfilling Prophesies," in *The Invented Reality: How Do We Know What We Believe We Know? (Contributions to Constructivism)*, Paul Watzlawick, ed. New York: W. W. Norton, 1984.

Watzlawick, Paul, et al. *Teoria de la comunicación humana*, Carlos Sluzky, trans., 3rd edn. Buenos Aires: Editorial Tiempo Contemporaneo, 1974.

————. Janet Beaven Bavelas, and Don D. Jackson. *Pragmatics of Human Communication: A Study of Interactional Patterns, Pathologies and Paradoxes*. New York: W. W. Norton, 1962.

Wechsler, Lawrence. *A Miracle; A Universe: Settling Accounts with Torturers*. New York: Penguin, 1990.

Weil, Simone. "The Iliad: Or the Poem of Force," Mary McCarthy, trans. *A Pendle Hill Pamphlet*, no. 91, Wellington, Penn., 1956.

Williams, Bernard. *Shame and Necessity*. Berkeley, Calif.: University of California Press, 1993.

INDEX

Abelard, Peter, 76

Acosta, Jorge, 64

Agosti, Orlando, 46, 179

Alfonsin, Raul, 3, 4, 5, 19, 42, 47, 50, 57–59, 64–68, 88, 112, 151, 168–76, 187, 190, 199n.3, 205–206n.66, 214n.23

Amnesty International, 95–97

Anaya, Jorge Isaac, 56, 98

Anchorena, Thomas de, 115, 211n.25

Anti-Argentine campaign, 88, 97, 116

Aramburu, Pedro E., 29

Arendt, Hannah, 128–29, 212n.5

"Argentinity," 81

Arguindegui, Jorge, 176

Arigos, Carlos, 135

Articulating power. *See* Power

Asamblea Permanente por los Derechos Humanos (APDH), 58, 205n.61

Auel, Heriberto, 206n.n.72, 76
Authoritative. *See* Authority
Authority 8, 9, 18–20, 27, 63, 92, 129–30, 140, 157, 179, 181, 184–85, 194, 196, 212n.5
Averbury, Lord, 95

Badie, Pierre, 207n.7
Ballester, Horacio, 75, 207n.12
Banco de Intercambio Regional (BIR), 55
Banzer, Hugo, 171
Barrionuevo, Luis, 154
Bateson, Gregory, 147, 200n.9
Becerra, Elsa de, 217n.21
Bergalli, Roberto, 103–104, 109
Bignone, Benito, 57
Blame, 4, 8, 21, 23–26, 117, 128, 139–46, 153, 162, 171–72, 188, 192, 200n.15
Blameworthy. *See* Blame
Blaming. *See* Blame
Boffi, Jorge, 209–10n.80
Bonafini, Hebe de, 49, 217n.21
Born, Jorge, 32
Born, Juan, 32
Borrino, Raul, 149
Brandt, Willi, 97, 211n.29
Breide-Obeid, Captain, 207n.15
Brito Lima, Alberto, 155
Bussi, Domingo, 5, 6, 153, 169, 191
Bustos Ramirez, Juan, 109

Cabildo, 52, 85, 93
Cafiero, Antonio, 45
Campora, Hector J., 31–32, 117–18
Camps, Ramon, 44, 48, 63, 95
Carrio, Genaro, 94
Carter, Jimmy, 117
Castro, Fidel, 31, 34–35
Catholic Church. *See* Roman Catholic Church
Catholic clergy. *See* Roman Catholic Church, clergy
CEMIDA, 11, 51, 200–201nn.22, 23, 24; 204n.45, 205n.52, 207n.12
Central Confederation of Labor (CGT), 56
Cerruti, Victor, 50–51

Cesarsky, Jorge E., 155

Cesio, Juan Jaime, 11, 204.n45

Chamorro, Ruben Jacinto, 64, 81

Chevigny, Paul G., 152, 200n.8

Christian tradition, 74

Cité Catholique, 74–75, 207n.6

Civilization, western. *See* Christian Tradition

Clairvaux, Bernard de, 76

Cold War, 41

Comision Nacional Sobre la Desaparicion de Personas. *See* CONADEP report

CONADEP report, 47, 50, 59, 82, 85, 203n.15, 205n.51, 217n.24

Conference of American Armies, 93

Consejo de Seguridad Nacional, 153

Conspiracy, 91, 161; conspiratorial, 90; "conspiratorials," 160–67, 188, 190, 196

Corradi, Juan E., 120

"Cosmic justice," 144

Cox, Robert, 95, 103

Cuba. *See* Cuban Revolution

Cuban Revolution, 34

Curuchet, Alfredo, 39

D'Alessio, Andres, 209n.69

Desaparecidos. *See* CONADEP report

Diaz, Alejandro, 204n.42

Diaz Losa, Florentino, 206n.77

Dirty war, 90, 93, 184

Disarticulating Power. *See* power

Doctrine of National Security. *See* National Security, doctrine of

Dominguez, Carlos, 11

Drinan, Robert, 95

Due Obedience Bill (or Law), 64, 66, 168, 173, 179

Duhalde, Eduardo, 150, 154

Dupont, Gregorio, 142

Dupont, Marcelo, 142, 212n.30

Durieu, Roberto, 142

Easter rebellion, 66

Ejercito Revolucionario del Pueblo (ERP), 30, 32–39, 42–43, 49, 73, 116, 186, 190

Epistemological. *See* Epistemology

Epistemology, 158–59
Ezeiza airport, massacre, 36–37, 155

Falkland/Malvinas Islands, 3, 26, 56–58, 67, 70, 97, 99, 106, 121–23, 168, 171, 177, 190
Feeney, Patricia, 95
Fanaticism, 92, 95
Farer, Tom, 97
Fascists, 38, 82
Fatalistically. *See* Fatalists
Fatalists, 160, 162, 167, 181, 187–88, 196
Fatherland, 84, 86, 182
Feced, Agustin, 91
Feeney, Patricia, 95
Ferradas, Carmen, 53, 205n.56
Financial Hiroshima, 55
Flathman, Richard, 129, 200n.16
Floriani, Carmen, 50, 205n.50
Fraga, Rosendo, 217n.26
Franco, Francisco, 52, 155
Frondizi, Silvio, 40
Full Stop Bill (or Law), 64, 65, 168, 179

Gainza, Maximo, 102–103
Galtieri, Fortunato, 56–57, 98, 122
Game without end, 187
Garcia, Jose Luis, 48, 51, 200–201n.23
Garcia Lupo, Rogelio, 206n.4
Garzon Maceda, Lucio, 208n.48
Gassino, Luis, 69
Ghio, Jose-Maria, 202n.44
Gingold, Laura, 152, 161, 164, 215n.63
Giussani, Pablo, 38
Gonzalez, Felipe, 97
Graziano, Frank, 207n.13
Grecco, Jorge, 202n.41
Guerre Revolutionaire, 40, 43
Guevara, Raul ("Che"), 34–35
Guglielminetti, Raul, 175, 216n.14
Guzzetti, Cesar, 81

Harguindeguy, Albano, 45–46
Hart, H. L. A., 14
Hitler, Adolph, 83, 209n.59
Hodges, Donald C., 38
Holmberg, Elena, 142, 212n.30
Human rights, organizations, 26–27, 147; trials, 5, 18, 20, 25, 27, 58, 88, 111, 166, 168–69, 178, 181–82, 189

Illia, Arturo, 73, 75
Interamerican Commission on Human Rights (IACHR), 96–97
Isabel. *See* Peron, Isabel

"Judicialization" of politics, 185, 197
Juventud Peronista (JP), 30, 38–39

Kant, Immanuel, 14

Lacoste, Alberto, 116
Landaburu, Laureano, 137
La Opinion, 93
Lastiri, Raul, 37
La Tablada, Regimiento de, 214n.23
Le Monde, 93
Ley de Pacificación, 58
Locke, John, 52
Lopez Echagüe, Hernan, 154
Lopez Meyer, Ernesto, 201n.24
Lopez Rega, Jose, 22, 36–39, 119, 191
Luder, Italo Argentino, 35, 46, 57, 62
Luque, Guillermo, 150

"Mad Mummies." *See* Madres de Plaza de Mayo
Madres de Plaza de Mayo, 13, 18, 113, 116, 178–79, 190, 197, 202n.40, 206n.2, 217n.21
Magdalena, Argentina, military prison, 217nn.16, 19, 20
Martinez, Mercedes, 112
Martinez, Tomas Eloy, 203n.16
Massera, Emilio, 46, 61, 80, 102–103, 182, 186, 212n.30
Maurois, L. de, 207n.7
Mendia, Luis, 80

Menem, Carlos, 6, 7, 11, 27, 72, 98, 148–54, 163, 165, 168–69, 199n.2, 215n.55

Menendez, Luciano Benjamin, 47, 63, 95, 113, 201n.29

Mercado, Pedro, 203–204n.31

Metal Workers Union, 190

Michelini, Zelmar, 102

Mignone, Emilio, 105, 210n.13, 217n.23

Miguel, Lorenzo, 36, 39, 45, 119

Mill, John Stuart, 52

Mitterand, François, 97, 211n.29

MODIM party, 6, 170

Molina, Sosa, 186

Montoneros, 29, 30–39, 42–43, 49, 73, 93, 118, 186, 190

Moore, Barrington, 84, 141

Morales, María Soledad, 140, 164

Mothers of Plaza de Mayo. *See* Madres de Plaza de Mayo

Mugica, Carlos, 32–33

Muzzio, Jorge, 83

National Commission for the Disappearance of Persons. *See* CONADEP report

National Security, doctrine of, 40–41, 73, 181

Naval School of Mechanics, 64, 104

Neilson, James, 192

Neruda, Pablo, 86

Nino, Carlos S., 4, 176, 211n.35

Noriega, Manuel, 67

Nunca Mas, 59, 111, 142. *See also* CONADEP report

Ochoa, Fermin, 96

O'Donnell, Guillermo A., 41, 20

Ongania, Juan, 73, 75, 207n.13

Ortega, Ramon ("Palito"), 169

Ortega Peña, Rodolfo, 39

Osinde, Jorge, 36, 39, 155

Ottalagano, Alberto, 52

"Pacification Bill," 60

Page, Joseph A., 39

Pascariello, Hugo, 86

Patti, Luis, 149, 150–54, 164–65, 191

Pencil children (niños de los lápices), 48

Perez, Mariano, 49
Peron, Isabel, 33–40, 44–49, 51–54, 105, 118, 138
Peron, Juan Domingo, 22, 29–39, 45, 51–52, 72, 117
Peron, Maria Estrela de. *See* Peron, Isabel
Pla, Norma, 154
Plaza, Antonio, 49
Ponce de Leon, Bishop Carlos, 48
Popper, Sir Karl R., 76, 80
Power, articulating, 125–32, 138–39, 145–46, 198; disarticulating, 125, 126, 138–39, 158; structural, 127–29, 138, 144–45, 158
Primo de Rivera, Jose Antonio, 155, 214n.34

Rajneri, Julio, 180
Ramayo, Raul, 216n.8
Rattembach, Augusto, 204n.45, 207n.9
Rattembach, Benjamin, 98
Rattembach Commission, 98
Rawls, John, 201n.31
Resumil, Sergio, 213n.6
Retributivist emotions, and the victim's dignity, 189
Revenge, collective, 197
Rey, Carlos, 209–10n.80
Ricchieri, Ovidio, 63
Rico, Aldo, 5, 6, 170–71, 215n.55, 216n.2, 217n.17
Rocca, Gustavo A., 208n.48
Roman Catholic Church, and Catholicism, 23, 34, 52, 59, 76, 82, 159; clergy, 32
Romero Mundani, Hector, 217n.16
Rosas, Carlos Jorge, 73–75, 207n.6
Rosenhan, David, 134–35
Roualdes, Roberto, 64, 105, 158
Rousseau, Jean Jacques, 52
Rucci, José, 36
Ruiz Guiñazú, Magdalena, 210n.5
Ruiz Palacios, David, 169, 192

Sabato, Ernesto, 59, 79
Sabato Commission, 111. *See also* CONADEP report
Saint-Jean, Iberico, 86, 93
Sanchez de Bustamante, Tomas, 209–10n.
Santos, Horacio, 150–51, 191
Santucho, Roberto, 30

Sartre, Jean Paul, 52
Sassiain, Juan, 110
School of Infantry, 69
Seineldin, Muhamed Ali, 67–70, 174–75, 203n.31, 206nn.71, 72, 73;
    207n.14, 216nn.5, 9, 11; 217nn.17, 19
Self respect, and democracy, 15–18
"Self sealing proofs," 90–92, 196
Shakespear, Ronald, 137
Sigal, S., 80
Soccer. *See* World Cup, soccer
Sociedad Rural Argentina, 56
Sola, Felipe, 154
Soldan, Silvio, 213n.10
Stalinism, 209n.59
State terror, 7
Suarez-Mason, Guillermo, 95–96, 209nn.75, 78
Szasz, Thomas S., 91, 92

Tacuara, 165
Taylor, Maxwell, 207n.6
Timerman, Jacobo, 93–95
Tito, General, 44
Toccalino, Jorge, 206nn.75, 78
Triple A, 22, 40, 81, 118, 165, 186, 190
Troccoli, Antonio, 151
Trotz, Ernesto, 44
Truman, Harry, 105
Tse-tung, Mao, 31

Union Industrial Argentina (Argentine Industrial Union), 56

Vago, Alberto, 209–10n.80
Vañek, Antonio, 81
Vega, Oscar, 208n.58
Veliz, Gustavo, 153, 214n.24
Veron, Eliseo, 80
Videla, Jorge Rafael, 46, 56, 58, 81, 86–87, 93–94, 102, 113, 158, 172, 190,
    203–204n.31
Viet Cong, 35
Vietnam War, 34
Vilas, Acdel, 157, 208n.50
Vilas, Guillermo, 114–15

Villa Martelli, 69
Villar, Alberto, 32
Viola, Eduardo Roberto, 46, 56, 172

Walter, Max, 211n.25
Warren, Kay, 85, 110
Washington Post, 93
Watzlawick, Paul, 83, 107–108
Weil, Simone, 126
World Cup, soccer, 115–17, 211n.25
World War II, 42, 172, 182, 203–204n.31